Italian Grotesque Theater

Italian Grotesque Theater

Translated with an Introduction
by Michael Vena

Madison • Teaneck
Fairleigh Dickinson University Press
London: Associated University Presses

Associated University Presses
440 Forsgate Drive
Cranbury, NJ 08512

Associated University Presses
16 Barter Street
London WC1A 2AH, England

Associated University Presses
P.O. Box 338, Port Credit
Mississauga, Ontario
Canada L5G 4L8

The paper used in this publication meets the requirements
of the American National Standard for Permanence of Paper
for Printed Library Materials Z39.48–1984.

Library of Congress Cataloging-in-Publication Data

Italian grotesque theatre/translated with an introduction by Michael Vena.
  p. cm.
  Includes bibliographical references and index.
  Contents: The mask and the face/Luigi Chiarelli—A man confronts himself/Luigi Antonelli—The bird of paradise/Enrico Cavacchioli.
  ISBN 0-8386-3894-5 (alk. paper)
  1. Italian drama—20th century—History and criticism. 2. Grotesque in literature. I. Vena, Michael. II. Chiarelli, Luigi, 1880–1947. Maschera e il volto. English. III. Antonelli, Luigi, 1877–1942. Uomo che incontrò se stesso. English. IV. Cavacchioli, Enrico, 1885–1954. Uccello del paradiso. English.

PQ4145 .I73 2001
852'.912'08—dc21   2001018952

To my mother and father.

Contents

Acknowledgments

I wish to acknowledge the constant support I received from my wife Anna in the use of our computer, for without her patience energy and guidance the manuscript would never have been completed.

A number of friends, colleagues and teachers come immediately to mind for their impact on these translations and the encouragement they gave. Barbara Folsom went through my first draft of *The Mask and the Face* and the late Lowry Nelson, Jr. read *The Bird of Paradise,* providing helpful suggestions for improvement. Olga Ragusa and Umberto Mariani have supported consistently my initiatives on the grottesco ever since I edited *La maschera e il volto* in the original Italian for use in high schools and universities, while Mario Moffa reviewed the same text for *Italica.* Prof. Mariani was also kind enough to read and comment on my introduction to Cavacchioli. I am equally grateful to Giuseppe Mazzotta, who read my introduction on Chiarelli and Antonelli and contributed valuable criticism. Reinhold Grimm has seconded the work throughout with cheerful suggestions.

A special word of appreciation goes to Emanuel Paparella whose comments have enriched our dialogue on contemporary civilization and enhanced the quality of this book. Gratitude is likewise due to Anthony Julian Tamburri who supported this publication, to Giose Rimanelli who gave me the incentive to do it in the first place, and to Jacques Guicharnaud for his later reading of the plays. Neither they nor others bear any responsibility for errors and omissions. On the other hand, let me acknowledge anyone whose ideas may have been unconsciously absorbed but I remain unaware of unaccounted borrowings. Indeed, I wish to thank the Connecticut State University System for a research grant that I received in the form of a summer stipend related to this project, and the Southern Connecticut State University Faculty Development Office whose progressive views and efforts to advance research, even with limited means, must be publicly commended.

I am indebted to Dr. Ugo Chiarelli for permission to reproduce and translate *La maschera e il volto,* to the estate of Enrico Cavacchioli, and to Grazia Antonelli Cascella especially for her extraordinary courtesy in assisting with illustrations. Luciano Paesani has been very generous with in-

9

formation on his own stage activities regarding Antonelli. In addition, special thanks are due to Mario Mignone, editor of *Forum Italicum*, for permission to reproduce in this book the contents of my notes " The 'Grotteschi' Revisited" from the Summer 1997 issue of that journal, and to Anthony Verna, editor of *Rivista di Studi Italiani*, for permission to reproduce the article "Cavacchioli's *The Bird of Paradise* and Metatheater" from the Summer 2000 issue. Finally, I thank the two readers for the Associated University Presses, managing editor Christine Retz for her skill, wisdom, and patience through the entire process, and Sue Kittek whose comments on the manuscript were most helpful.

Laura Sabatino helped with photo development and Nicholas Orsini contributed suggestions for the cover.

Last, but not least, I like to thank my students, who listened with patience, and who taught me over the years. This book was written with them in mind.

Introduction:
Twentieth-Century Italian Grotesque Theater

W E HAVE WITNESSED WITHIN THE LAST TWO OR THREE DECADES A SURGE of critical attention aimed at reassessing the work of playwrights who produced a genre of drama called *grotesque* or the "new Italian school" as it came to be known in France at the turn of the century. Their importance needs hardly be stressed both in terms of their relation to Pirandello's own theatrical production and the role they played in the rejuvenation of European stage. More specifically, we owe a debt of gratitude to Giancarlo Sammartano who, with his 1994 volume on Luigi Antonelli, completes an itinerary on twentieth-century grotesque theater, begun with a similar publication on Luigi Chiarelli in 1988, and a subsequent one on Enrico Cavacchioli in 1990. All three volumes include an extensive introduction and bibliography, a chronology of the author's life, all the most important plays, and other jottings. As an assiduous cultivator of the theatrical field, Sammartano captures with remarkable clarity some significant innovations of these *grotteschi* both in terms of ideas and in the relationship between author, actor, and the public, thereby suggesting that the time is ripe for a systematic reassessment of such works: to look and listen again to these three and other voices of that brief but significant early-twentieth-century current, widely acclaimed then, certainly underestimated now, and perhaps all along misunderstood.

The Mask and the Face by Luigi Chiarelli is historically important as the first successful attempt at grotesque theater, while two plays that follow, *A Man Confronts Himself* by Luigi Antonelli and *The Bird of Paradise* by Enrico Cavacchioli, exhibit further innovations in content and form as their authors sought to forge a more radical, irreverent, even violent linguistic medium. The new style, which reflects also the developments of futurism and surrealism, turned to an assertion of that spirit of revolt driven by the philosophical influence of Friedrich Nietzsche. Although Antonelli and Cavacchioli shared pretty much the same vision of reality, they are vastly different from one another, as the first brought to the stage an aura of fairy tale and magic whereas the second parodied, through the lenses of science

11

or rather science fiction, a world obsessed with particular views of self and other. To be sure, all three dramatists—Chiarelli included—showed life as a grotesque farce full of contradictions; all three played important roles in a renewal of the European stage, and although they were eclipsed by their great contemporary Pirandello, it is no coincidence that the successful performance of these plays paved the way for the early successes of Pirandello as a playwright.

In a short span of seven or eight years the grotesque theater produced some of the most significant works of the twentieth century. If the early Pirandellian plays of the same period—also categorized as grotesque— were included, we would have a clear, comprehensive view of the importance of this dramatic, theatrical mode and its influence upon succeeding generations down to the present. To grasp the substance and impact of the grotesque theater we should focus, however briefly, on some of its representative texts. In 1916, following Chiarelli's *The Mask and the Face,* we also have *Better Think Twice About It* by Pirandello; in 1917 Chiarelli successfully staged *The Silken Stairs,* while Pirandello—as a result of feverish activity— produced at least four works: *The Jar, Caps and Bells, It Is So (If You Think So),* and *The Pleasure of Honesty.* In 1918, along with Antonelli's success, Rosso di San Secondo staged his masterpiece, *Puppets of Passion!.* What these texts share, aside from an obvious critique of positivism and naturalism, is the belief that the apparent order of bourgeois society was a tissue of arbitrary conventions and false assumptions, as well as the conviction that theater— as the arena of fictions, simulations, postures, and so on—essentially represents the privileged art form for their social and moral concerns. Through these works the conception and development of grotesque theater becomes firmly established. Certainly Chiarelli, Pirandello, and Rosso set the parameters of inquiry for other playwrights.

While Chiarelli is polemical and subversive of old theatrical practices, Antonelli breaks away from the past by the infusion of elements reminiscent of the fantastic dream play, and of course he also dissects the classic love triangle according to what we might call grotesque poetics: thus the triangle is turned into a vicious circle, with no exit or solution for the characters disoriented by passion and lust. Whereas in *The Mask and the Face* the grotesque uncovers a conflict primarily between self and society—even though Paolo experiences his own evolution—in this play of Antonelli's the ambivalence originates and stays within the individual, in man's unconscious; hence we have a drama dealing with a division of the self or the problem of disintegration of personality: in this sense, the difference between the two plays is noticeable and brings to mind the evolution from Pirandello's *It Is So (If You Think So)* to the masterpiece yet to be written *Henry IV.* At any rate, all three playwrights play a pivotal role for an under-

standing of the genre they represent. They forge links with the most avant-
garde contemporary thinking and, some of them at least, set the pace for
what becomes surrealism and much later the theater of the absurd. Also,
they are important for the broader implicatons they carry in the area of
scholarship, as clearly accomplished dramatists involved in the whole process of reassessing and preserving good literature.

Luigi Chiarelli (1880–1947)

Luigi Chiarelli's contribution to modern theatre was acknowledged in his
day by many authoritative witnesses including Thomas Mann, Filippo T.
Marinetti, Antonio Gramsci, while Luigi Pirandello not only supported the
concepts of the grotesque but extended them in the multifaceted variations
of his own production. Chiarelli's plays were translated into many languages
and performed on the stages of Europe and the Americas almost as quickly
as in Italy. In 1921, while riding the crest of popularity, the playwright
concluded his humorous " In anticipation of my memoirs: pages of the
year 2021" with a great deal of subtle ironic foresight.

> Great news has come from London. A distinguished researcher has discov-
> ered in that wonderful head of Homer which is at the British Museum the
> manuscript of an unknown comedy by Willy Shakespeare. It's entitled *The
> Mask and the Face*. The action takes place on Lake Como. It deals with a
> husband who . . . Alas! Now everything unfolds.

> [È giunta una grande notizia da Londra. Un illustre cercatore ha scoperto in
> quella meravigliosa testa di Omero che è al British Museum il manoscritto di
> una commedia sconosciuta di Willy Shakespeare. La commedia s'intitola *La
> maschera e il volto*. L'azione si svolge sul lago di Como. Si tratta di un marito
> che . . . Ahimé! Adesso tutto si spiega.] (L. Chiarelli, "Anticipo alle mie
> memorie . . . ")

The upshot of this statement has a double significance now. In the first
place Chiarelli remains indeed an author to be discovered; his works deserve more critical attention in Italy and also in the English-speaking world.
There are very few entries, if any, under his name in our major American
and English encyclopedias. Secondly, in the passage above, Chiarelli seems
to imply a rapport in dramatic primacy between his own age and the Re-
naissance tradition, superbly exemplified by Shakespeare but also by
commedia dell'arte and pastoral drama down to the origins of melodrama.
   Chiarelli was an innovator and he knew it. One might call him the contrary voice of his age; yet his lively intelligence and sharp artistic sensitivity

mellowed the polemics in which he engaged, whether he was dealing with his grotesque portrayal of reality, his conception of the eternity of myth, or his antiexistentialism. Thomas Mann was not off the mark when he stated that the theater of succeeding generations would follow the patterns set by two great playwrights: Chiarelli and Pirandello. As a progressive voice of the new theater, here is how Chiarelli characterized the genesis of his little masterpiece at the beginning of the grotesque movement:

> *The Mask and the Face* was born of a critical as well as philosophical and polemical position . . . critical because it was subversive of all the rules of the old theatrical practice, shattering the prevailing threadbare norms on which European dramatic literature is based.
>
> [*La maschera e il volto* nacque da una posizione critica oltre che filosofica e polemica . . . critica perché sovvertiva tutte le regole della vecchia tecnica teatrale, infrangendo i logori schemi imperanti sui quali si modella la letteratura drammatica europea.]

The author breaks away from the stale models of nineteenth-century bourgeois situations which, except for the very special works of D'Annunzio and Verga, had conditioned or even plagued the theatergoing public for decades. Chiarelli is concerned with ideas and problems of a philosophical nature; but what strikes us most is the originality of his approach: from his a priori distortion of reality to his *demonstratio per absurdum* of his theses.

The Mask and the Face

The Mask and the Face is generally considered Chiarelli's masterpiece. It is an ironical comedy in three acts, written during the summer of 1913 in the manner of the modern Italian grotesque. Chiarelli satirizes here the conventional attitude toward marital infidelity and the differences between what we preach and what we actually do. The plot centers around the dilemma of a betrayed husband who, to avenge his honor, pretends he has killed his wife.

Count Paolo Grazia and wife Savina, typical members of upper-middle-class Italian society, are having a reception in their villa on Lake Como. While the group is engaged in a discussion on the subject of infidelity, Paolo states that if he were betrayed by his wife he would kill her, because a "husband who forgives is subject to ridicule" and "for such a husband there is nothing left but suicide." That same evening he discovers that his beautiful wife Savina is indeed betraying him. His natural impulse would be to forgive her, but he dismisses such a solution for it would belie his public pronouncements. He therefore compels her to leave Italy in secret and to live abroad under an assumed name, while he tells everyone that he has thrown

Portrait of Luigi Chiarelli. Courtesy of the Chiarelli family.

(Entrambi si guardano con 47/c
angosciosa intensità; poi ella, con
uno slancio improvviso, fa qualche
passo tendendo le braccia a Paolo
in un supremo gesto d'amore.)

Paolo — (accogliendola fra le sue braccia e
stringendola forte, forte) Ah, sei qui!...
qui!... qui!... (la bacia con grande
tenerezza sui capelli.)

(le note della marcia fu-
nebre illanguidiscono.)

Sipario

Luigi Chiarelli

Milano
10 agosto 1913
ore sei del mattino.

"LA MASCHERA E IL VOLTO..

L'ultima pagina del manoscritto

Last page of the manuscript of *The Mask and the Face*

the adulteress in the lake. Paolo is taken into custody, but later is acquitted thanks to a glowing defense presented by Luciano, a lascivious lawyer who happens to be Savina's lover. Paolo is welcomed home with public honors by his friends and the authorities; as a result of this sorry spectacle which society has imposed on him, he is overcome by disgust and repulsion as he realizes the absurdity of "killing" for the opinion of others. "Doesn't anything serious exist in this world? Even the most grievous experiences become ridiculous. What fools! . . . And to think it was for these people that I . . . Oh, fools!"

But Paolo pays still another price for his fictitious murder. One day, the corpse of a woman is recovered from the lake. Everybody identifies it mistakenly as Savina's. Paolo feels obliged to concur in their opinion. Consequently, the corpse is brought to his house and a lavish funeral is arranged. In the intervening time, the real Savina returns and Paolo begins to feel the true nature of their love, as the image of death gives meaning and value to their lives. His impending catharsis signifies also the triumph of the philosophy of Cirillo, the most positive character in the play, who from the beginning has questioned the validity of conventional attitudes.

Unfortunately, some guests attending the funeral surprise Savina in the house. Her appearance —there—is, for them, no laughing matter, nor is it a good joke in the eyes of the law. Marco, a magistrate, points out to Paolo that this time he faces a prison term for simulation of a crime and falsification of documents. To avoid that, Paolo and Savina must run away—as outlaws—toward an authentic freedom. They make their furtive departure while burial services begin with Chopin's funeral march. Clearly, Chiarelli's social concerns and moral angst become an emblem of his theatrical self reflexiveness; and the theater, as the place for simulations, improvisation and conflict, offers the obvious artistic setting to exemplify such concerns. So, in dramatic form, he makes his attack on empty social conventions. His polemic, verging at times on tragic farce, is skillfully tinged with humor, fraught with paradox, and full of surprises. It lends itself to a rich development, typical of the postwar drama of the twenties. In fact, the play is considered one of the first successful attempts to rejuvenate Italian and European theatre and to free it from the trammels of the customary "triangle" (husband, wife, lover) situations inherited from the nineteenth century. An important aspect of the polemic presented by Chiarelli is the contrast between *form* and *reality*. Form here is not used in a Crocean sense, but rather as signifying an outward appearance, a stereotype, a mask. Chiarelli operates therefore in an intellectual sphere closely related to Pirandello's. But *The Mask* is less pessimistic than most of Pirandello's plays: Chiarelli's conclusion seems to imply that a tolerant acceptance of life can be won though an understanding of its contradictions.

Scene from a 1926 stage performance of *The Mask and the Face*, Madrid.

Chiarelli would be prone to follow this logic: other people can't really judge us for what we are; they tend to judge us by isolated instances or specific acts. They impose a mask on us which we cannot strip off, either because that is the way they can best deal with us or because our principles prevent us from showing our true faces when it might be dangerous to do so. Thus we become a form. If form, then, is the only reality which counts for others, we might just as well create our own form and impose it on others as a mask that would allow us to follow our inner feelings in the most free and emancipated ways.

The necessity of pretending is justified as a means, not as an end. (In addition, by now the theories of the subconscious are also telling us that we hardly determine the nature of our own souls). Undoubtedly, *The Mask and the Face* is a product of that deep intellectual crisis and moral disorientation which marked the years preceding and immediately following the First World War. In this respect, the drama gives character and direction to a brief but significant current called grotesque. By this term we refer to a genre of theater wherein the passions and tragedies of life are mechanically simplified and shockingly distorted. The grotesque incorporates positivistic disenchantment, social criticism, and an unusual concept of ethics which denies traditional values and leans toward a relativistic philosophy. Authors adhering to it scorn such a miserable mode of existence. They expose contradictions, absurdities, vanity, hypocrisy, but generally leave their protagonists in the midst of unresolved conflicts. In such a situation, in this seeming confusion, life itself becomes a laughingstock to them or tragically hopeless. This view of the world is made manifest in the works of Rosso di San Secondo (*Puppets of Passion!*), Luigi Antonelli (*A Man Confronts Himself*), and Enrico Cavacchioli (*The Bird of Paradise*), who, along with some aspects of Pirandello's literary personality, represent the main authors of the grotesque. As for *The Mask and the Face*, we notice some positive developments which change the lot of the protagonists and show what power love can have as a

Scene from a 1924 stage performance of *The Mask and the Face*, **London.**

catalytic agent in the elimination of the conflict between form and reality, between the mask and the face.

Other Works by Chiarelli

The remainder of Chiarelli's literary production can be categorized mainly along the lines of the grotesque. *La scala di seta* (*The Silken Stairs*, 1917) presents the contrast between two men: a decent one doomed to failure and an unrepentant ballet dancer named Desire'. Desire' enjoys the life of pleasure and success, allegorically portrayed as a silken stairway that leads to the height of fame. By means of outrageous extortions, he becomes a minister in the government, while his honest and capable opponent is forced into humiliation. Ironically, he begins to display his temper in a seemingly uncompromising situation; he becomes an object of ridicule by insulting, in a speech, a cheering crowd, and then breaking into a wild waltz.

In *Chimere* (*Chimeras*, 1919) Claudio and Maria cherish a dream to be a devoted lover and a pure soul, respectively. They slowly descend to the most debasing concessions, thus disclosing the thoroughly superficial nature of their ideals. *Morte degli amanti* (*Death of the Lovers*, 1919) is a parody of conventionalism of two melodramatic lovers who dream up headlines newspapers will use to extol their relationship, after they have consummated their romantic existence in suicide. Luckily, they will be saved by the woman's husband. *Fuochi d'artificio* (*Fireworks*, 1922) deals with an old theme in a modern fashion. It depicts the plight of a destitute man, Gerardo, whom everyone believes to be very wealthy. His reputation for nonexistent wealth is skillfully fabricated by his secretary Scaramanzia. This play was widely acclaimed. It completes the cycle of Chiarelli's grotesque.

However, his creative efforts are not limited to the grotesque. As early as 1917, he produced *La portantina*, a political satire, and *Le lacrime e le stelle* (1918), a morality play of the war years. Subsequently, we have *Jolly* (1928),

Un uomo da rifare (1931), *Carne bianca* (1934), *Cerchio magico* (1937), *Pulcinella* (1939), and *Enrico VIII* (1940), in addition to various one-act plays and a substantial number of short stories, which from 1932 appeared in *La Stampa* and were later collected in two volumes, *La mano di Venere* (1935) and *La figlia dell'aria* (1939). We also have *Enea come oggi* (1938) and *Ninon* (1940), representing a type of drama Chiarelli characterized as mythical. Finally, toward the very end of his life, he gave us *Essere* which is in marked contrast to his previous plays. *Essere* is an allegorical drama (performed posthumously in 1953) in which the author reveals his need for faith in a supreme being.

Biographical Note

Luigi Chiarelli was born at Trani in the province of Bari on 7 July 1880. He received his secondary education at the Liceo Viconti in Rome, but the early death of his father prevented him from attending a university. Nevertheless, he soon became well known in literary circles, and contributed verse as well as prose to periodicals such as *L'Alfiere* and *La Patria*. His first attempts as a playwright also belong to this period (1895–1910). In 1911 Chiarelli joined the Milanese newspaper *Il secolo* as a reporter. It was in Milan that he became acquainted with the most important theatre groups in Italy. The following year he succeeded in having two one-act plays performed, *Una notte d'amore* and *Er Gendarme*, the latter in Roman dialect. Later, he went on to Turin to direct the review *Armi e Politica* (1914). With the outbreak of World War 1, although he was drafted, Chiarelli was allowed to continue his literary activities and his work as a journalist. But recognition was yet to come. Not before 29 May 1916, did Chiarelli establish his position as a dramatic writer; that night a theatre company from Rome, the Compagnia Drammatica di Roma, staged his *The Mask and the Face* at the Teatro Argentina. The play was an immediate success throughout Italy, and soon after in America and Europe. That same summer the renowned actor Virgilio Talli insisted upon another production at the Teatro Olimpia in Milan, and assumed its direction. This was the first of several successful cooperative ventures between the famous actor and Chiarelli. By the end of 1918 Chiarelli had founded the troupe Ars Italica, and entrusted its artistic direction to Talli; Goldoni's *La Locandiera* and Morselli's *Glauco* were staged. In 1921 Chiarelli organized another company, Comoedia, which presented *The Merry Wives of Windsor*. Two years later while continuing his activity as playwright he also joined the *Corriere Italiano* as a drama critic. He was instrumental in proposing the establishment of a state theatre at the First National Congress of the Theatre (1924). As president of the Playwrights Union (Sindacato Autori Drammatici) Chiarelli exerted a great deal of influence within and outside Italy; indeed his commitment to the theater continued until the last years of his life.

Aside from his plays Chiarelli also wrote short stories and essays, and translated a number of works from Latin, English, French, Spanish, including Plautus' *Aulularia* and *Menaechmi*, Shakespeare's *The Merry Wives of Windsor*, Mauriac's *Asmodée*, and Zorrilla's *Don Juan Tenorio*. He regularly reviewed films for the Roman daily *Il Tempo*. Chiarelli also enjoyed some success as a painter. He died in Rome on December 20, 1947.[1]

LUIGI ANTONELLI (1877–1942)

If Chiarelli begins the process of grotesque theater with an *a priori* distortion of reality, Antonelli moves further away from literalness and through the visionary power of his imagination advances into a novel way of representing reality on stage with the many phases/faces of our respective Self. So the role of the single character and even the action in the play can become negligible as the author deals with time as an endless succession of moments and as dissolution of the single existential experiences. As a result, the action gets broken into a series of brief events, and characters are hardly developed before they are reabsorbed by the totality of life in art; directing and commenting on the play, by allowing himself to stop it, begin again, backtrack or preannounce it at the right moment, the stage director becomes the "poetic voice" of the work of art. Also, by overlapping life and death (something already tried by Chiarelli with Savina's simulated murder), and giving a sense of uselessness and blindness of human beings who hardly learn from their mistakes, Antonelli seems to be a forerunner of much intellectual and artistic life of the twentieth-century, and one example of such literature can be found in Thornton Wilder's *Our Town*.

Antonelli defines the main points of his art in a "confession" for his audience:

> My theater deals with the conflict between illusion and reality in the fantastic mode, and that fits perfectly my nature as a writer. I see the theater as an over-all compound of drama, comedy, farce and the lyrical. I enjoy merging all these elements because, after all, the same thing happens in life. I have often made use of such elements of the fantastic as a point of departure in order to reach my own conclusions. And I have done so to broaden the significance of that situation and to give it a dose of dramatic tension and a wider appeal. . . . I insist that what takes place onstage must go beyond the physical confines of the scene. The small event must open up the world to the eyes of spectators. The significance and effect of my drama must be magnified by the imagination.

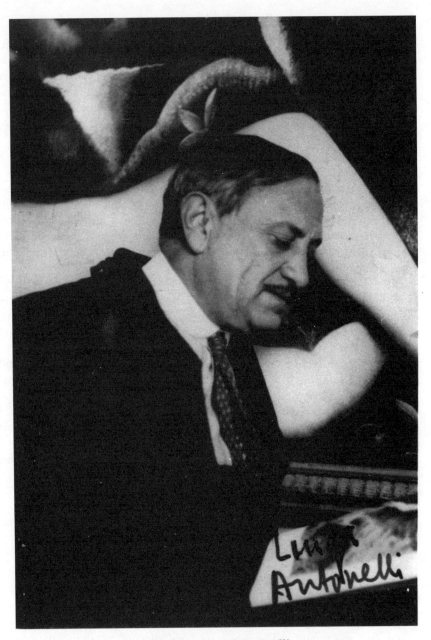

Portrait of Luigi Antonelli

[Il mio è teatro dell'umorismo fantastico, e risponde perfettamente alla mia natura di scrittore. Vedo il teatro come un insieme di dramma, di commedia, di farsa, di lirico; a me piace fondere tutti questi elementi perchè la stessa cosa infine avviene nella vita. Spesso mi sono servito di elementi fantastici come punto di partenza per arrivare alle mie conclusioni. E l'ho fatto per allargare il significato della mia vicenda e darle un'ansietà e un più vasto respiro . . . Io voglio che l'azione teatrale sia più vasta del suo arco scenico. La piccola vicenda deve aprire un mondo dinanzi agli occhi degli spettatori. La significazione del mio dramma deve essere ingrandita dalla fantasia.][2]

A Man Confronts Himself

The premiere of *A Man Confronts Himself* occurred on 23 May 1918, at the Olympia Theater in Milan, with great success. The play, defined by the author as a "fantastic adventure" in three acts, offers a subtly ironic reflection of our wretched human condition. Its central theme deals with the attempt to recreate or confront one's past in order to go on with one's life. The plot centers around the dilemma of an older man who is allowed to relive his youth, but will soon discover that life can hardly be fashioned according to his wishes, and that what he eventually finds out doesn't really help him that much, although it may be valuable to others as a general statement on human nature, considering that one of the essential components of modern psychology, from Freud down, is the analysis of one's past in order to shed light on old wounds that may be festering there.

The initial description of the backdrop stresses, immediately and in unequivocal terms, a radical departure from any traditional or realistic setting: "Unreal landscape, marked with synthetic crudeness and characterized by violet-colored cypresses, which give the scene a violent aspect and set the tone for a fairy tale nightmare." Here the expressionistic context, dealing with distortion of form, color, and space, seems to aim at the destruction of external reality to cut quickly to the truth or emotional essence of the matter. Does the figurative backdrop suggest that this is a representation? That we are living in a fictional world? Where are we, anyway? What is the plot? Who is involved?

At age forty-five, in the prime (or the end?) of his life, Luciano de Garbines loses his memory in a shipwreck, regains it after two months, and thus lands, as in a dream, on an island—a strange, mysterious island "outside the bounds of geography." (There are no hotels here, you are either a visitor to or an employee of the island, which is privately owned by a certain Dr. Climt.) Is the island to be seen as a stage (theater itself) or simply as the world at large? As a visitor (or spectator?) Luciano's behavior seems inexplicable: He has no idea how or why he got to the place, except that he was rescued on board a sinking ship, following in the footsteps of all the shipwrecked visi-

Front cover of the theater journal "Il dramma," with Antonelli referring to his masterpiece *L'uomo che incontrò se stesso (A Man Confronts Himself)*.

tors who ever landed here, inductees in need of epiphany or enlightenment (catharsis?) or simply hapless characters imprisoned in their ambivalence and unresolved conflicts. Or does the visitor/outsider represent man's obscure and ominous double, that unconscious part of his self that is unacceptable to the rest of society?

Yet Luciano still manages to maintain a certain degree of normalcy in a strange environment. He will soon discover that, indeed, Climt is not just the owner, but the all-powerful master on a different level of reality, a magician in control of his environment, who created this island "as a marvelous piece of fiction between immortality and farce," who deals with the likes of people as a child plays with toys. Before his visit with Climt, Luciano meets a beautiful but somewhat crazy (folle), young lady, Rosetta, who warns him: Dr. Climt is very dangerous, he could easily have Luciano embalmed (read: will turn him into a puppet!?). Beautiful Rosetta happens to be an ultracentenarian. Interesting here is the way in which Antonelli develops and twists the myth of the feminine fear of aging and eventually resolves Rosetta's case in a totally unexpected way. Climt had heard her lamenting that she would grow old in time and endowed her with eternal youth (an improved version, one might think, of the myth of the Sibyl who asked for immortality but forgot to ask for youth, so she was immortally old). Hence, what appeared to be a beautiful gift soon turned into an atrocious torment, "because my life no longer holds any excitement," Rosetta explains. "Could you love a statue? Nobody loves me. None of my friends can stand my eternity."

Celebrating a return to mortality seems to defy the laws of logic, but confirms as well the island's nature "between immortality and farce," as Antonelli satirizes the fickleness of human beings, who never learn from life, while paving the way for Luciano's confession and eventual repetition of mistakes just like Rosetta's. She is indeed a charming and dangerous character, whose episode could serve as a key to understand the play. Through her disquisitions she manages to displace the logical by the unexpected, which gives way to the incoherent, the irresponsible, the ridiculous—in short, the absurd. But her wisecracks also carry ironic and allusive references, a double meaning, that blur the line between levels of reality, the literal and the figurative, the comic and the tragic. Ultimately, we get the message that the world is not what it appears to be, that it is governed by something that eludes the logic of the moment, that it is being manipulated, that new values and new myths are in the making.

Eventually Luciano is relieved to meet Climt, the affable scientist who has made a startling discovery: he can replace death by eternal youth. So Luciano has ended up on the island all right, but does he truly believe that the place belongs to the real world? Indeed, Rosetta had concluded that "if Climt could do good he would be like God, assuming of course that God can do good." Her conclusion implies a Nietzschean influence in its rejection of traditional values and traditional belief systems in God and a call for a transvaluation of values on the part of humankind. It is obvious that Antonelli, like Nietzsche, is satirizing a bourgeois world where respectability has become the only value. Also, given Rosetta's words about Climt and God, it may be worth mentioning here Nietzsche's understanding of Man as God's co-creator, hence his call for man to create new worlds and new realities. So, how does an author imitate God's creativity when he creates his artistic world?

Climt, indeed, is operating at a level of inner reality. As the impeccable puppeteer who pulls the strings of the action, he diligently gets down to removing Luciano from contingent reality, and in fact suspends time by showing that all watches have stopped and telling Luciano that a watch is no longer necessary. Time and timelessness: as Eliot says, "To be conscious is not to be in time." Further indication of such inner reality is given in Climt's own words, when on this island we meet, for example, "survivors of great tragedies. Queens, poets, murderers of passion, men driven by curiosity about the future, vagabonds who looked like kings, kings disguised as vagabonds, all of those shipwrecked people picked up by my men on the high seas have been reconciled to their dreams by Dr. Climt."

But what is Luciano's dream? Luciano confesses that he is chasing his own past: an old-fashioned, innocent happiness he had enjoyed before an earthquake killed his wife, Sonia, who was eventually found under the ruins in nightclothes, clasped in the arms of his best friend, Rambaldo. Her loss and the discovery of her betrayal have tormented Luciano for twenty years. Ever since, he has been racked by soul-shattering queries: "What did I really know about her?" He still feels deeply the tearing and unsuppressable need to go back in time, to pin down the moment in which the mistake was made and what he should have done to avoid it: a recurring, tormenting idea, a fixation. The stranger may be providing a suitably Freudian interpretation of his existence: "You understand now, Dr. Climt, the pain that is still tearing me apart inside! Sometimes when I wander distractedly down the street in search of my youth, I find it headed hastily toward the same old mistakes . . . as I run after my youth, panting somewhat, with my eyes bulging and my heart pounding." From these words we have a premonition of what will happen to Luciano in the process of reliving his existence (and we detect the changing view toward adultery as it was first presented in *The Mask*).

The puppeteer Climt reassures Luciano that his dream will be fulfilled: soon he will meet his own past; he will encounter his self of twenty years ago, along with his young wife, Sonia, his mother-in-law, Mrs. Speranza, his friend Rambaldo . . . and feel the same emotions experienced then. Here they come in fact, in the brilliant sunlight of the enchanting isle, young

Luciano and the others, who are introduced by Climt to old Luciano under the name of Gregory, "a millionaire, illustrious scientist, bachelor, my guest."

As Gregory socializes with the newly arrived visitors, he observes that young Luciano and Sonia indeed make a lovely couple, he also discovers that Mrs. Speranza (ironically hopeless character!) doesn't think much of her son-in-law, indeed, and that she—inspired by Gregory's presumed wealth, to which Climt had referred—seems to appreciate and even favor his interest in Sonia. Later, left alone with Sonia, Gregory realizes that she is quite different from what he knew, or thought he knew, of her: a coquette, interested, available, experienced. Their surreptitious encounter turns into a strange kind of courtship in which his carnal desire struggles with his hope that she will reject him and prove to be a worthy woman. On the contrary, she is very much attracted to this experienced old man. She is candid and provocative: "We notice instinctively when a man is an expert in feminine sexuality, and so we approach him more frankly . . ." Sure enough, Sonia and Gregory are unable to restrain the latent forces that harken back to our animal roots, and engage in the rituals of sexual interlude. Unfortunately, he is still left with an uncomfortable feeling of ambiguity when he asks her not to see Rambaldo any more, while her cute but frivolous retort is: "How can I promise? I never know what's going to happen to me from one day to the next!" His disappointment continues through insults such as "Coward! Coward!" and again, her comical refrain: "Sure, insult me. I like it." The dialogue consequently falls prey to an absurdly perverted wit dominated more by violence and passion than by sexuality, and slips into moments of ridiculous melodrama and pseudo-meaningful rhetoric.

As the play moves along, Old Gregory is in despair over what has taken place. Baffled and disappointed, he seeks guidance from Climt, whose response reminds us of Cirillo's answer to Paolo in *The Mask and the Face* ("You lost a wife but gained a lover"). Climt tells Gregory: "Not only did she take you as a husband twenty years ago, she is taking you again as a lover today. What else can a woman do for the same man?" By now Climt's objective has been accomplished; allowing Gregory to relive his life was like placing him in front of a mirror: The "real" identity of the self cannot be seen directly but is instead indirectly reflected through an other. As a spectator of his own and his family's performance, he has also become aware of the double life that characterized their personalities: Sonia was pretending to be faithful while carrying on an affair with Rambaldo, who in turn pretended to be his friend just to mess around with Sonia, while Mrs. Speranza claimed to be a woman of irreproachable moral character but was condoning her daughter's relationship behind the back of her son-in-law. There was, on the one hand, a true reality (the face) and, on the other, a different reality, believed by him and played out by others (the mask).

Despite his second lesson, Gregory is still unable to learn from experience, to distinguish between appearance and reality, and to understand that it is not always advisable to separate the face from the mask (the fact that they are in antithesis may not mean there is no interaction) in order to protect the multiple nature of our own selves. So by now he is being branded a madman, even by Sonia, and he does not dispute her claim as he becomes conscious of his double failure, which excludes him from the game of life: being in love with a woman by whom he would love to be rejected and looking forward to a future that belongs entirely to the past, unable to do anything but meet Luciano and tell him to watch his wife and his best friend. At first Luciano reacts violently to such a suggestion, but then he begins to look at the stranger more sympathetically, as Gregory accepts—so to speak—the challenge to prove his point: "I agree to be a madman until we have established whether I am a madman for warning you about the danger you run, or whether you are a madman for not listening to me." And Gregory warns him that, within half an hour, on the same spot, Sonia will meet Rambaldo; and he—Luciano—hiding behind a hedge, can personally see proof of their betrayal. Luciano agrees, but Sonia has overheard their conversation and accordingly can manage to foil such a plan. Also, she takes full advantage of the unusual situation ruthlessly to play the part of the faithful wife totally trusted by the man she loves. As a result, not only will Luciano undergo the same betrayal by Sonia as Gregory endured twenty years before, but—ironically—Luciano will even thank Gregory for having tested Sonia: "I thank you, sir . . . for having gotten me to listen to this conversation . . . because by sheer coincidence you have been able to offer the best proof of the one thing about which I was sure even before. . . . I mean, sir, the purity, the innocence, the nobility of my wife!"

Once more, truth can be manipulated, perverted, turned into a farcical play of illusion. Although Gregory doesn't give up and reveals to Luciano that Sonia made love with him right there on the island, it's too late for his revelation to become credible. Luciano doesn't want to hear anything, by now he is convinced that Gregory is a madman, whereas Gregory makes no attempt to strip off the mask being imposed upon him: "You don't believe me? You don't believe me because I am a madman . . . Since you're leaving, and I won't see you again, listen to the last word of a madman. Do you know who I am?" Luciano: "A poor wretch." Gregory: "Maybe. But you know that you and I are the same thing." Luciano: "Ah ! No ! Let's not play games! I am a respectable person! *(He leaves.)*"

Gregory is left alone, while his twenty-five-year-old self hurtles unresisting toward his own freedom in life. The conflict between Luciano and Gregory in fact presents the difference between life and art, time and timelessness. The events of life can hardly be anticipated or even stopped because life is a continuous stream of possibilities, flux, illusions, even traps set for the unaware and inexperienced. So Gregory's words can carry no meaning for young Luciano until *after* he has had his own concrete experiences with things. Real knowledge comes with experience, and from it consciousness is derived. For that precise reason Luciano cannot identify with Gregory, an existential victim of the games people play. As Giorgio Pullini points out, Gregory is a victim of his inability to defend himself, which results from his inability to assume those masklike attitudes and expressions we need to be continuously readjusting to protect ourselves from revealing our innermost feelings or the moods of our personalities. In order to survive in the jungle of human society, one must have the same ability and the same weapons that others use. Gregory's good nature is another dirty trick played on him by Mother Nature, as it does not protect him from pain and heartache (Pullini, 292). He certainly lacks what Paolo learned in *The Mask and the Face*, which is the necessity of using both the mask and the face as protection against others and as a way to regain the love of his wife. Instead, Gregory's inaction brings him back to the point where he began. He has gone full circle in his own immobility. The only difference now is his full awareness of life's duplicity. "A horrible laugh shakes him." He falls on the stage. "A mocking horselaugh that slowly turns into a desperate sob." We can assume that his life is pinned in the form of consciousness.

The fictional world thus created, the world of mad characters like Rosetta "crazy," of the island referred to as "one big crazy asylum," and the rest of the folks "an asylum of gracious madmen and you, Dr. Climt, the most conspicuous of all," the fictional world of which Gregory has become an integral part is now a fitting refuge from the reality of a life where he would remain a stranger, an exile. References to and images of madness form a common thread that runs through the play. Although not stated, the implication is that Gregory will find in madness and in a fictional, static past a necessary and convenient evasion. The theme of insanity of course is closely identified with Pirandello. To be sure, Gregory is cast after and perhaps modeled on Signora Frola and Signor Ponza of *It is So (if You Think So)*, but his lot as an abnormal madman is quite different and more tragic than the other two. As a divided, isolated self, Gregory is a close relative of Rosso's puppets and a forerunner of the schizoid emperor in *Henry IV*. To conclude, we need to stress a marked difference between Chiarelli's and Antonelli's work: in the first case, we have a drama of revolt against societal conventions; in the second, the author concentrates on the disintegration of personality in a drama of existential revolt, set against the absurdities of a civilization fast approaching the cycle when, according to Vico, everyone goes crazy.

Other Works by Antonelli

A man of great intellectual curiosity, Antonelli produced poetry and a wide variety of plays, while working as actor, stage director, entrepreneur and journalist. *A Man Confronts Himself* won him wide critical attention and eased his entry into the ranks of acclaimed playwrights, as this play sets the tone and the pace for a number of other significant works that searched for the new and the contemporary, both in aesthetic terms and in stage design. As a result, Antonelli had developed a bold new style where reality and fantasy, reason and the absurd combine to give a personal impulse to the theater of revolt in a "fantastic mode." In addition to *A Man Confronts Himself*, often labeled as a drama of those who wish to regain youth, Antonelli later produced *La bottega dei sogni (The Dream Shop)*, a drama of those who want to recapture illusion, and *La rosa dei venti (The Weathervane)*, a drama of those who hope to recreate public opinion. These plays constitute a trilogy of his grotesque.In 1919 he staged another play, *La fiaba dei tre maghi (The Fairy Tale of the Three Magicians)*, under the artistic direction of Virgilio Talli at the Teatro Carignano in Turin. From this point on, Antonelli's writings, much in demand, are published consistently in Lettura, Il Dramma, Comoedia and other avant-garde journals that contribute to the flow of ideas and to the circulation of theatrical works focusing on current disquietude and critical of the inability to change and understand the contemporary world. In another masterpiece, *La casa a tre piani (A Three-Story House)*, Antonelli opens up toward a European ambiance set between the visionary power of Maeterlinck and the violence of Strindberg (1924).

Soon thereafter Antonelli published *Il dramma, la commedia, la farsa (Drama, Comedy, and Farce)*, a satire of nineteenth-century theatrical practice. *Il maestro (The Teacher)* can be justly regarded as a high expression of his art and career, a unique work of naturalistic background yet brilliantly developed around the ambiguity of the theater within the theater, staged under the extraordinary direction of Luigi Pirandello, with a major role by Marta Abba.

Antonelli cultivated his fascination with theater to the very end of his life, as he parodied a world where the sublime and the preposterous are mixed together. His plays are still à la mode and being staged in the best world theaters.

Biographical Note

Luigi Antonelli was born at Castilenti (Teramo) on 22 January 1877. He began his theater experience early in school plays: in those days one of his classmates was Luigi Tonelli, the future author of a history of drama. Antonelli studied medicine and the humanities at the University of Flo-

Photo of Luigi Pirandello, Luigi Antonelli, and Marta Abba; stage director, author, and interpreter of *The Teacher***, at Teatro Argentina in Rome on 19 December 1933.**

rence, but quickly turned to journalism as a drama critic and to the writing of one-act plays. While serving as a correspondent for an overseas publication, he managed to visit and live in Argentina for a number of years. Upon his return in 1914, Antonelli settled in Milan where he became deeply involved with theater, poetry, and the general debate about the renewal of the Italian stage. He began to write and stage one-act and three-act plays which led to the successful production of *A Man Confronts Himself* in 1918 and the beginning of his fame. Later, the playwright took Maria Cascella as his second bride and a daughter named Grazia was born in 1924, the second of his three children. A return to his birthplace also prompted a rearrangement of D'Annunzio's *La figlia di Iorio* in the local dialect, staged in Pescara under his direction. By now he enjoyed a significant influence over the national theater and attracted the best actors and directors to stage his plays.

Around 1925 Antonelli had moved to Rome, a city teeming with new theatrical companies as well as ideas and discussions about the new experimental theater. He felt at home here. From 1931 on, he regularly contributed a commentary on theater to the daily *Giornale d'Italia*. As of 1932, he established a new theater club called "La baracca e i burattini" (The Playhouse and the Puppets) that sought innovations in ideas, sets, and production for the stage. As he retired in Pescara, Antonelli cultivated his fascination with one-act plays to the very end of his life. He tells us that his final act—last will and testament—was his selection of a burial plot overlooking the shores of his beloved Pescara, where he could relish the whistle of the train and the roar of the sea because, as he claimed, "it's not true that the dead can't hear." He died on 21 November 1942.

ENRICO CAVACCHIOLI (1885–1954)

The Bird of Paradise and Metatheater

Given the outcome of *A Man Confronts Himself*, a few key questions may be appropriate as we undertake the reading of the third play, *The Bird of Paradise* by Cavacchioli, long-standing questions that would go all the way back to Plato: Is the work of art in the author's mind as the cosmos is in God's mind before creation? Does the work change as it is made? Even more to the point, do the author and the reader change at the end of the work? Does the fact that this is an evolutionary cosmos teach us something about the nature of the self? Hence, paradoxically, can a play such as this one help the reader meet one's authentic self? Hence the urgent need for new myths and paradigms to apprehend reality. Be that as it may, such questions will make the reader more aware of how existentially modern these plays are, and how even theoretical questions of theater and stage remain fundamentally coherent to a philosophy of life.

Enrico Cavacchioli came to the theater after an early experiment with the futurist movement, of which he was a charter member along with Filippo T. Marinetti. That background is manifest in his early poetry as well as in a number of his plays, including *The Bird of Paradise* which completes an important first cycle of grotesque drama and poetics.[3] This particular work, written as a "confession in three acts" in 1918 and staged at the Teatro Carignano in Turin on 19 March 1919, is widely regarded as the most important play by Enrico Cavacchioli. It deals with a theme of anguish and frustration over the mechanical nature of its characters or a tragically farcical theater where the split between life and art is dramatized by the introduction of a symbolic intruder referred to as *Him*, who places all the others on trial. Eventually *Him* concedes his failure to introduce them to the magic world of art and to give purpose and form to the existence of such characters who are thus reduced, by his assessment, to the condition of human puppets. To register his disapproval he withdraws into a world of his own, and for him the performance is over, while the characters carry on the play at the existential level only to confirm their interpretation or preconceived notions of what it's supposed to be. Therefore we shall see how Cavacchioli begins to bring forth on stage some of the same theoretical concerns about art and life even before they are pursued and elaborated by Pirandello in his *theater within the theater*.

As the curtain rises, we view the study of a distinguished ornithologist, Giovanni Ardeo, a sullen hall crowded with books and collections of stuffed birds, glass cases and people who are as mummified as the animals they embalm. We meet some colleagues of the scientist, visiting him during a science congress. From the comments of this first group we learn much about them and their host; a gossipy society, these conventioners are equally entrapped by social conventions and prejudice as they are given to a peculiar view of science as something ossified by imitation. Ardeo himself is referred to by a colleague as a "strange character, stuffed behind the display of his eyeglasses." These folks bring to mind the stock masks of commedia dell'arte and patterns of ancient Greek comedy. As members of a professional society, they are in character with what we might call *poseurs*, people who think highly of themselves, who pretend to be wise and smart whereas they really are educated nonentities.

They inquire about and indeed intrude into Ardeo's family life. They become so curious about his marital problems that he is led to comment, in a self-deprecating, pathetic tone: "I ended up being happy with the solitude that grew out of my suffering." This invasion of privacy must be seen as a first attempt to strip off the mask from Ardeo's face. His socially oriented wife, Anna Corelli, has left the household, rebelling against the stuffy environment of her methodical husband, who feels betrayed, whereas she is romantically searching for a great, true love. Anna periodically visits their daughter Donatella in Ardeo's house, always with a different lover in tow: there is a marked contrast between her freewheeling life and that of her husband, who is completely immersed in his work. During one such visit, we are introduced to an unassuming escort whom Anna calls "my aspiring porter"; this nameless intruder, *Him*, becomes the master manipulator who pulls the various strings of the plot and explains: "Ecco dunque che con un pò di ordine costruisco" [Let me then construct (create) in some orderly fashion]. He goes on to say: "I told that dowager [referring to Anna]: Take your child back with you! Donatella, the delight of our soul!", and later tells us that the whole plot can be easily anticipated, because "a prophecy is the distillation of logic" (in polemical reference to the theater of the immediate past?).

In fact, as *Him* has predicted, following a stormy encounter with Giovanni, Anna does decide to take Donatella away from her husband. But here the complications begin. Things are not what they appear to be. Anna's apparent self-assurance masks the strain of an unrequited and jealous love for a licentious man, Mimotte. Her suffering becomes intolerable when Mimotte announces that he wants to break off the relationship because he is in love with young Donatella. Though Anna manages to keep her lover away from Donatella, who has no idea of her mother's affair with Mimotte, she is nevertheless unable to free herself from feelings of rejection and despair and a sense of loss and loneliness. Donatella goes through her own baptism by fire, as she is shocked by the revelation and her first disillusionment. Lastly our dissolute Mimotte is swept along in a whirlwind of passion—first enmeshed in the vagaries of Anna and then dazzled by the innocent beauty of Donatella. So, this part of the cast can be characterized as victims of the habits and passions that erode the fibers of existence. They are sufferers, or *pharmakoi*, that is, incapable of controlling their feelings and desires with a dignified sense of moderation, and unaware of their masks or hidden secrets.

Now what about *Him*? Cavacchioli drops among his characters this symbolic intruder, who is more than a *raisonneur* like Cirillo (Chiarelli) or the magic puppeteer Climt (Antonelli), in directing the action of the play as well as harboring some strange ideas. More so than any one before, *Him*, albeit not an integral part of the intrigue, manipulates the characters like a puppeteer the strings of the action. What follows is a drama that questions and repeatedly undercuts old myths as the impulse persists to break old rules and find new forms that more accurately reflect a changing world and contemporary aesthetics. As an ironical type, the *eiron* of ancient comedy, *Him* confronts, prods, mocks (the cast), while masking his cleverness under the guise of a strange, peculiar chap. He is the ironist at work.

Yet, in the prefatory note to the first act, the playwright stresses the importance of such character: "This stage setting revolves around *Him*," and goes on to define his nature: "an unreal, philosophical, abstract character. A old centenarian. His body lives on. His spirit has a life beyond. His head is cadaverous. But his behavior is still youthful, impeccable, very elegant. The tone of his voice—ironic, sharp, pleasing—is made of contrasts: slow and deep, or thin and unevenly high-pitched. He is a braggart, a mocker, a demon. Only in the third act does he reach a tragic pitch, but after having reached the highest intensity he falls back on his impassive and arrogant mask." Obviously this introduction is an attempt to emphasize a level of philosophical or higher reality, the wisdom of the seer or cocreator who acts on various situations, "predisposes" people and seeks to turn things around. He represents a separate entity, an individual of superior intellect, who asks questions and simulates ignorance as a way to extract answers (by dialectical means) in a world not used to believe in anything beyond one's own immediate experience. Thus, the *raisonneur* or puppeteer here becomes even more clearly the spokesman for the dramatist, who operates in the abstract, or the artist in action.

From time to time, *Him* gives us glimpses of what he does: "I crisscross life like the threads of a skein, till the skein becomes tangled." Being imbued with philosophical relativism, he moves from the premise that truth is multifaceted, that is, subjective, relative, pluralistic; there are as many truths as there are people: "Because truth is not, but is made," that nothing is certain and therefore not worth taking seriously ("I don't rush impulsively because I have no ideals to defend. I have no remorse because I have no virtue to follow. I don't swear because I don't believe. All I do is produce life . . ."). *Him* sets thus an ironic philosophical distance from existential realities and gives from time to time clues about his Pirandellian ideology. Such clues recur in the play with some consistency as when, referring to Anna's inner contradictions, *Him* will say that she is "Ready to believe anyone and with an objectivity that's downright repulsive! That's why she's the protagonist of the most delightful live novel that I've ever produced. For those who do not know it, I have a weakness for literature in action. It's just that I hate newsprint." And later he will add: "I represent the four stages of cadaverous putrefaction of feelings. I stand before you, and you see me sometimes at the green stage, sometimes at the gaseous or skeletal stage, at the mercy of the eight light migrations of insects that someday, God willing, will wear out even your own honorable carcasses."

We have said that the rest of the cast is made up of victims, the sufferers still engaged in building their experiences and exploring their unknown secrets; they could be called also realistic characters, Anna, Donatella, Mimotte, and we might include Giovanni (Ardeo) although he has been all along in his own artistic realm. They all pursue, each in their own way, an ideal they believe, mistakenly or not, they can achieve or have achieved. An indication of their differing notions is provided by the scene in which Ardeo, who has found his own peace of mind in having become a perfectly methodical man, explains the title of the play by expounding on the traits of the bird of paradise: "People had thought about the strangeness of this 'bird of paradise' condemned from its origin never to alight and always to fly . . . myth of eternal restlessness," a characterization of the bird that seems to reflect perfectly Anna's character and lifestyle, which are certainly not acceptable to Ardeo, for whom all that is a lot of nonsense accumulated from science fiction. Ardeo tells us: "In truth, of the whole pack of lies so lightly assembled about this creature, the only accurate fact is that it lives isolated and haughty. And under the blows of hurricanes, whipped by rain and tossed by wind, it rises in a vertical course and darts out of the inclement zone toward the calmer regions of the skies—above the storm." While this second description of the "paradise" fits, rather, Ardeo's own views and way of life, it becomes signicant as it proves once more how such varied interpretations of myth bring about differing attitudes and values, with the ensuing result that, as Gigi Livio tells us, both lifestyles and ideals will clash and be proven inept in their existential struggles (78);[4] furthermore, we shall see how the split that developed between Anna and Giovanni comes down to a conflict between life and art. Anna's ideals and pride will be also totally shaken in an unsatisfactory dialogue with Mimotte, her young and beautiful lover, during which the woman is trying to salvage a hopeless relationship, while Mimotte's calculated and cruel answer is, "Did you think I would be tied forever to the vice that wears you out ? . . . I made myself the thickest mask but I'm tearing it off. My face is cheap. . . . I am an adventurer without a future."

Yet, even Mimotte's psyche is getting eroded. He becomes a pathetic character and as a result makes only a weak attempt to win Donatella. The dialogue at the end of the second act between him and Donatella, seemingly taking place through a wall near the canopy with *Him* as mediator, becomes a peculiar setting, in fact a symbolic theatrical device, reminiscent of the Greek concept of fate, a hidden presence and yet all powerful as a mouthpiece for the author. Cavacchioli may also be making skillful use of the setting as an attempt to destroy the fourth wall, that is, the barrier separating the reality of stage characters from that of the audience. And what effect does it have? Mimotte is made an object of ridicule, henceforth a helpless victim under cross-examination from *Him* who has referred to the practice above as popular theater. By the same token we can see the classical oracular myth of the inspired seer, benevolently passing on his revelation to the world, here being undermined and reversed: *Him* had divined in the first place the natural love between Donatella and Mimotte, but then the relationship is quickly nipped in the bud. Other myths about love and family are shaken as well. For instance, we are not convinced by Anna's attempt to reaffirm, frustrated as she is in her womanly pride, the ideal of motherly love, while in reality she has been her daughter's rival. As for Ardeo, whose apparent rigidity can be equally deceiving, he stands for the misunderstood idealist everyone picks on, who has lived all along in a world of artistic concerns and, as a result, totally uninvolved and unprepared to respond to his family needs. Actually, none of these folks learn much as they come to grips with their existential woes. They simply remain intrepidly set in their unresolved conflicts. So *Him* can justifiably conclude, having tried in vain to stir up each character, as it is most fitting: "That's it. The story has come to an end. It's necessary to change the subject because catastrophe is near and the knot is untied. I made every effort to infuse a soul into all these puppets, and all I could squeeze out of them was words—a false love, false maternal compassion, male egotism, a few violent little quarrels. But nothing that would get even two centimeters off the ground."

This mocking, ironic comment theorizes on the passive, mechanical nature of the characters while it formulates the poetics of Cavacchioli: people are mere puppets incapable of true and deep feelings, lost creatures with lost ideals and, worse yet, unable to create new ones. It's a commentary on society but especially on theater; the advent of *Him* on stage as a conscious spokesman for the author gives a clear signal of departure from past tradition. Unlike the chorus/coripheus of ancient classical drama, in this play *Him* dramatizes the encounter/confrontation with different types of characters, set in their own ways and therefore unable to represent a theater that should produce or invent and express the multifarious feelings, emotions, experiences, and aspects of life. For Cavacchioli a representation which lends its artistic flavor, force, and depth to the human dimension cannot ignore that characters and situations are continuously evolving, and what really matters to the stage is that magic moment never quite so easily defined and constantly changing.

Not by coincidence even some of the titles given by Cavacchioli and others to their works suggest (polemically) mechanical devices which translate into oversimplifications and even distortions: masks, puppets, mannequins, tools, even a Pinocchio in love is still a piece of pine—a whole series of cases which prompt Cavacchioli to declare: we just keep on simulating, on acting out our parts, until he concludes: "I have been unable to give a soul [feelings] to those puppets [actors]" and he stops right here. Hence the dismissal of the characters and the unraveling of the plot. Thus the figure of *Him* becomes emblematic of Cavacchioli's polemics in so far as his presence on stage is to show how easily he can anticipate and therefore expose what the action of the other characters is going to be, thereby seeing the essence of the creative process in the theatrical experience shattered. Needless to say, we are now in the midst of a developing consciousness by which stage representation no longer holds to the idea of an objective imitation of reality but stresses instead the many and multifaceted fictions of life and art, the contrast between character and actor, life which does not tolerate theatrical abstractions or (the paradox of) art being more real than life (because art does not change), in short Cavacchioli advances and tackles in this play some of the problems that Pirandello will elaborate in his *theater within the theater* (plays such as *Six Characters in Search of an Author, Tonight We Improvise, Each in His Own Way*), but had dealt with in his earlier theoretical work *On Humor*.

Regarding the title of the play: through the myth of this splendid animal first brought to Europe as a stuffed bird by the crew of Magellan's fleet, the playwright sheds some light on the necessity to wonder beyond the realities of the human condition, fraught with contrasts and woes, in order to give some coherence to the world around us. So in the fantastic and fairylike atmosphere of the bird of paradise the allegory is transposed to construct [create] a certain ideal of life or the realm of art. While a symbol of the power of the imagination, the bird stands as a propitious omen for calm and naturalness removed from and antithetical to an existential condition obsessed by passion and antagonism. Through the soaring, visionary power of his imagination the author seeks a pathway to the world of timelessness. Cavacchioli's answer to the flux and frustrations of existential involvement is to contemplate a beautiful mythical bird in a world set "above the storm" where time is suspended: Ardeo gives clear signs of having created for himself a fixed and immutable world (of art) through the stuffed specimens of birds in his study, to which Anna refers as "carcasses garnished with feathers" while he rebuts: "how can you say that? You enter the realm of beauty, coming here," and again continuing his discussion with her:

ARDEO: Life stopped here in its very best attitudes and its most diverse manifestations . . .
ANNA: (*ironically*) Are you really sure?
ARDEO: Yes, from the moment we caught it in its shapes, colors, changes: a mixture of dream, harmony, suggestion, snatching from death everything that could survive it! . . .
ANNA: I would love to see this surviving harmony.
ARDEO: Look around you!

As Anna is left alone to face her own drama, the conflict between real life and the world of art persists with the estrangement and withdrawal of *Him* as a spokesman for the dramatist. While *Him* makes a bold attempt to generalize human life in abstract terms, he does so outside of any concrete involvement of live and real characters. Anna's own experience proceeds at the existential level of the play where her romantic urge towards freedom crumbles in the reality of life; we hear her last call for help, we feel her loss (husband, daughter, lover), and her sense of despair and terrifying emptiness. As a key figure in the drama, she becomes a pityful antihero with the only capacity to be crushed by reality or doomed, as it were, to a life of anguish and isolation. "Sì, ora sono veramente sola" [Now I am really alone] are her last words in the play.

We might say that Cavacchioli deals here with three key issues: a polemic about the old theatrical practice and the need to stress the centrality of the creative process in the theatrical experience; the fundamental question of human freedom and the relationship between self and world, a concern which all three authors share and which links their works through a common thread—starting in our case with Chiarelli's *The Mask and the Face* (individuals want to live in the most free and emancipated ways), continuing in Antonelli's *A Man Confronts Himself* (individuals cannot be free the moment they face society and its existential woes), to complete the cycle with Cavacchioli (individual freedom can be achieved only in an inner world or level of reality (art) or else defeat is inevitable); and theoretically the most important issue is the problem of the twin opposite poles of artistic creation : reality and illusion, time and timelessness, life and art. How to find a link between these twin poles is the problem of the modern dramatist, a problem underscored in *The Bird of Paradise* as *Him* spurns reality and withdraws into a world of his own invention, while the characters bring the play to an end according to their notions of what it's supposed to be. So *The Bird of Paradise* still feeds on the conflict between the ideal desires of the creator or stage director and the somber world of matter; as the drama remains divided at its core, *Him* clearly takes on an important metatheatrical function where theater comments on itself, where the comments about the play are as insightful as the play itself in our search for meaning, whether we are dealing with the trials of human personality or the identity of art. Actually, among the ancient Greeks, plays were viewed indeed as trials that would cut to the very essence of the matter through dramatic representations of human conflict. Likewise in the trial introduced by *Him*, Cavacchioli seeks to raise the audience's consciousness about the meaning and value of theater and life, and advances some of the dialectic that will be elaborated in Pirandello's theater trilogy and later production, in particular as it pertains to the problem of the absence of the creator's will operating in the characters and to the disintegration of personality defined and seen as a mirror of distorted images. Clearly, *Him* is beginning to address some of the same concerns that will be later tackled by Pirandello from *Six Characters in Search of an Author* to the end of his poliedric production. As a metaphysical rebel *Him* stresses the idea of a theater conceived as a pretext and as a platform to organize the representation, theater seen as testing ground of a work in the making, which becomes text or (the life of) art only with the concrete experience of stage performance.

It is certainly interesting that this nameless intruder *Him* as a figure for the author/director is the forerunner of another nameless protagonist, the old and famous writer identified as *** (three asterisks) in Pirandello's *When Someone is Somebody*, where the playwright is concerned about his art being pigeonholed by the public and expresses the hope that this young Someone (himself writing under a pseudonym) can eclipse the old and famous Somebody, confident as he is in the fresh creations of his dramatis personae. Not by coincidence this play and other grotesque performances contributed to the exchange of ideas and transfusion of experiences at the beginning of the century, and paved the way for the early success of Pirandello's theater and metatheater dealing with his insights about character, actor, audience, and all the arguments about his dramatic conception. Furthermore, Luigi Antonelli will stage a play in 1925—*Drama, Comedy and Farce*—dealing with metatheatrical concerns and in 1933 none other than Pirandello will take over, with the extraordinary participation of Marta Abba, the stage direction of Antonelli's *The Teacher*, a play that deals with the ambiguities of the theatrical genre as it reflects on disquietude, questions, and compromises between the will of the author and the need of the actor, styles of writing and stage directions, artistic taste and moods of the public, with all the concerns of the writer who is also actor and stage director. Be that as it may, Cavacchioli carries forward the important cycle of grotesque theater while he begins a process of metatheatrical dialectics just as the clash between the twin opposite poles of artistic creation remains wide open and sustains the longstanding conflict still at the core of modern drama.[5]

Other Works by Cavacchioli

The first phase of Cavacchioli's creative efforts consisted mainly of poetry, ranging from symbolist verse, collected in two volumes, *L'incubo velato* (*A Veiled Nightmare*, 1907) and *Le ranocchie turchine* (*Blue Frogs*, 1908), to his futurist experiments in free verse, *Cavalcando il sole* (*Riding the Sun*, 1914). Only during the postwar period did Cavacchioli bring his full attention and energy to the theater. His first significant play, *La campana d'argento* (*Silver Bell*), which presaged a shift toward grotesque theater, was staged at the

Olympia Theater in Milan. *The Bird of Paradise* followed in 1919 with much success through the renowned theater company headed by Virgilio Talli, and later in the year there was an equally successful production of a second work, *Quella che t'assomiglia (The Lady Who Resembles You)*. Subsequently, a number of other plays made their mark on stage: *Belly Dancing*, a three-act play with a wildly expressive plot (1921), *Pinocchio in Love* and *A grotesque Fairy Tale* staged by a theater company headed by playwright Dario Niccodemi (1922), *Allegory of Spring* (1923), *Miracle Court* or *The Glass Man* (1927), and *Circle of Death* (1927), all attesting to the high caliber of Cavacchioli's art and versatility as a writer for the stage, along clearly distinguishable forms of grotesque, futurism, surrealism, and strands of decadence typical of his whole generation. In addition, he published two novels, *Vamp*, a grotesque in narrative form, and *Celestial Serenade*, which contain strands of his early futurist experience. Cavacchioli exercised great influence on the Italian cultural scene, a standing that was partly diminished when he joined the Fascist Party in 1926. Yet, his commitment and contributions to the stage, scholarly journals and popular magazines continued unabated during and after the fascist period.

Biographical Note

Enrico Cavacchioli was born on 15 March 1885, at Pozzallo in the province of Ragusa, Sicily, the same year that Ezra Pound came to the world. Cavacchioli had written already a number of lyrics by the time his family moved to Milan in 1905, where he continued his studies and managed to become introduced into avantgarde literary circles and the world of journalism. Cavacchioli's quick adjustment to the new environment and his successful career remind us of the pattern set by other Sicilian writers such as Verga, Capuana, and De Roberto. During the 1906 and 1907 period Cavacchioli joined the futurist movement and, under the auspices of that group, later published two collections of poetry. But his involvement with the theater would not be long delayed. As early as 1909 a three-act play, *I corsari (The Buccaneers)* and a second one-act play were staged, while he signed along with Marinetti and others the *Manifesto of Futurist Playwrights* (1911). These activities constituted the beginning of a long association with various literary journals and daily newspapers, including *Il Secolo*, by way of articles and interviews as a drama critic. In fact, his third and last verse collection in the futurist vein, *Cavalcando il sole (Riding the Sun)*, was published in 1914. He would turn now his full attention to the theater, for four uninterrupted decades of activities. His first significant play, *La campana d'argento (A Silver Bell)*, which presaged a shift toward grotesque theater, was staged at the Olympia Theater in Milan, followed by *The Bird of Paradise*, and a vast repertoire of plays, great actors, directors and famous theaters. He belonged to the Executive Council of the National Association of Authors (and eventually Publishers, future copyright office), became in 1928 a director of *Comoedia*, a prestigious bimonthly theater magazine published by Mondadori, and directed, from 1934 on, a popular magazine, *L'illustrazione italiana*, as well as a number of other local periodicals. He died on 4 January 1954.

NOTES

1. This introduction appeared in *Connecticut Review* 7, no. 2 (1974). For Chiarelli and the *grotteschi* see also the *Dictionary of Italian Literature*, edited by Peter Bondanella and Julia Conaway (Westport, Conn.: Greenwood Press, 1979), and the *Columbia Dictionary of Modern European Literature*, article by Olga Ragusa (N.Y.: 1980) Under "Italy," see *The Reader's Encyclopedia of World Drama* edited by John Gasner (1969), and the *Oxford Companion to the Theater* (1951), 407–8. All translations from Italian texts are my own.

2. "Lo scrittore si confessa," Teatro Università, 1943, 270–71, quoted by Giorgio Pullini, 289.

3. On this aspect of Cavacchioli's production, see M. Guglieminetti, "Dal futurismo al 'grottesco': Enrico Cavacchioli," *La contestazione del reale* (Napoli: Liguori, 1974).

4. Gigi Livio, "Esplode l'avanguardia nel grande teatro: il grottesco", *Il teatro in rivolta* (Milano: Mursia, 1976).

5. For basic information and orientation I have benefited as well from Giorgio Pullini, *Teatro italiano tra due secoli* (Firenze: Parenti, 1958); Luigi Ferrante, *Teatro italiano grottesco* (Bologna: Cappelli, 1964); and Giancarlo Sammartano's introduction to Cavacchioli's Works (Roma: Bulzoni, 1990).

Selected Bibliography on Chiarelli, Antonelli, Cavacchioli, and Twentieth-Century Grotesque

Antonini, Giacomo. *Il teatro contemporaeo italiano*. Milano: Corbaccio, 1927. 105–24.

Antonucci, Giovanni. *Storia del teatro italiano del Novecento*. Roma: Studium, 1988.

Bakhtin, M. *Literatur und Karneval*. Munchen: Carl Hanser, 1969.

Barasch, Frances K. *The Grotesque: a Study in Meanings*. The Hague: Mouton, 1970.

Bevilacqua, Giuseppe. "Essere" (review). *Il Dramma*, 77 (15 gennaio 1949).

Calendoli, G. *La suggestione del Grottesco*. Padova: Delta Tre, 1976.

———. "Chiarelli." *Enciclopedia dello Spettacolo*, vol. 3.

Casella, A. "Furono soltanto due gli autentici grotteschi." *Scenario* 11 (1953).

Chiarelli, Luigi. *La mashera e il volto e altri drammi rappresentati (1916–1918)*, a cura di G. Sammartano. Roma: Bulzoni, 1988.

———. "Ricordi e progetti," *Maschere* 1 (1945).

———. "Anticipo alle mie memorie," *Il Dramma* 53 (15 gennaio 1948).

Curato, Baldo. *Sessant'anni di teatro in Italia*. Milano: Denti. 237ff.

D'Amico, Silvio. *Il teatro dei fantocci*. Firenze (1920): 5–133.

———. *Il teatro italiano*. Vo. 1. Milano: Treves, 1933.15–61.

Eifler, M. Thomas Mann. *Das Groteske in drei Parodien.*. Bonn: Bouvier, 1970.

Ferrante, Luigi. *Teatro italiano grottesco*. Bologna: Cappelli, 1964.

Firth, F. "The Mask as Face and the Face as Mask: Some of Pirandello's Variations on the Theme of Personal Appearance." *YBPS* 2 (1982): 1–27.

Forlani, M. "Futurismo, grottesco, varietà." *Tes.* 12 (1986): 68–91.

Gassner, John. Chapter 12 of *Masters of the Drama*. New York: Random House, 1940. 434ff.

Gobetti, P. *Opera critica*. Torino 2 (1927): 156–68.

Gramsci, Antonio. *Letteratura e vita nazionale*. Torino (1950). 286ff., 376ff.

Grimm, R., Garofalo, S., "Il teatro del grottesco." *Rivista Italiana di Drammaturgia* 8 (agosto 1978). (An Italian version of Grimm's study which appeared originally in *Sinn oder Unsinn?* . . .).

Grimm, R., W. Jaggi, and H. Oesch, eds. *Sinn oder Unsinn? Das Groteske im modernen Drama*. Basel, 1962.

————. *Smysl nebo nesmysl? Groteskno v modernim dramatu.* Praha: Orbis, 1966. (A Czech translation of *Sinn oder Unsinn?* . . .).

Heidsieck, A. *Das Groteske und das Absurde im modernen Drama.* Stuttgart: W. Kohlhammer, 1971.

Jacobbi, R. *Guida per lo spettatore di teatro.* Messina-Firenze: D'Anna, 1973.

————. *Teatro di ieri e di oggi.* Firenze: La Nuova Italia, 1972.

Jennings, L. *The Ludicrous Demon:* Aspects of the Grotesque in German PostRomantic Prose. Berkeley and Los Angeles: Univ. of California Press, 1963.

Kassel, N. *Das Groteske bei Franz Kafka.* Munchen: W. Fink, 1969.

Kayser, W. Chapter 5 of *The Grotesque in Art and Literature.* Bloomington, Indiana: 1963. 130ff.

Livio, Gigi, *Il teatro in rivolta.* Milano: Mursia, 1976.

————. *La scena italiana:*Materiali per la storia dello spettacolo dell'Otto e Novecento. Milano: Mursia, 1989.

————, ed. *Teatro grottesco del Novecento (Chiarelli, Rosso di San Secondo. Cavacchioli, Antonelli).* Milano: Mursia, 1965.

Lo Vecchio Musti, Manlio. *Il teatro italiano del Novecento.* Roma, 1942.

————. "L'opera di L. Chiarelli nel teatro moderno." *Il Dramma* 53 (15 gennaio 1948).

————. *L'opera di Luigi Chiarelli.* Roma, 1942.

Lodovici, C.V. "Chiarelli smontò la macchina del teatro borghese," *Scenario*, 1953, n. 7.

MacClintock, Lander. Chapter 6 of *The Age of Pirandello.* Bloomington, Indiana:1951. 138ff.

March, M. E. *Forma e Idea de los Esperpentos de Valle-Inclan.* Chapel Hill: University of North Carolina, Estudios de Hispanofila 10, 1970

Pirandello, Luigi. "L'umorismo." *Saggi,* a cura di Manlio Lo Vecchio Musti. Milano: Mondadori, 1952.

Pullini, Giorgio. *Cinquant'anni di teatro in Italia.* Bologna: Cappelli. 68–84.

————. *Teatro italiano fra due secoli* (1850–1950). Firenze: Parenti, 1958. 269ff.

Radice, R. "La vita teatrale e i successi di Luigi Chiarelli." *L'europeo* (4 gennaio 1948).

Sergeeva. N. N. "Ital'iankii teatr 'groteska." *VLU* 4 October1989: 105–8.

Terzi, C. "Le poetiche del grottesco," in AA. VV., *L'idea del teatro e la crisi del naturalismo.* Studi di poetica dello spettacolo, a cura di Luciano Anceschi. Bologna: Calderini, 1971.

Thomson, Phillip. *The Grotesque.* London: Metheun, 1972.

Tilgher, Adriano. *Studi sul teatro contemporaneo.* Roma: 1923. 91ff.

Tonelli, Luigi. *Il teatro contemporaneo italiano.* Milano: Corbaccio, 1936. 233ff.

Vena, Michael. "The 'Grotteschi' Revisited." *Forum Italicum* 31, no. 1 (1997): 153–62.

————. "Enrico Cavacchioli: *The Bird of Paradise* and Metatheater." *Rivista di Studi Italiani* 17, no. 2 (1999): 89–98.

Verdone, Mario. *Teatro del Novecento*, Brescia: La scuola, 1981.

Wright, T. *A History of Caricature and Grotesque in Literature and Art.* Introduction by Frances K. Barasch. Revised edition, New York: Frederick Ungar, 1968.

Zetti. W. "Vom Grotesken-Spien zur Aktion." *Muk* 30, no.3–4 (1984): 285–94.

See also entries in the *Dictionary of Italian Literature*, P. Bondanella and J. Conaway, eds., Westport: Greenwood Press, 1979, and in the *Columbia Dictionary of Modern European Literature*, N.Y., 1980 (article by Olga Ragusa).

See under Italy *The Reader's Encyclopedia of World Drama*, J. Gasner, ed., 1969 and *The Oxford Companion to the Theater*, 1951, pp. 407–8.

Italian Grotesque Theater

The Mask and the Face
Luigi Chiarelli

Translated by
Michael Vena

Cast

Count Paolo Grazia, thirty-five years old
Luciano Spina , a lawyer, thirty years old
Cirillo Zanotti, a banker, fifty years old
Marco Miliotti, a judge, forty years old
Giorgio Alamari, a sculptor, twenty-five years old
Piero Pucci, twenty-five years old
Savina Grazia, twenty-eight years old
Marta Setta, twenty-five years old
Elisa Zanotti, thirty years old
Wanda Sereni, twenty years old
Andrea
Giacomo   Servants
Teresa

Today. On Lake Como[1]

Act One

A spacious room on the ground floor of Villa Grazia overlooking Lake Como. Through very wide French doors one exits onto a broad garden terrace extending to the lake. On the right and left, stairs lead down to the shore. On the terrace, in the background, some small tables; just in front of them is a card table. On each table is a lamp with a colored shade.

The room, richly and tastefully furnished, is in semidarkness. Two doors on the right and two on the left. The full moon is shining on the lake.

(As the curtain rises, Marta *is playing an Argentinian tango on the piano.* Wanda *and* Piero *are dancing. The others are talking among themselves while watching the dance.* Savina *and* Luciano *are on the terrace. Now and then, while playing,* Marta *turns around and looks at them.)*

ELISA. How charming! . . . They dance divinely! . . .

GIORGIO. See? What graceful movements! They look like Tanagra.[2]

ELISA. Did Tanagra invent the tango?

MARTA. It ought to be outlawed; it's immoral!

CIRILLO. My friend, nothing is immoral! We would have to outlaw men.

MARTA. (*Turning away*) That's a good idea.

CIRILLO. So that women might appear to be moral.

MARTA. How impertinent!

ELISA. (*To* Giorgio) Do you like to dance?

GIORGIO. No.

ELISA. Too bad! . . . (*She sighs.*)

WANDA. (*Stopping suddenly, to* Marta) Stop, stop! (Marta *stops playing.* Wanda, *pointing to the lake.*)

ELISA. The lovers? (*In fact, one can hear, rising from the lake, a man's voice modulated in the slow rhythm of an American song. For a moment everyone listens in silence.*) They must be greatly in love with each other.

CIRILLO. Who knows! It would seem that those two youngsters need too many props for their love: Lake Como, the moonlight, a sentimental song . . .

ELISA. I won't let you say anything against them.

CIRILLO. I'm not talking against them; I pity them.

ELISA. You're a heretic. (*To* Giorgio) Don't they seem appealing to you? (*She goes away with him, talking.*)

PIERO. Exported love.

MARTA. Italy has become a haven for runaway adulterers.

WANDA. The word is that they were compelled to run away because she has a dreadful husband.

PAOLO. Any self-respecting husband wouldn't let his wife run off with her lover.

MARTA. What would you do, then? (*Glances toward* Savina, *laughing.*)

SAVINA. (*Vexed*) Marta? (*She walks away toward the terrace.*)

MARTA. I'm enjoying this.

PAOLO. What would I do? I'd kill her; oh yes, I would kill her! On the other hand, this is a well known fact (*To* Savina, *who is coming back.*) Isn't that true, Savina?

SAVINA. Of course, dear!

PAOLO. There you are!

MARTA. And what would you do with the lover?

PAOLO. Nothing. A husband must see in every man a possible lover of his wife.

MARCO. A man is always within his rights!

MARTA. Oh yes! Duty was invented for women!

CIRILLO. To give their sins more spice.

ELISA. To excite men's imaginations, rather!

CIRILLO. Poor women, if men didn't have great imaginations, they would seem very poor creatures.

WANDA. (*From the terrace*) There they are, down there. I can make them out perfectly. How happy they must be!

ELISA. Dear things! . . .

WANDA. Which of you knows them?

ELISA. I saw them one evening on the beach.

WANDA. Is she beautiful?

ELISA. I couldn't say.

MARTA. Young?

ELISA. Very young. He, on the other hand, is very handsome, like one of those young men you see on billboard displays.

WANDA. They don't leave each other for a minute.

ELISA. Dear things!

WANDA. And the blinds of their villa are always shut!

CIRILLO. They're probably counterfeiting money!

WANDA. And they come out only late in the evening; and they just drift along, lulled by a song, dreaming . . .

CIRILLO. Yes, till one day they wake up . . . like what happened to those two last year.

MARTA. What happened last year? I wasn't here.

CIRILLO. Here's what happened . . . Two young Americans had come here to the lake, two lovers . . . And one fine day the husband appeared.

MARTA. And then?

CIRILLO. Nothing. He forgave her and took her back to the States.

PAOLO. Ridiculous!

CIRILLO. Why?

PAOLO. Why? Because a forgiving husband is ridiculous, a hundred times ridiculous. And there is nothing worse than ridicule. For a husband like that, nothing is left but suicide, later on.

PIERO. They say the lover paid the husband twenty thousand dollars, plus travel expenses.

PAOLO. Aha, so he was making a profession of it!

ELISA. But it seems that as soon as she arrived back there, she died of a broken heart.

WANDA. That's enough, otherwise you'll make me lose any desire to get married.

PIERO. Alas, it's a desire that passes only with marriage.

WANDA. Dumbbell!

ELISA. Husbands are a necessary misfortune for us women! . . .

WANDA. (*To* Piero) And if I were unfaithful to you would you kill me?

PIERO. That implies that you're sure I'm going to marry you.

WANDA. (*Softer*) Oh, you know very well that nothing else is possible.

PIERO. Everything is possible, even that I might marry you.

WANDA. Also, that I might tear your eyes out.

CIRILLO. What are they saying to each other, these two sweethearts? They're bickering already! That's bad . . . There won't be anything left for you to do when you're married. There's no need to jeopardize the future joys of matrimony.

PIERO. She was asking me if I would kill her the day that she betrays me!

CIRILLO. And what did you answer? . . . No, no! Killing them would mean taking them seriously, and this you shouldn't do; they are just too appealing!

ELISA. Are you still talking about fidelity in love?

PIERO. They do have such poor taste, my lady!

ELISA. Fidelity is not virtue, it's ignorance!

MARTA. That is why ladies who are unfaithful should be taught a lesson.

WANDA. By killing them? And how could they learn from such a lesson?

MARCO. Others will learn from it.

CIRILLO. Yeah, go on . . . with such ideas you'll make very foolish mistakes in life!

PIERO. It's precisely for our foolishness that women love us. Only if a man is very stupid does he manage to be forgiven by women for his feelings of enormous superiority over them.

SAVINA. Well, gentlemen, have you finished lynching women? Are you forgetting about poker this evening?

PIERO. Are you making fun of us? Fair enough, you have nothing to fear.

PAOLO. That would be the last straw!

CIRILLO. (*To* Savina) And what do you think of the bold assertions of these gentlemen?

SAVINA. A small slave rebellion . . . (*Looking at her husband*) led by a miniature Spartacus.[3]

PAOLO. Savina, I don't like this subject . . . you know that! . . . Gentlemen, who will play poker?

MARCO and other VOICES : I will, I will . . .

PAOLO. Too many, no more than five. (*Rings the bell*) So, are you playing?

MARCO. Yes.

PAOLO. *(To the* waiter *who has just entered)* Prepare for the poker game on the terrace.

(The waiter exits. He returns with the cards and chips, goes out onto the terrace and sets up the card table. Paolo *to* Piero*)* Are you playing?

PIERO. Yes.

PAOLO. *(To* Giorgio, *who is conversing with* Elisa, *and who answers positively.)* You? . . . And . . .

WANDA. And I?

PAOLO. *(Indecisively)* You, no.

WANDA. I'm going to play. Last evening I lost 120 *lire* [4] and I want to make it up.

PAOLO. Okay. Now we have enough players. *(He sets out, followed by a few others, toward the terrace.)*

ELISA. *(Softly to* Giorgio) Are you going to leave me to play poker?

GIORGIO. Yes.

ELISA. *(To* Cirillo) The sculptor Alamari has asked me to go to his studio to pose . . . only for the head. Will you let me?

CIRILLO. Of course! . . . Go to his studio to pose and . . . to repose.

ELISA. Thanks. *(She leaves).*

CIRILLO. That way I'll rest too. *(He lights a cigar, dims the light, and calmly sinks down into an easy chair. A lamp, remaining lit in a corner, casts just enough light to relieve the darkness. Meanwhile, the players have begun the game.* Elisa *is standing at* Giorgio's *shoulder, watching.* Marta *is thumbing through a newspaper.* Luciano *is looking at the lake, smoking a cigarette.)*

MARCO. *(Playing)* Open! . . . *(To* Savina) Madame Savina, we're thirsty! . . .

SAVINA. What would you like to drink?

MARCO. Something cool. — Chip.

PAOLO. Raise ten.

SAVINA. Some iced tea?

MARCO. Gladly . . . — Raise twenty.

PIERO. I pass. — I pass.

MARCO. Flush to the King.

PAOLO. Oh, this is too much! And he even took three cards.

ELISA. *(To* Marco) You'll never be lucky in love!

(Every so often one can hear the players' voices.)

SAVINA. *(After having asked the others)* I'll have the drinks brought in at once. *(She enters the room. To* Cirillo) What are you doing there, Mr. Philosopher? *(She exits from the left.)*

CIRILLO. Nothing at all, like all true philosophers. (*To* Luciano, *who has come forward.*) What do you think about that, Mr. Lawyer?

LUCIANO. About what?

CIRILLO. About philosophers, by George!

LUCIANO. Oh! . . .

CIRILLO. So?

LUCIANO. We were saying?

CIRILLO. How distracted you are!

LUCIANO. Oh, excuse me, I was thinking . . .

CIRILLO. About a woman?

LUCIANO. Who said that?

CIRILLO. You must be the passionate kind!

LUCIANO. About philosophy?

CIRILLO. However you wish it! . . . Okay, okay! On the other hand, philosophers and women resemble each other; they both tend to complicate the simplest things.

LUCIANO. Do you think so?

CIRILLO. You should know something about it since you are the lawyer for women! How come you haven't said even a word in their defense this evening?

LUCIANO. Defend them? Not at all necessary. They don't need it, not even in court.

CIRILLO. You are right. We men already have enough to do to defend ourselves from them.

SAVINA. (*Reentering from the left*) Here is something for thirsty souls. (*To* Cirillo *and* Luciano) What are you two plotting in the shadows?

LUCIANO. We were talking about philosophy.

SAVINA. You'll go to hell! (*The* butler *enters from the left, carrying a big tray loaded with refreshments.* Savina *to the* butler.) Serve Mr. Cirillo; philosophy makes people thirsty. What would you like to drink?

CIRILLO. Who knows! You put me on the spot. I never know what I should drink! . . .

SAVINA. Iced tea?

CIRILLO. It keeps me awake. Shoot! . . . I think it's more difficult to choose a drink than to choose a wife.

SAVINA. Imagine that!

CIRILLO. Oh yes. Wives . . . are all alike . . . and so! . . .

SAVINA. But you can't complain! You have a model wife.

CIRILLO. I don't deny that. It's the philosopher in me speaking . . .

SAVINA. Help yourself then . . . (*Approaching* Luciano) And you?

LUCIANO. I'm not thirsty, thanks. (*Lowering his voice*) I'm leaving. Have you opened the veranda door?

SAVINA. Yes.

LUCIANO. I'm going to wait for you in your room. Join me soon!

SAVINA. Be careful, I beg you.

LUCIANO. Don't worry; (*Alluding to* Paolo) he'll be busy for a while yet, as usual! He prefers poker!

SAVINA. (*To* Cirillo) Well, then, what would you like?

CIRILLO. Iced tea. But I won't sleep. (*He goes out on the terrace with* Savina . *The butler, after* Cirillo *has served himself, goes out on the terrace and serves the refreshments.*) I'll have my wife sing me a lullaby.

ELISA. Darling!

MARTA. (*She steps into the room sipping her drink. To* Luciano, *who is immersed in thought*) You haven't said a word all evening.

LUCIANO. The others have more than made up for that!

MARTA. Are you worried about something?

LUCIANO. Me?

MARTA. Why aren't you playing?

LUCIANO. I'm going to leave.

MARTA. Right now?

LUCIANO. I promised the Salvuccis I'd drop by.

MARTA. At this hour?

LUCIANO. They, too, usually stay up until four in the morning; playing, dancing.

MARTA. And so you won't take me home again tonight?

LUCIANO. If you are still here when I get back, gladly.

MARTA. You're acting as if we were already married.

LUCIANO. Let them say that about Piero.

MARTA. Piero is always near his Wanda.

LUCIANO. Even too much.

MARTA. Wicked words!

LUCIANO. It's their business.

MARTA. Let it be. But what about us? Doesn't it seem to you that we go to the other extreme? It was decided that we would marry now, in September; instead, you've put it off again until next year.

LUCIANO. I explained to you that my business situation at this point is not at all promising . . .

MARTA. Yes, I know! Meanwhile our marriage has become an endless bingo game. We move ahead by postponements.

LUCIANO. Our day will come . . .

MARTA. You don't strike me as being very enthusiastic.

LUCIANO. I will be at the time.

MARTA. Meanwhile . . .

LUCIANO. Meanwhile what?

MARTA. Meanwhile . . . you're going to the Salvucci's tonight.

LUCIANO. What does that have to do with it?

MARTA. Oh! . . .

LUCIANO. (*Trying to hide his irritation*) . . . What a way of reasoning! I beg you to explain yourself!

MARTA. Explain myself? Are you or are you not going to the Salvucci's?

LUCIANO. Well?

MARTA. Enough. What do you want me to explain? . . . Have a good time.

LUCIANO. They're my clients. It's a call I have to make.

MARTA. At midnight?

LUCIANO. They invited me.

MARTA. I'll come with you.

LUCIANO. (*Startled*) Where?

MARTA. (*She laughs briefly*) No, no, I'm not coming. Relax!

LUCIANO. I don't see why you should.

MARTA. Right.

CIRILLO. (*Entering*) I can't take the night humidity. (*Turns to sit in the armchair.*)

LUCIANO. (*To* Cirillo) Good-bye.

CIRILLO. Are you leaving? What's the hurry?

LUCIANO. I'll probably see you all later. Good-bye. (*To* Marta) Good-bye, dear.

MARTA. Good-bye.

LUCIANO. (*Goes out on the terrace. To* Savina) Good-bye, Signora Savina.

SAVINA. Are you leaving?

PAOLO. I pass. (*To* Luciano) So soon?

LUCIANO. I'm going to the Salvucci's for a bit. I'll see you later perhaps; I'll come to take Marta home.

SAVINA. You're sure to find these fanatics still here. But I'll see you tomorrow. I'm going to bed; I'm tired. (*She rings the bell.*)

MARCO. We're overdoing it somewhat, aren't we?

SAVINA. Not at all. But you well know that at a certain hour my eyes close on me. So I must ask you to excuse me.

LUCIANO. (*Telling the others good-bye, to the* butler *who has appeared*) My hat and walking stick, please. (*The* butler *goes out, and returns with* Luciano's *hat and walking stick.*)

PAOLO. (*To* Luciano) Luciano, we'll wait for you, then. And give my greetings to Signora Teresa.

LUCIANO. Fine; I'll see you later. (*Goes out by the terrace.*)

SAVINA. Good night, my friends; have fun. (*She says good night to the guests, one by one.*)

GIORGIO. A card.

PAOLO. Three cards. (*Kisses* Savina *on the forehead.*) Good-bye, dear, good night.

SAVINA. (*Enters the room followed by* Marta) Good-bye, Signor Cirillo.

CIRILLO. Good night, Signora Savina. Oh, how I envy you!

SAVINA. Come and keep me company.

CIRILLO. It's obvious that you're firmly determined to remain a virtuous woman.

SAVINA. Oh, I wouldn't trust myself at all with you.

CIRILLO. Thanks, you leave me some illusions.

MARTA. (*Who is smoking a cigarette, to* Savina *who is moving to the right*) I'll finish my cigarette in your room, so you can show me the two hats you got yesterday.

SAVINA. At this hour?

MARTA. Why not?

SAVINA. No, no. I'd rather you saw me wearing them. Tomorrow I'll put one on . . . that mauve velvet one.

MARTA. Ah, velvet! . . .

SAVINA. It's the fashion this year? Velvet in the summer! . . . I know it's not logical. But, on the other hand, our heads are not logical, so how can we expect hats to be logical? Good-bye . . .

MARTA. Hats, at least, can be changed.

SAVINA. Even too often. You should see the bill I got from my dressmaker!

MARTA. What can we do? We have to please the men!

SAVINA. We're slaves of fashion.

MARTA. Ladies' fashion is dictated to some extent by their lovers' tastes.

SAVINA. They are so crazy in Paris!

MARTA. Here too!

SAVINA. (*Trying to get away from* Marta) And now . . .

MARTA. Now I'll start reading, and wait for Luciano to return.

SAVINA. Good girl. (*Handing her a magazine*) Take a look at this, it arrived today.

MARTA. Who knows what time Luciano will come back. He went to the Salvucci's.

SAVINA. They're very nice.

GIORGIO. That's it; I'm paying and quitting. I've had enough for tonight. (*He gets up*)

MARTA. Of course! . . . They are very nice! . . . And he left me here to wait for him!

SAVINA. It's right that you should wait for him; you're his fiancée. But as for me . . . I'm dying to go to sleep. Bye, I've got to run now. (*She quickly exits to the right.* Marta *watches her go, makes a scornful gesture, and goes out on the terrace.*)

GIORGIO. (*Followed by* Elisa, *enters the room. They don't see* Cirillo *stretched out on the easy chair.*) What do you have to tell me?

ELISA. Dear! . . . My husband gave me permission to come to your place. I can hardly wait till tomorrow to throw myself madly into your arms!

GIORGIO. Fine.

ELISA. At three, then?

GIORGIO. At . . . (*Turning, he sees* Cirillo, *who suddenly pretends to be asleep.*) It's your husband!

ELISA. Oh! . . . He's sleeping . . . always sleeping! . . .

GIORGIO. But, if he heard us! . . .

ELISA. No! On the other hand . . . he is so good!

GIORGIO. Are you complaining about it?

ELISA. Of course! . . . And unfortunately, it's always someone else's virtue that drags us all down the primrose path of evil.

GIORGIO. Perhaps! . . .

ELISA. There is no fun whatever in betraying a husband like him! And to think that the only thing that can make married life interesting is precisely the risky necessity of deception, lying, and subterfuge . . .

GIORGIO. So if you . . . it's his fault?

ELISA. Of course. I . . . should have married a man like Savina's husband, like Paolo. A man passionate and strict, ardent and pitiless; who would have held me as his very own, who would have subjugated me with caresses and with fear, who would have instilled in my life a red tinge of sensuality and tragedy! But instead . . . look at him, he's sleeping! . . . Do you know, once I let him catch me on purpose, to provoke some terrible thing . . . Nothing happened! He forgave me! Oh God, there's no drama in my life! And without drama love is banal, sad, vulgar!

GIORGIO. I say, let's not play tricks!

ELISA. But your kisses will make up for the disappointments I have had to bear.

PAOLO. Oh, I can't play anymore. This is the height of bad luck. (*The players protest and would deal him in again.*)

MARTA. (*Extremely nervous, comes from the terrace, crosses the room, and exits left. Passing in front of* Cirillo) Sleep well.

CIRILLO. (*Pretending to wake up suddenly*) Who's that? . . . Oh! . . . (*Sees his wife.*) Excuse me . . . I must have dozed off.

ELISA. Rest, dear, sleep . . . Sleeping does you a lot of good. (*She goes out with* Giorgio *on the terrace.*)

CIRILLO. Sure!

MARCO. (*To* Giorgio *and* Elisa) Take your places. Only for a half hour. (Elisa *and* Giorgio *sit down at the card table.*)

PAOLO. (*Enters the room*) Ah, enough for this evening!

CIRILLO. I must have dozed off! . . . (*Gets up*)

MARTA. (*Enters from the left and goes out on the terrace, still more nervous. Passing in front of* Cirillo) Good morning! Did you sleep well?

CIRILLO. What's the matter with Marta? She looks down in the dumps.

PAOLO. She's waiting for Luciano! She is waiting for her fiancé! . . . Ah, love!

CIRILLO. Ah, marriage!

PAOLO. It seems to me that marriage is an overly maligned institution. I'm extremely happy, for example.

CIRILLO. So am I! It's a question of getting used to it!

PAOLO. To what?

CIRILLO. To your own wife.

PAOLO. It's also necessary to try to understand women.

CIRILLO. There's only one way to understand women; love them! . . . The more they're loved, the more they feel understood!

PAOLO. Don't you love your wife?

CIRILLO. Me! Oh, well!

PAOLO. What?

CIRILLO. I didn't say that my wife felt misunderstood . . . in life!

PAOLO. Well then?

CIRILLO. Well . . . life is something . . . much greater than marriage. Life . . . encompasses everything . . . everyone! . . .

PAOLO. I don't understand . . . I don't know!

CIRILLO. (*Smiling sadly*) Go on, you understand very well, you know! Why bother to pretend? . . . Yes, even you know . . . they all know . . . we all know . . .

PAOLO. What?

CIRILLO. Of course! . . .

PAOLO. You mean . . .

CIRILLO. Sure!

PAOLO. Oh!

CIRILLO. Eh!

PAOLO. Your wife?

CIRILLO. My wife!

PAOLO. And you . . .?

CIRILLO. And I . . .!

PAOLO. Oh, magnificent!

CIRILLO. One can't imagine how great men's capacity to adjust is!

PAOLO. And you let her betray you, just like that . . .

CIRILLO. Let's be fair; I was the first to betray her; I married her and I am almost twenty years older than she is.

PAOLO. But she knew this when she married you; she should have thought about it first.

CIRILLO. But I knew it too; and it was I who should have thought about it beforehand; because it was in my interest, because I would run the risk of becoming . . . what I am! . . .

PAOLO. So you married her, already prepared . . .

CIRILLO. And even if that is so? All men, if they had any guts, should marry with this favorable disposition, to . . . to avoid disappointments later on!

PAOLO. Ah, I would not have stood for it!

CIRILLO. And then? You see, if I had been a terrible husband, she . . .

PAOLO. She wouldn't have betrayed you.

CIRILLO. . . . she would have betrayed me just the same and I would have been ridiculous; perhaps much more ridiculous! . . . and then . . . why ridiculous?

PAOLO. Look, don't you ever feel ridiculous?

CIRILLO. Me? No! . . . We are too many in the same situation . . . And when there are so many of us in the same boat, we feel normal! . . . I am a normal husband!

PAOLO. Ah, at the first sign I would have been ruthless!

CIRILLO. Oh, I know! You would have killed! Well . . . if I had killed her the first time . . . I would find myself in the same situation today with my second wife or my tenth mistress.

PAOLO. The other or the others would no longer have dared, then.

CIRILLO. Women dare anything, dear boy! . . . Nothing but danger tempts them. And the man they really love is the one who induces them to commit enormous, irreparable follies. Oh, you know so little about women!

PAOLO. I know myself! I know I'd kill her!

CIRILLO. I know it, too. I know you. But why?

PAOLO. Why? Because marriage is a pact for life, and it's right that anyone who breaks it should pay with life! . . .

CIRILLO. That sounds like something Napoleon would say! . . .[5] You are the Napoleon of husbands . . . But even the great Napoleon, you see, was not lucky in marriage. Undoubtedly women hold nothing sacred.

PAOLO. Ah, you are a cynic; you almost make me . . . (*Makes a gesture of disgust*).

CIRILLO. At times I have felt that way about myself . . . But then, when we look at mankind a bit closely, we end up being indulgent with ourselves. And besides what I've already told you . . . truly . . . deep down in my heart, there's something I don't say . . . because if I said it . . . then perhaps I might become ridiculous. Who knows! . . . Weariness, boredom, disappointment will come even for her . . . she will realize that even the ashes of love are a bit sad, a bit depressing like all other ashes . . . and perhaps . . . perhaps she will then come to me, and will be a good companion, sweet, very faithful, because even she will have lived her life, as all we men have lived it before getting married! Who knows!

PAOLO. (*Ironically*) And so you, the husband, resign yourself to be the last one, if at all!

CIRILLO. If at all! . . . On the other hand, women, who are more experienced than we are, and keep less pride in their feelings, want to be the last possession of the man they love! . . . And in this desire of theirs there is great wisdom and exquisite refinement!

PAOLO. (*Nauseated*) Ah, enough, enough! It's nauseating! . . . (*He goes off, disgusted and nervous.*)

MARTA. (*Who has entered at* Cirillo's *last words, very agitated, seeking to control herself; to* Paolo) Ah, you're here?

PAOLO. Obviously!

MARTA. (*To* Cirillo, *indicating* Paolo) What's wrong with him?

CIRILLO. (*Smiling*) He is a husband too . . . susceptible!

MARTA. (*Pretending to have understood something else, and feigning great surprise*) Oh! What on earth are you saying?

CIRILLO. Try to calm him down.

MARTA. (*Hesitating*) Come, come, Paolo . . . You're wrong!

PAOLO. What?!

MARTA. But yes; don't make a mountain out of a molehill!

PAOLO. Ah, you call it a molehill.

MARTA. Certainly! You can't judge by appearances.

PAOLO. (*Looking at* Marta *who turns away from his glance*) Eh?!

MARTA. I know; perhaps a bit of foolishness, a little flirting, but from this to . . .

PAOLO. To what?

CIRILLO. (*Who is beginning to be uneasy, seeing the turn the conversation has taken*) Marta!

MARTA. (*To* Paolo) No, no, don't get so upset. I assure you that you're making a mistake. I . . . know her well, and she's beyond suspicion . . . I feel I can speak for her . . . (*She meanwhile puts herself in front of the second door on the right as if she wanted, without letting* Paolo *understand her purpose, to prevent him from entering* Savina's *room.*)

PAOLO. (*Jumping up*) She . . . who?

CIRILLO. (*To* Marta) What are you saying?

MARTA. (*As though dumbfounded and bewildered*) But, weren't you talking about . . .

PAOLO. About? . . .

CIRILLO. About no one!

PAOLO. (*To* Cirillo) Hush! . . . (*To* Marta) About whom?

MARTA. I don't know . . .

PAOLO. Say it!

MARCO. (*From the terrace*) Be quiet, in there!

MARTA. (*To* Cirillo) But what did you tell me?

CIRILLO. Me? (*To* Paolo) But don't listen to her; don't you see? She doesn't know what she's saying . . .

MARTA. I can't make any sense out of this . . .

PAOLO. (*Approaching, with a hoarse voice*) You were talking about . . . about her . . .

MARTA. But I thought that . . .

PAOLO. . . . about Savina . . .

CIRILLO. But there's been a misunderstanding, don't you see?

PAOLO. Oh God! . . . I want to know!

MARCO. Will you be quiet? What's got into you? (*The players get up and come as far as the threshold of the room.*)

PAOLO. (*To* Marta) You know, tell me.

MARTA. You're mistaken, no . . .

PAOLO. You don't want to? Very well, she'll be the one to tell me . . . (*Tries to enter* Savina's *room*)

MARTA. (*Barring the way*) No! . . .

PAOLO. (*Startled*) Eh?! . . .

CIRILLO. Paolo, don't do anything rash.

PAOLO. Let me by! (*He frees himself from* Cirillo *and exits through the second door on the right. Everyone runs after him anxiously, and goes out right behind him, except for* Marta *who remains alone, terrified, in a state of tension at what is going to happen. Angry voices in an uproar come from within, and above all that of* Paolo *shouting:* "Open up, open up—or I'll break the door down! Open up!." *He knocks furiously at the door of his wife's room. Several seconds pass in this fashion; then again the furious voice of* Paolo *is heard:* "Open up, for Christ's sake, open up!" (*Finally* Paolo *flings himself against the door, which opens with a crash. More screams, more commotion.* Marta, *who has stayed still, is completely rigid, then falls into a nearby armchair. After a few minutes everyone enters from the right.* Paolo *is surrounded by his friends, who hold and try to calm him; he is still in a state of frenzy, emitting inarticulate sounds.*) Ah, for Christsake, what do you still want from me? Are you glad you've given her time to get away?

MARCO. By now your frenzy is useless. Try to find another way to defend your honor. (*He places on a table the revolver he has wrested away from* Paolo.)

PAOLO. My honor? Oh, yes . . . say hello to my honor for me, if you run across it.

MARCO. What does your honor have to do with it? Barbaric ideas!

PAOLO. Shut up, it's better, shut up, don't say anything to me. You're all in on it; you all knew; I was the only blind one, like any husband, stupid . . . ridiculous, there it is, ridiculous!

MARCO. Calm down, calm down! We'll see later what's the best solution.

PAOLO. Sure . . . later . . . I'll face the court, isn't that right, the court . . . to hear a judge tell me which article of the code authorizes a husband to be ridiculous! Right? Later! While she . . . she laughs at me! And I couldn't even have the satisfaction of seeing who he was, that bastard! But of course, he follows his masculine trade and he does well to, seeing how women are all . . . all . . . wide open doors!

MARTA. (*To* Elisa) Take me away, take me away! Take me back home! My God!

ELISA. Yes, you'll come with us; take it easy.

PAOLO. (*To everyone*) And what are you doing here now! Huh? You've already expressed your condolences; get out! Do you plan to spend the night here watching over the corpse of a husband? Huh? (*To* Cirillo) Are you happy? Are you happy?

CIRILLO. Me? What are you saying?

PAOLO. This . . . I'm a normal husband too! I'm the Napoleon of normal husbands! You make me sick!

CIRILLO. Come now, leave!

ELISA. Why?

CIRILLO. He's suffering.

ELISA. Poor thing!

CIRILLO. Yes!

PAOLO. Leave me alone! Get out!

MARCO. Okay, Okay, we'll leave . . . when you're calm.

PAOLO. At once!

MARCO. When you've promised us not to do anything crazy.

PAOLO. Right now! Don't you understand you're irritating the hell out of me?

MARCO. Okay. We're leaving.

PIERO. (*To* Wanda) Take care!

WANDA. You take care!

(*Someone shakes hands with* Paolo; *the others, not knowing how they should behave, go away quietly. All exit by the terrace.* Marta *clings to* Elisa's *arm.*)

PAOLO. (*When all have left he violently shuts the glass door. The* butler *appears outside on the terrace, clearing the tables and turning the lights out.*) Oh! . . . (*He walks about the room in a state of excitement, then suddenly lets forth with a deep and aggrieved voice.*) But why, why, why? (*He collapses into an armchair; remains there for a while. All of a sudden, behind the big glass door in back appears* Savina, *who remains still behind the panels, watching* Paolo. *Then she opens the door without making a sound, enters, closes it again, stands leaning against it.* Paolo *turns, sees his wife, jumps to his feet, and remains still for a moment, rigid, staring at her. Then he rouses himself and goes toward her; he seizes her and pushes her back brutally for a few steps.*) Ah, you, you . . . ! (*She is entreating and anxious. It seems that she wants to speak.*) Not one word! . . . it's useless!

SAVINA. (*In a stifled voice*) Paolo!

PAOLO. Ah, you came back!

SAVINA. Listen!

PAOLO. You came to challenge me?

SAVINA. To humble myself.

PAOLO. But if a short time ago you managed to escape from me, now, I have you here . . .

SAVINA. If you have loved me, if you won't . . .

PAOLO. Ah, here is how I love you. (*He grabs her by the throat and squeezes. Savina doesn't resist; she turns pale, gives a little cry; he immediately releases his grip and pulls away with an instinctive gesture of horror for the deed he was about to do. Both remain silent, facing each other, bewildered. Paolo clearly has the sensation that he can't, that he will never be able to commit the crime.*)

SAVINA. (*After a very long silence*) Paolo! (Paolo, *with a desperate gesture, commands her to be quiet. Another very long silence*) Paolo, do with me what you want!

PAOLO. (*After a silence, with great bitterness*) You permit yourself to be ironic! But don't think you're safe yet . . .

SAVINA. (*Who has understood that he won't ever be able to kill her*) No!

PAOLO. (*Looking at his hands, he stretches them toward her neck*) This . . . I can't do. (*Makes a gesture of horror*) One touch of your flesh . . . oh, God, why have they disarmed me? (*Threateningly*) But . . .

SAVINA. (*With a gesture of great audacity, takes the revolver that's on the table and hands it to him*) Take it; here's your revolver.

PAOLO. (*Makes a frantic gesture to get hold of the weapon, but he vacillates; the gesture dies in mid-air. Angrily*) Oh, you're a bitch! (*And he sinks down into an easy chair.*)

SAVINA. (*Replacing the revolver on the table*) No. No! You won't kill me!

PAOLO. Oh no? Don't be so sure!

SAVINA. You won't kill me!

PAOLO. You've risked everything to get the better of me!

SAVINA. I've risked less than you think!

PAOLO. Sure, your life, from now on will be worthless.

SAVINA. Life! What does it matter? It's the least important thing! And now I understand that perhaps it's exactly the only thing I haven't risked!

PAOLO. You're insane; I would have killed you if . . .

SAVINA. No! Take off this mask of crime, be sincere with yourself, look into your heart, and don't be a slave to your words and conventional attitudes! Our future's at stake, Paolo, right now; don't put this barrier between us. Think, Paolo, we can still save something of our life together.

PAOLO. No, No! You're dead as far as I'm concerned.

SAVINA. It will be as you wish, but first think about it . . .

PAOLO. (*To himself*) As far as I'm concerned . . . But what about others?! "Dead as far as I'm concerned" is nothing but a stupid expression!

SAVINA. (*With profound sorrow*) And it's for this reason that you suffer, not for having lost me! . . .

PAOLO. (*Laughs bitterly*) Ridiculous! . . .

SAVINA. How terrible!

PAOLO. (*After a very long silence*) Oh well, there's only one thing to do!

SAVINA. Whatever you wish.

PAOLO. You'll leave.

SAVINA. (*With sad surprise*) Ah!

PAOLO. You must disappear!

SAVINA. You're casting me out?

PAOLO. Forever!

SAVINA. Forever!

PAOLO. Nobody must suspect your departure. An hour from now at the most you'll go out to the car with me; I'll accompany you to Switzerland; from there you'll take a train to Paris . . . London . . . I'll take care of the rest.

SAVINA. What will you do?! . . .

PAOLO. None of your business!

SAVINA. You scare me right now! What are you plotting?

PAOLO. So you're afraid? No, don't worry! See, I'm calm!

SAVINA. I'm not afraid for myself, but for you.

PAOLO. For me?! . . . You shouldn't have done what you did if you were afraid of me! . . .

SAVINA. What plan are you hiding from me? I'll leave tomorrow! Let me have time to speak—to explain—

PAOLO. It's useless! What are you hoping for?

SAVINA. Give me time until tomorrow—

PAOLO. No! Do I have the right, yes or no, to throw you out of my house after what's happened? Do I? It's the least I could do! . . . that's it, then, then I ask you to do me a favor, by going far away and changing your name. Is that too much? Look; I'll spare your life on this condition.

SAVINA. That I take another name?! . . .

PAOLO. I demand it. I'll give you money so that you can provide for yourself at first. Afterward I will find a way for you to have what you need.

SAVINA. But then it is really forever!

PAOLO. What did you expect? And let's understand each other . . . No one must know . . . not even him! . . . so that he won't be able to join you!

SAVINA. (*With hope in her voice*) That . . . that would displease you?

PAOLO. Only because I want no one to know where you are. You must be dead for everyone.

SAVINA. (*Disappointed*) Ah! . . . don't doubt it. And then it seems possible to you that I would be here now, in front of you, if I still had something in common with that man? . . . No, no! It's finished.

PAOLO. Keep your regrets to yourself.

SAVINA. What I regret is something quite different!

PAOLO. It doesn't interest me. Surely you see that I don't even ask his name!

SAVINA. What good would that do?

PAOLO. I have nothing else to say to you.

SAVINA. You're adamant then? It's decided?

PAOLO. Decided!

SAVINA. Think, Paolo!

PAOLO. Go!

SAVINA. Think!

PAOLO. Enough . . . And don't let anybody see you. (*He turns his shoulders*)

SAVINA. (*Looking at him with great pity, somewhat ironic*) He commutes death penalty to exile. (*Exits slowly right*)

PAOLO. (*Rings the bell, then sits down at a table and writes. The* butler *enters from the first door on the left.*) Who is still awake?

ANDREA. Only me. Giacomo and Teresa have already gone to sleep.

PAOLO. Bring the car onto the road at once.

ANDREA. Should I phone the chauffeur?

PAOLO. There's no need. I'll drive myself. After you have the car ready, jump on a bicycle and go immediately to Como to send this telegram. Here you are . . . (*Gives him a written piece of paper*) If you don't feel like coming back you can sleep in Como. Do everything well and quickly. Go. (*The* butler *bows and exits by the first door on the left.* Paolo *watches him go.*) He was trying not to laugh in my face . . . There, it's beginning . . . Ah!

LUCIANO. (*Enters from the second door on the left; trying to be at ease*) Has everyone left? . . . And Marta?

PAOLO. (*Assuming a tragic expression, and advancing toward him*) Ah, it is heaven that has sent you!

LUCIANO. What's happening?

PAOLO. I need you.

LUCIANO. Why?

PAOLO. Why? Because . . . (*Trying to produce the desired effect*) I have killed my wife!

LUCIANO. (*Wavering*) Eh! . . .

PAOLO. She betrayed me . . . I killed her!

LUCIANO. (*Terrified*) How? . . . When?

PAOLO. An hour ago, while we were all together here, she was in her room with a man!

LUCIANO. With a man?!

PAOLO. I surprised her, but she managed to get away just on time!

LUCIANO. (*Anxious*) And then? . . .

PAOLO. Then . . . I was staying here alone . . . when she returned . . . and appeared behind those glass doors . . . she came in . . . she was hoping perhaps that I might pardon her . . . (*Becoming more and more excited in his description*) Huh! . . . pardon her . . . she was able to hope! She said something that I don't remember; I rushed to her . . . I seized her . . . then . . . I don't know exactly how she managed to run away from me . . . I took her by her throat . . . That's it . . . I remember clearly the sensation in my fingers, my nails sinking into the soft whiteness of her neck . . . she leaned against the railing . . . she was struggling . . . desperately . . . becoming more and more pale . . . and for a certain moment I was completely beside myself . . . I pushed her . . . I pushed her. She fell down . . . a scream . . . a splash . . . two white hands in a frantic gesture at surface level . . . then rings . . . rings . . . bigger and bigger . . . then—nothing more . . . silence. Look! I killed her! (*He falls exhausted into a chair.*)

LUCIANO. (*Annihilated*) It's atrocious! . . . It's horrible.

PAOLO. It was inevitable!

LUCIANO. (*After a silence, with poorly feigned trepidation in his voice*) And—he?

PAOLO. He —who? The lover? I don't know who he is, I don't know anything about him. I don't give a damn either!

LUCIANO. (*With a sigh of relief*) Ah! . . .

PAOLO. And now it's your turn . . .

LUCIANO. (*With a jump*) Eh?

PAOLO. Aren't you my best friend? Tomorrow morning I'll give myself up at Como. You'll be my lawyer.

LUCIANO. Ah, no! . . .

PAOLO. Why not?

LUCIANO. I don't know, I feel I wouldn't know how to . . .

PAOLO. You're the only one who can, on the contrary. You've known me for many years, you know my character, my ideas, you alone could convince the jury to acquit me. My fate is in your hands.

LUCIANO. It's too much. (*He puts his head between his hands and remains silent.*) No, I can't do it!

PAOLO. You can't? It's a question of saving me and you refuse? Why?

LUCIANO. Saving you? Look, I don't know if I would succeed . . .

PAOLO. They will acquit me, there's no question. You think perhaps that I didn't have the right to kill that miserable woman?

LUCIANO. I don't know!

PAOLO. What reason do you have for defending her? Eh? Do you perhaps have some reason? Explain yourself!

LUCIANO. None, none! I agree she was . . . an unworthy woman. Alright, I'll do it.

PAOLO. At last! Then we'll both go to Como tomorrow morning to turn me in. Good-bye! (*He holds out his hand; Luciano, distracted, doesn't see it.*) You don't want to shake the hand of a murderer?

LUCIANO. (*Giving him his hand*) Oh, sorry . . . of course, I'm used to it.

PAOLO. See you tomorrow.

LUCIANO. (*Starting to leave*) How calm you are!

PAOLO. After a great tragedy one no longer has any feelings. (*The song of the Americans can be heard rising from the lake: and it will last until the end of the act.*) Sing . . . sing. (*To* Luciano) Do you want to go out by the gate? It's quicker. (*He opens the glass door in the back and lets* Luciano *pass through it. The latter sees the lake and stops, overcome by a vague fear. He would rather* Paolo *went first, and between the two passes a brief scene of silent invitations to lead the way. Finally,* Paolo, *irritated, pushes* Luciano *ahead and they exit. The song is heard more clearly.*)

SAVINA. (*Enters cautiously from the door on the right. Takes several steps, looks outside, leans on the glass door, then, with great bitterness*) I've only been dead for an hour, and to my lover I am already an unworthy woman!

ACT TWO

The same setting as the first act. The room is filled with flowers: bouquets, baskets, vases, scattered all over the floor and on the furniture. Each floral arrangement bears a card, a ribbon, a token that adds meaning to each offering. Hanging from the terrace, a large flag flutters in the wind.

(A bright, festive sun shines through the open glass doors. Andrea, Giacomo *and* Teresa *are on the terrace.)*

ANDREA. Wait, wait. I think I see some people down there.

TERESA. Yes, yes . . . Can you hear? . . . Music! (*In fact, the gay notes of a band can be heard, and the sporadic shouting and applause of a crowd of people.*)

ANDREA. They're escorting him here with music.

TERESA. His acquittal is everyone's celebration.

ANDREA. How happy our boss must be to return here, to his house, after so long! . . .

TERESA. And in the meantime, Savina, oh, the poor woman . . .

ANDREA. May her soul rest in peace.

TERESA. She couldn't even get a decent burial. She's left to rot on the bottom of the lake.

ANDREA. If she had done her duty all this would not have happened.

TERESA. Oh, you men—you're all alike!

ANDREA. Here he is, here he is!

(The band is very near, as well as the shouting and applause. Andrea *and* Giacomo *clap their hands enthusiastically;* Teresa, *exuberant, waves her handkerchief. The music continues to play under the terrace.* Andrea, Giacomo *and* Teresa *rush down the*

stairs, which are imagined to be on the left, shouting excitedly and joyously. After a few seconds, Paolo *appears followed by his three servants. He enters the room quickly, somewhat annoyed by all the cheering.)*

PAOLO. (*Addressing his three servants*) Thank you, thank you, people . . . You are so kind. (*He shakes the emotional servants' hands*) And I must also thank you all for your loyal testimony before the grand jury.

ANDREA. We only told the truth, sir.

TERESA. Nothing but the truth.

PAOLO. Good, good!

ANDREA. (*Taking* Paolo's *hat and coat*) Would you like anything?

PAOLO. Wait a minute . . . wait a minute! . . .

ANDREA. We have made you an excellent lunch.

PAOLO. I've already eaten. (*Letting out a deep breath*) Oh! (*After a brief silence*) But enough of this—do they expect to continue with this music until dark? (*He takes some money from his wallet and gives it to* Giacomo) Here, thank them for me and tell them to leave. (Giacomo *exits through the terrace.*) Well . . . (*Suddenly he realizes that the room is full of flowers*) What the . . .? What's all this stuff?

ANDREA. Flowers sent you this morning.

PAOLO. (*Really amazed*) For me?! (*Remaining astounded and meditative for a long while, he finally goes up to one basket, then to another, and reads*) "A secret admirer." . . . "Without the shedding of blood, there is no forgiveness." . . . (*He walks around the room, shaking his head. The music finally stops; the cheering and applause dies down. Seeing the flag*) And that? . . .

ANDREA. We put it up as a sign of our happiness.

PAOLO. Oh I get it! . . . a national celebration! . . .

ANDREA. Sir, I would like you to meet her . . . my wife! . . .

PAOLO. Who? Teresa? You've married Teresa? (Andrea *and* Teresa *nod their heads.* Paolo *is embarrassed.*) Oh, good, good . . . I give you my congratulations! . . .

ANDREA. Thank you.

TERESA. Thank you.

PAOLO. (*To change the subject*) And . . . what else is new around here? . . . Any mail? . . .

ANDREA. Any mail! (*Exits to the left, followed by* Teresa.)

PAOLO. Oh, my God! I can't get used to being home yet. (*Looking at the flowers*) It looks like the dressing room of a ballerina. (*Seeing* Andrea *and* Teresa *reentering the room carrying with great effort a large basket of mail.*) What's that?

ANDREA. (*Placing the basket on a chair*) The mail.

PAOLO. (*Terrified*) All that stuff?

ANDREA. There's even more? (*Exits again followed by* Teresa)

PAOLO. (*He approaches the box, almost with fear, examines it, picks out a few letters and telegrams, opens one slowly and reads*) "I have seven million, an ardent heart, a spotless past. Can I be yours? . . . Miss Emily" . . . Oh! . . . (*He tosses the telegram away, opens a letter*) "I too have murdered someone. I killed my husband with a gun because he betrayed me." What good taste that fellow had! (*Opens another letter*) "Have you ever seen, on the bank of a clear, silent stream, a lily, all by itself, standing straight on its slender stalk? Such am I." What trash! (*Seeing* Andrea *and* Teresa *approaching from the right with another basket of mail*) More? . . . Enough! . . . Enough! . . . Get rid of all this trash, get rid of it! (Andrea *and* Teresa *leave again, carrying the basket.*) Doesn't anything serious exist in this world? Even the most grievous experiences become ridiculous. What fools! And to think it was for these people that I . . . Oh, fools! . . . (Andrea *and* Teresa *return, pick up the other basket of mail and carry it away.*)

MARCO. (*Entering from the terrace*) May I?

PAOLO. Oh, it's you?

MARCO. I'm here to embrace you once again.

PAOLO. Ah, go ahead! (*He submits passively to* Marco's *embrace*)

MARCO. I can't tell you how happy I am for you!

PAOLO. Thank you!

MARCO. But I hear you really aren't so satisfied.

PAOLO. Why shouldn't I be?

MARCO. (*Catching a glimpse of the flowers*) This display of admiration should make you feel proud.

PAOLO. To a degree.

MARCO. What do you mean? It shows the esteem of so many noble and generous souls.

PAOLO. Perhaps. But all this makes me a bit . . . uneasy.

MARCO. Why?

PAOLO. Oh, I don't know.

MARCO. I think I understand. It's just that you weren't prepared for all this, you've been swept up on an unexpected pedestal and today you've emerged as a highly exemplary figure. But men, in the grandeur of their court of law, have legalized your actions. Therefore, make peace with your conscience, just as you are at peace with the rest of society.

PAOLO. (*Somewhat annoyed and inattentive*) All right, all right. I'll follow your advice.

MARCO. My wife is also in full agreement with me. She'll be along any minute now to give you her congratulations.

PAOLO. (*Surprised*) Your wife? . . . You've gotten married? . . .

MARCO. Yes. I thought Luciano might have told you.

PAOLO. No. To whom? . . .

MARCO. I married Wanda.

PAOLO. Is that so . . .

MARCO. Yes, Wanda.

PAOLO. (*More and more stunned*) Wanda?

MARCO. That's right. Don't you remember her?

PAOLO. Of course, I remember her very well!

MARCO. It's been six months! . . .

PAOLO. (*After staring silently at him a while with a subtle, ironic expression, he extends his hand*) Congratulations!

MARCO. Thank you, dear Paolo.

PAOLO. My heartiest congratulations!

MARCO. Thank you . . . Needless to say, it is a magnificent match! . . .

PAOLO. Oh, no doubt!

MARCO. And we are very happy.

PAOLO. Of course.

MARCO. A creature of such pure and delightful charm. I couldn't have married a better woman.

PAOLO. Certainly, and what about . . .

MARCO. Piero, you mean? Her ex fiancé?

PAOLO. Precisely.

MARCO. He is an irresponsible boy. No, he would not have been able to understand her, and would have made her very unhappy.

PAOLO. True.

MARCO. They parted, but are still good friends. No harm, you see, when things are done correctly.

PAOLO. Oh, surely. Well, um, I'm delighted to hear all this.

MARCO. Thank you. (Wanda *enters from the terrace, followed by* Piero.) Here she is!

PAOLO. (*Shaking her hand*) Wanda. (Marco *shakes hands with* Piero.)

WANDA. I am so very, very happy to see you again! — here! . . .

PAOLO. You are very kind.

PIERO. (*To* Paolo) Hello, you jailbird. (*He shakes hands*) We've already wallowed in the conventional effusions.

PAOLO. (*Annoyed*) Yes, already!

PIERO. And all these flowers? It looks like the backroom for a call girl!

PAOLO. Even worse!

PIERO. Then, of a woman of integrity. (*He laughs*) When do you plan to remarry?

PAOLO. (*Pointedly*) When you show some respect for women!

PIERO. So you're going to wait till I die, eh? What a shame! . . . (*Laughs and turns to speak to* Marco)

PAOLO. (*To* Wanda) And so now I find you a married woman! . . .

WANDA: Well . . .

PAOLO. Be wise . . . and above all very shrewd.

WANDA. Why do you say that?

PAOLO. Because during this long period of solitude I've had time to really think, and I now understand, my young friend, that life does not consist of formulas.

WANDA. I think I understand what you mean.

PAOLO. That's a good start. Be cautious. People should never be forced to confront their own convictions directly. Through the lightness of our words and ideas we take on so many obligations that, certainly, it is a good thing we aren't reminded of them in the moment of necessity, because if that happened it would be an inevitable disaster. But don't worry, this does not occur because it would require people to have more courage than they do in their thoughts and actions, they would have to do away with the convictions which their egoism and pride have nurtured, they would have to stop lying to other people, to become really and truly honest with themselves. But this is not an easy thing to do, especially in the moment when one is overcome by violent emotions. And so . . . and so . . . one follows the so-called plan of life, and like all plans, it is very logical, and therefore completely unsuitable for life.

WANDA. (*Who has listened to him with great interest*) So you . . .

PAOLO. (*Upset*) I, I don't enter into the picture. I have told you this for your sake and for those who are close to you. Be cautious . . .

WANDA. Now it's all over. (*She glances toward* Piero.)

PAOLO. So much the better! . . . And then . . .

WANDA. (*Shrugging her shoulders*) Then? (*She walks toward* Marco. Cirillo *and* Elisa *enter from the terrace.*)

ELISA. (*Running toward* Paolo) Darling, darling! Let me give you a hug! (Paolo *passively submits to her embrace.*) It is so hard to express in a single word to you how I feel. What can I say? Well, you've put on weight!

PAOLO. (*Smiling*) Relaxation!

ELISA. Darling, did you get my flowers?

PAOLO. Yes, thank you.

ELISA. Well, now, tell me all that happened to you there.

PAOLO. Of course, this winter. In fact, to simplify things, I plan to write a book entitled *My Stay in Prison*.

ELISA. Darling . . . and I will reciprocate by bringing you up to date on everything that's happened here during your absence. Some weddings, for instance: Marco and Wanda (*She glances toward them, speaking more softly*) The poor man!

PAOLO. Sshh—For heaven's sake! These comments . . . you . . . shut up!

ELISA. You're right . . . Then, Luciano, your lawyer, and Marta.

PAOLO. I know that! And also Andrea, my butler, married Teresa. It seems that my example had little effect in discouraging any would-be aspirants to marriage. In fact, not at all! (Giorgio *enters from the terrace*)

GIORGIO. (*Coming towards* Paolo) Dear Paolo . .. words are useless . . . so (He *heartily shakes* Paolo's *hand*)

PAOLO. Terrific, thank you. *(He walks away to get a cigarette)*

ELISA. (*To* Giorgio) Well then? Can I at least see you today? It's been fifteen days! What's bothering you?

GIORGIO. All right. Today at five. I'll be waiting for you. I have something to tell you.

ELISA. Why not right away? What do you have to tell me?

GIORGIO. At five. *(He walks away)*

PAOLO. *(Approaches* Elisa *again)* Well, where were we?

ELISA. I am unhappy my dear, so unhappy.

PAOLO. *(Sarcastically)* Chin up, chin up. There's always time to begin again in life!

ELISA. Alas! . . .

PAOLO. Yes, yes.

ELISA. You certainly can!

PAOLO. Me—begin again?

ELISA. If not in marriage then at least in love.

PAOLO. Oh, what are you thinking of?

ELISA. But I, by now . . .

PAOLO. For you, if not in love, at least in your marriage!

ELISA. (*Surprised*) Why do you say that? (*Sighs*) In marriage! . . . If I had married a man like you, then I could see it. You were the perfect man for me! You have all the qualities for . . . But fate!

PAOLO. (*Harshly*) . . . Fate made me marry a woman like you . . . and . . . it was bad!

ELISA. (*Moves away from him, hurt*) My God, how coarse! . . . (*She turns to look at him*) And yet I like him! . . . (*She goes toward the others.*)

CIRILLO. (*Followed by* Piero, *approaches* Paolo) Be brave!

PAOLO. Oh, it's you?

PIERO. (*To* Paolo) Do you know, today the mayor is coming here with the administrative council to share officially in your joy of your acquittal?

PAOLO. The Mayor? . . . But have they gone crazy in this town? . . . Don't they understand that everything will end up being grotesque? I don't want to see anyone! . . . Enough with the congratulations!

CIRILLO. Have courage!

PIERO. And tonight there's going to be a big banquet in your honor. The mayor will invite you to attend.

PAOLO. (*Startled*) A banquet? . . .

PIERO. Yes, at the Hotel Splendid. A great many people have accepted.

PAOLO. Ah, this is too much! . . . Don't let them dare propose such a thing to me! . . . Do they think, perhaps, that I've become their fool?

PIERO. The mayor is going to read a magnificent speech.

PAOLO. I don't want to know anything!

PIERO. He came to my house this morning and asked me to write it.

PAOLO. A banquet! Ah, that's fantastic!

PIERO. You don't want to go?

PAOLO. Go? . . . Ah, by God, no! . . . Let them enjoy their banquet! . . . I don't want to serve as the pretext for their indigestions! Clowns!

PIERO. What a shame; such a beautiful speech! . . . (*He goes off smiling*)

PAOLO. But what do they want from me?

CIRILLO. These are the inconveniences of fame! . . . (*Smiles*)

PAOLO. (*Irritated*) You too? . . . I beg you! . . .

CIRILLO. Yes, me too, naturally!

PAOLO. Why?

CIRILLO. Because if I didn't extol you . . . I would have to pity you.

PAOLO. For what reason?

CIRILLO. For the same reason that you feel forced to be irritated . . . so as not to pity yourself.

PAOLO. I beg of you not to torment me with useless plays on words.

CIRILLO. I'm not here to torment you . . . but to give you courage!

PAOLO. To give me courage?

CIRILLO. Ah yes! You need it!

PAOLO. Why?

CIRILLO. To stand all this! . . . (*Silence*) The acquittals of the courts, in certain cases, have this terrible aspect: they abandon the accused to the crowd so that they can deliver justice in the way that pleases them most! . . . And in your case they are stoning you with blows of enthusiasm! . . . And you cannot escape!

PAOLO. In your opinion, what should I have done?

CIRILLO. Left, immediately, and gone far away. But I understand! That was impossible!

PAOLO. As a matter fact it was impossible!

CIRILLO. Because you felt the need to return and show yourself to your ten friends who knew, and in whose honor you had killed, for fear that they would not know how to hush up the unfortunate incident that you were forced to witness that night.

PAOLO. What I did was right!

CIRILLO. Oh, our misery!

PAOLO. It was right!

CIRILLO. Today it's useless for you to still say that! . . . What good does it do you, now, today that the members of the jury, the judges, and the people have repeated it to you? What good? Maybe to convince yourself.

PAOLO. Of what?

CIRILLO. That it was right?! . . .

PAOLO. Let's not talk about it. You know how far apart we stand on this.

CIRILLO. Today, not so far, maybe.

PAOLO. (*Mockingly*) Oh! . . . (*Silence*)

CIRILLO. Tell me: if you had been here all alone that night, in your house, and if you could have been absolutely sure that no one would ever find out, would you have killed her?

PAOLO. Would I have killed her? Perhaps you doubt it?

CIRILLO. I doubt it.

PAOLO. How's that? . . . And my principles, are you forgetting about them?

CIRILLO. No. But you have forgotten yourself, you have betrayed yourself, for your principles.

PAOLO. Are you trying to say that I'm not sincere?

CIRILLO. Right . . . At best you are in good faith; this I believe.

PAOLO. Ah! . . . No! . . .

CIRILLO. And so these flowers, the music, the flags, the speeches, the applause, the fame, the triumph, are all deserved! . . . Undoubtedly today you're living your finest day . . . Enjoy all this deification; and, want some advice? Go to the banquet tonight. It's logical that you go!

PAOLO. Enough, enough!

CIRILLO. Ah, you see! . . .

PAOLO. Well then, what are you driving at? What are you trying to show?

CIRILLO. Nothing! . . . In life there's nothing to show because everything is evident.

PAOLO. For example?

CIRILLO. That you're a weakling.

PAOLO. I? . . . After what I've done? . . . Ah! . . . Maybe you are!

CIRILLO. Leave me out of it. Maybe one day you'll understand even me! . . . But we were talking about something else now.

PAOLO. Me, a weakling? . . .

CIRILLO. You lack the strength, the courage to overcome the terror of ridicule. You killed for fear of being a ridiculous husband! And the funny thing is this: that ridicule always and only hits those who fear it!

PAOLO. Not me!

CIRILLO. Then tonight you'll go to the banquet!

PAOLO. But don't you understand?

CIRILLO. What?

PAOLO. That I'm disgusted by all this exaggeration today!? . . .

CIRILLO. I love you for this moment of sincerity. You feel the ridiculousness of today, of this glorification: you demolish your past!

PAOLO. That's not it, you misunderstand me.

CIRILLO. No, no; acknowledge that you are beaten. The husband who forgives is not always ridiculous; sometimes it can be the one who has killed, as you see!

PAOLO. I don't understand anything anymore! . . . (*Silence*) The truth is that I feel a great sense of disappointment!

CIRILLO. Ah, I understand! You're beginning to see all the absurdity that lies in our conventions! . . . But prepare yourself to bear more subtle and tormenting states of mind.

PAOLO. Still more? It's impossible!

CIRILLO. Yes. All this will pass, and relatively soon; but . . .

PAOLO. But? . . .

CIRILLO. But it's from today on that you will really begin to kill your wife. To kill her within yourself! . . . Day by day, hour by hour, feeling by feeling . . . What you've already done is nothing! . . . The crime was only a point of departure!

PAOLO. You're hurting me! . . .

CIRILLO. You're right, forgive me! . . . Let's not talk about it anymore! . . . (*He goes off toward the terrace*)

PAOLO. (*After a long silence*) What will she be doing down there?

CIRILLO. (*On the threshold of the terrace, to* Luciano *and* Marta *who appear*) Oh, here's the hero of the day! . . . (Luciano *and* Marta *greet the friends on the terrace,* Paolo *turns, sees them, and makes a sharp gesture of disgust.* Luciano *and* Marta *come toward* Paolo.)

LUCIANO. How are you, then? Do I see your face a little more serene today?

PAOLO. Why today more than yesterday?

LUCIANO. What do you mean, why? . . .

MARTA. (*Who is walking around the room looking at the flowers and reading the messages*) What beautiful flowers, and how many! . . . A real demonstration! . . . (*After wandering about the room, she goes out on the terrace among the others.*)

PAOLO. (*Who has seen a newspaper in* Luciano's *hands*) Ah! You've bought the special edition!

LUCIANO. Why not? . . .

PAOLO. (*Ironically*) Naturally! . . . Certainly your magnificent speech is printed there in its entirety.

LUCIANO. Oh, not for that reason!

PAOLO. You're among the princes of the forum, now . . . And you owe it all to me . . .

LUCIANO. Don't talk to me about it, I beg you. Remember what I suffered for this; that I didn't want to do it; and had it not been for friendship! . . . But in any case I'm not at all satisfied.

PAOLO. Ah, neither am I!

LUCIANO. (*Surprised*) You?

PAOLO. I beg you to give me your bill tomorrow. I intend to pay you . . . right away.

LUCIANO. Pay me? . . . Ah, no!

PAOLO. No? Why not?

LUCIANO. Because it would disgust me to take money from you . . . from a friend! . . .

PAOLO. And it disgusts me to owe you gratitude for an acquittal obtained by such means.

LUCIANO. What means?

PAOLO. Slandering in open court . . . that unfortunate woman! . . .

LUCIANO. I told the truth!

PAOLO. (*Wincing*) Eh?! . . .

LUCIANO. As a lawyer would speak in open court in order to obtain the desired effect! Rhetorical necessity!

PAOLO. You were supposed to uphold my legal rights and nothing else!

LUCIANO. With a jury one must appeal to the emotions.

PAOLO. To what is right!

LUCIANO. I would have allowed them to convict you!

PAOLO. You should have affirmed that I was within my rights when I . . . killed! . . .

LUCIANO. My duty was to get you acquitted.

PAOLO. No. You had the duty of not doing me a larger wrong. That is why I chose a friend! . . . Instead you only thought of your own success! . . . Ah! . . .

MARTA. (*Reentering from the terrace*) Well then? What are you arguing about?

PAOLO. I will expect your bill tomorrow. (*Crosses the threshold of the terrace*)

MARTA. What a good client! . . . (*To* Luciano) What's the matter? . . . You're upset.

LUCIANO. He says . . . he is displeased with me.

MARTA. (*Ironically*) Why in the world? . . . You got him acquitted! . . . You paid your debt.

LUCIANO. What debt?

MARTA. Of friendship! . . .

LUCIANO. On the contrary he thinks that . . . I have not been his friend.

MARTA. That's strange! . . . Where could he find a better friend than you?

LUCIANO. And he wants to pay me!

MARTA. It's only right!

LUCIANO. Ah, no! . . .

MARTA. (*With a slight smile*) You are a man of scruples! . . . One would say that you now, in exchange, are awaiting an acquittal from him; on the contrary, maybe it's the opposite!

LUCIANO. Exactly. It seems to me that you are making an excessive effort to please him. One would say that you want him to forgive you for something.

MARTA. For having married you, perhaps? . . . (*They remain looking in each other's eyes, then, all of a sudden,* Marta *bursts out in a shrill laugh.* Luciano *makes a gesture of anger and goes off.*)

PAOLO. (*Reentering the room*) I would like to know what all those people are doing in front of the gate. You would think they're waiting for the door of a theater to open.

MARTA. To see a great tragic actor who has returned to us after a long absence! . . .

PAOLO. Madam, I beg you! . . .

MARTA. And my husband has announced you to the public with such pompous words that . . .

PAOLO. Your husband . . . your husband! . . .

MARTA. My husband? . . . Isn't he perhaps your best friend?

PAOLO. My best friend? . . . Ah, no!

MARTA. No? That surprises me!

PAOLO. I'm telling you something unpleasant, I know, but . . .

MARTA. Unpleasant? . . . Not quite! . . . I don't care whether or not you're my husband's friend!

PAOLO. (*Mockingly*) Ah, you're afraid that I'll spoil him? . . . That I'll transmit my principles to him? You fear for yourself?

MARTA. The day on which it was my turn, I would be very calm . . . because you would be there to defend me! . . .

PAOLO. Me?!

MARTA. Because it could only be you.

PAOLO. (*After a silence, ironically*) Ah! . . .

MARTA. I prefer you not to be his friend; you can see very well that I'm a truly moral person!

PAOLO. Very moral!

MARTA. And you? How have you spent all this time? What did you do down there?

PAOLO. Nothing.

MARTA. That's very little: nothing! . . . And then . . . the loneliness! . . . always alone, isn't it true?

PAOLO. Once in a while your husband came!

MARTA. Certainly that couldn't have been a great comfort! . . . And always there within those four walls.

PAOLO. Almost always.

MARTA. (*Provocative*) My God! . . . I can imagine what an enormous burden of desires, accumulated in there, you must have brought with you when you got out! (*She moves closer to him*) Desire for sun, for movement, for life!

PAOLO. In my hurry to get out, I forgot everything, down there!

MARTA. Everything?

PAOLO. (*Looks at her with mixed irony and curiosity; moves away slowly, rings a bell, turns again to look at her, crosses the threshold of the terrace*) Friends, I beg you to excuse me if I leave you for a few minutes.

MARCO. If we're disturbing you, we'll leave.

PAOLO. No, no, please stay. (*To Andrea who has entered from the left*) Is everything in order, there, in my room?

ANDREA. Yes, sir. (Paolo *starts out slowly toward the left*) Do you want me to help you with something?

PAOLO. No, thank you.

ANDREA. (*He draws closer to him and in a lower voice*) If you pass by the room . . . of your wife . . . you will see that there are some flowers . . . Teresa put fresh ones there every day . . . and I didn't believe it right to prevent her from doing it . . . because the intention was good . . . I don't know if we've done something wrong . . . If you don't . . .

PAOLO. (*Who has listened to him, troubled, taps him affectionately on the shoulder*) No, no! . . . (*He again takes another step and stops on the threshold; then he gets hold of himself and exits by the second door on the right. Some of his friends who were on the terrace have entered the room and stopped to look at him in silence. Conversation is resumed. Among those who have entered the room are* Piero *and* Wanda.)

WANDA. (*To* Piero *in a subdued voice*) Well, those letters, when are you going to give them back to me?

PIERO. When you come to get them.

WANDA. Me? You're crazy!

PIERO. Tomorrow I'll be home at 4 o'clock; I'll wait for you.

WANDA. You'll wait a long time!

PIERO. I'll be patient.

WANDA. This is blackmail, what you are doing.

PIERO. No, a favor.

WANDA. You fool! . . . Bring back my letters as soon as possible, do you understand?

PIERO. Tomorrow I'll be home at 4 o'clock; I'll wait for you! (*He laughs and leaves her. She makes a gesture of anger*)

(*Suddenly, from the street come excited voices approaching the house. The people on the terrace peer outside with evident curiosity and signs of surprise. Those in the room stop talking, cock their ears, and move toward the terrace.*)

CIRILLO. Something must have happened!
MARTA. For sure. Let's go and see.

(All of a sudden everyone from the terrace rushes toward the left and disappears. The voices are very, very near. One distinctly hears phrases:—It's her . . . It's her! . . . This way . . . this way! . . .—Then the voices weaken.)

ANDREA. *(After a moment he enters precipitously from the terrace. He is very moved. Entering, he shouts)* Sir! Sir! *(and he moves toward the right)*
PAOLO. *(Enters from the right)* What's happening!
ANDREA. *(Perplexed and unable to overcome his emotion)* Sir! Master!
PAOLO. Well? *(Now the voices are very distinct, coming from a room on the left)* Who's out there? What is it?
ANDREA. There's . . . they've . . .
PAOLO. What?
ANDREA. A little while ago . . . in the lake, two boatmen passing in front of here. . . felt something knocking against the oar . . . and . . . and then . . .
PAOLO. And then?
ANDREA. It was a corpse!
PAOLO. Oh! . . .
ANDREA. Of a woman! . . .
PAOLO. I understand! . . .
ANDREA. Savina! . . .
PAOLO. *(Irritated and skeptical)* Ah! . . .
ANDREA. Savina! We recognized her.
PAOLO. *(Extremely surprised)* What? You have . . .?!
ANDREA. It's really her. There's no doubt! . . . And in such a state! . . . Unrecognizable!
PAOLO. But you're going crazy!
ANDREA. I assure you! It's her, her! . . . We all recognized her at first glance! And you will too, as soon as you see her . . .
PAOLO. I don't want to see anything!
ANDREA. What?
PAOLO. Nothing!
ANDREA. But, sir! . . .
PAOLO. Ah! Do you think perhaps that I want to take part in your whimsical games?
ANDREA. It's her!
PAOLO. That's absurd!
ANDREA. Why? They have fished her out from the same spot where . . . she fell!
PAOLO. *(Wringing his hands)* Oh! . . . This is too much! . . .

ANDREA. Come, sir, she's out there!

PAOLO. Where?

ANDREA. Out there!

PAOLO. Eh? . . . What is this, a morgue?

ANDREA. Poor lady, we brought her back to her own house. Did you want us to leave her on the beach?

PAOLO. (*To* Marco *who enters from the left*) Well then?

MARCO Oh, you know?! . . .

PAOLO. I know that you're a bunch of lunatics; that's what I know!

ANDREA. (*To* Marco) He doesn't believe that it's Signora Savina!

MARCO. You don't believe it? And who else could it be? It's obviously a body that's remained submerged for a long time. Undoubtedly her clothes were entangled in some rocks . . . But . . . it is she . . . they were all in agreement: it is she! And it is only natural that it should be! . . .

PAOLO. (*Desolate*) Natural! . . . (Cirillo, Piero, Elisa, *and* Wanda *enter from the left. The women have reddened, tearful eyes.*)

MARCO. (*To* Paolo) Come out here for a minute. I understand that it is a painful thing! . . . but it's necessary that you see her! . . . that you recognize her. Then, I'll take care of the rest so that the legal proceedings can immediately follow.

PAOLO. (*With sad irony*) It's necessary, so be it! . . . (*Exits with* Marco *from the left*)

WANDA. What an awful thing, my God!

ELISA. Poor Savina!

PIERO. Are you sure it's her?

ELISA. There's no doubt! I recognized her right away!

PIERO. How!

ELISA. From . . . everything.

PIERO. Oh, in that case! . . .

WANDA. And how impressionable Luciano is! He almost fainted when he saw the corpse!

PIERO. The poor lawyer's nerves are weak! . . .

MARTA. (*Enters from the left*) My God! My God! What a terrible thing! . . . I can't stay here! . . . I'm going away! Good-bye! My God! (*Exits by the terrace*)

WANDA. Imagine Paolo's agitation when he saw his wife!

ELISA. It was very cruel to drag him into that room!

WANDA. What remorse! . . .

ELISA. Here he comes! He looks like a dying man! (Paolo *reenters from the left followed by* Marco; *he is not at all disturbed; on the contrary, one would say that he has an urge to laugh.*)

MARCO. Well then, there's no doubt?

PAOLO. Well . . .

MARCO. It is she?!

PAOLO. (*With a gesture of resignation*) It is she!

MARCO. Very well! Now try to stay calm. I'll take care of everything. (*To Piero*) Are you coming with me? . . . (*They both exit left*)

ELISA. We'll take care of everything and . . .

PAOLO. (*Who walks without a word, motions her not to speak. Elisa and Wanda exit left. After a long silence full of gestures*) It's some mechanism! . . . God only knows where it will end . . . (*He stops in front of the entrance to the terrace. The second door on the right opens slowly, cautiously. The head of a woman appears wrapped in a very thick veil. After a moment of hesitation, the woman enters; she is enveloped in a large, light cloak of a flimsy gray color. She takes a few light steps into the room. Paolo turns abruptly.*) Who are you? . . . Lady?! Are you looking for me? . . . (*The woman nods her head in assent. Surprised*) For me?! Oh, I think I understand! . . . Perhaps you sent me flowers, perhaps you wrote me one of the many letters I have found here, but . . . (*The woman has removed the veil from her face. It is* Savina. *Paolo recognizes her and for an instant remains speechless. Then, furiously*) Hey?! You . . . you . . . here? What for? Why? Have you forgotten . . . Are you mad? (*Glances around in the fear that someone might be there*)

SAVINA. (*In a slow, sweet voice*) Don't be afraid! No one has seen me! I came by the veranda stairs. And after all . . . I'm protected by the veil!

PAOLO. Ah, she is mad! . . . (*He rushes to lock all the doors; he also closes the glass doors in the back and lowers the blinds*) What have you come for?

SAVINA. To see you! Aren't you going to ask me to sit down? I am Madame Séverine de Grèze, who lives in London. Mind you, I made a long trip for the pleasure of seeing you for a moment.

PAOLO. Don't talk nonsense!

SAVINA. A few days ago I went as far as Chiasso in order to follow your trial more closely. I heard of your acquittal and came here!

PAOLO. To do what?

SAVINA. I told you! . . . And then I thought that on this day of great joy for you, you would appreciate, amid so many compliments, also the . . . pardon of your victim! . . .

PAOLO. But, you wretch, don't you know that in there . . . is your corpse? . . .

SAVINA. (*Amazed*) My . . .?!

PAOLO. Yes!

SAVINA. My corpse?! I don't understand!

PAOLO. A while ago, some boatmen fished out here in front of our . . . of my house, a woman's corpse that had obviously been in the lake for a long time. It was unrecognizable . . . and yet everyone, immediately, recognized you! . . .

SAVINA. Me?!

PAOLO. They took you and carried you into the house, into that room; and now they're all there, around your corpse, weeping over it! . . .

SAVINA. And you?

PAOLO. Me? . . . What could I do? . . . They almost forced me to identify you!

SAVINA. Oh! . . .

    (*Silence*)

PAOLO. And now what do you intend to do?

SAVINA. Well then . . . am I really dead? . . .

PAOLO. In a little while all legal proceedings will be completed.

SAVINA. Dead . . . Even for you? You identified me!

PAOLO. What were you hoping for?!

SAVINA. Who knows! . . .

PAOLO. It's absurd! . . .

SAVINA. At least this: that the thought that I was still alive could perhaps—I don't know—comfort you.

PAOLO. It makes no difference to me! . . .

SAVINA. As I was comforted by the news of your acquittal.

PAOLO. It isn't the same thing!

SAVINA. Well then, I must go away again? . . .

PAOLO. Certainly!

SAVINA. Return to London?

PAOLO. Or wherever you please!

SAVINA. And live my life alone?

PAOLO. Well! . . .

SAVINA. Without ever seeing you again?

PAOLO. It's necessary!

SAVINA. All right! I will go back to being Madame Séverine de Grèze. And for the rest of my life! . . . Good-bye! . . . Good-bye, Paolo! . . .

PAOLO. (*Distressed and struggling with himself*) Now? Not now! . . .

SAVINA. Why?

PAOLO. It would be rash!

SAVINA. Don't be afraid; I will go as I came. And my veil will protect me from inquisitive looks! Good-bye!

PAOLO. (*Taking her hand*) No, they might recognize you!

SAVINA. Who will think of it? I am in there dead, I have been dead for such a long time!

PAOLO. All the more reason! . . . If someone were to recognize you, do you realize what would happen?

SAVINA. Ridicule?

PAOLO. I told you I don't want that!

SAVINA. (*Mildly*) You don't?! I'm Madame Séverine de Grèze! . . .

PAOLO. Look! . . . You will wait until dark!

SAVINA. And where?

PAOLO. (*Even more distressed*) Out . . . there! . . . (*The handle on the second door on the left creaks*) Go, go! . . .

SAVINA. (*In a subdued voice*) Well then . . . till I see you again!. . . (*Exits by the second door on the left.*)

PAOLO. (*Opens the second door on the left*) What is it?

LUCIANO. (*Enters, very pale*) I can't stand it any longer! I can't go on!

PAOLO. What's the matter with you?

LUCIANO. Oh, that corpse. (Paolo *makes a gesture of grief*) It's horrible! Paolo, I must tell you everything! . . .

PAOLO. Everything? . . . What else is there?

LUCIANO. A torment greater than my strength! . . . I can't go on living under these conditions! . . .

PAOLO. What's happening to you?

LUCIANO. Well, remember that night . . .

PAOLO. Which night?

LUCIANO. I've been a devoted friend of yours, a sincere friend, the dearest of friends.

PAOLO. Oh! . . . It's all over, now! . . .

LUCIANO. What?

PAOLO. Aren't you referring to my dissatisfaction with your defense?

LUCIANO. No!

PAOLO. What then?

LUCIANO. And yet the friendship that I felt for you was of no avail in protecting me from myself! The day on which I was overpowered by my wretched madness, it seemed that the most beloved friend and . . . the husband . . . had become two separate people! . . . To you as a friend I gave my whole heart, but . . . alas! . . .

PAOLO. (*Profoundly surprised*) What are you getting at?! . . .

LUCIANO. That night . . . it was I . . . in there . . . with her! . . .

PAOLO. (*Starting nervously*) You?! . . .

LUCIANO. It was I . . . who swept her to her death!

PAOLO. You?! . . .

LUCIANO. And now do what you like with me! . . .

PAOLO. Oh! . . . You miserable!

LUCIANO. I had to confess this to you, to alleviate my own remorse!

PAOLO. You?! . . . You took my wife, my love, my honor . . . You . . . my friend . . . Ah!

LUCIANO. You're right!

PAOLO. You bastard! . . . You had the nerve to assume my defense! . . . You even accused her, said obscene things about her! And you were her lover. How could you? . . . You're miserable! . . . Oh, no, she couldn't have loved you, no, she couldn't possibly have loved you.

LUCIANO. (*His vanity wounded*) Why not?

PAOLO. It must have been a moment of madness . . . You make me sick! . . .

LUCIANO. (*Wearily*) That's enough!

PAOLO. (*With deliberate cruelty*) And now let me tell you this: Today, your wife . . . offered herself to me! . . .

LUCIANO. (*Staggering*) What?

PAOLO. She acts as my revenge! . . .

LUCIANO. (*Trying to react*) Oh, not that! . . .

PAOLO. It disgusts me! . . .

LUCIANO. (*Reassured*) Oh, well! . . .

PAOLO. But for you it will be the same! . . . And now . . . get out!

(Luciano *slowly leaves by the terrace.* Paolo *closes the glass door, then makes his way to the second door on the right, and opens it.* Savina *appears in the doorway, and enters*)

SAVINA. Well?

PAOLO. Did you hear? . . . (*He flings himself at her with the clear intention of doing violence*) Ah! . . .

SAVINA. (*Quickly retreating*) What do you want to do? . . . kill me again? . . .

PAOLO. (*Suddenly stops, annihilated*) Again?

SAVINA. Just think, my body is in there.

PAOLO. (*Sinks down wringing his hands*) Oh, here I am, caught in my own net!

SAVINA. I am Séverine de Grèze!

PAOLO. Not even that night did I have such a clear and rending sensation of your betrayal as I do in this moment.

SAVINA. But you see very well that the man with whom I betrayed you wasn't worth the betrayal! . . .

PAOLO. Don't try to split hairs! . . . Oh, why didn't I really kill you that night?

SAVINA. If you had, you would be sorry today.

PAOLO. It's better, though, to experience any remorse rather than suffer like this! . . .

SAVINA. Love this "suffering," for it comes from my presence.

PAOLO. Go away, I don't want to see you ever again! . . .

SAVINA. If you had killed me . . . then . . . today your torment would be much greater.

PAOLO. It would have been a liberation.

SAVINA. How so a liberation? If you love me!

PAOLO. Who? I? . . . Ah!

SAVINA. You love me!

PAOLO. I hate you!

SAVINA. You love me!

PAOLO. Go away!

SAVINA. You held me back a little while ago!

PAOLO. Because I didn't want a scandal!

SAVINA. Because you love me! Because you still want me . . . with you! . . .

PAOLO. That's a lie! . . . Who said that?

SAVINA. You don't have to say it. But I know that I'll always be with you . . . You want me again, as before!

PAOLO. You're mistaken! . . . Look, nothing matters to me anymore—scandal, ridicule, nothing! Rather than have you here for one more minute, I prefer to pay any consequences! Even if they see and recognize you, I don't care, but not one more minute here, no! . . . Is that clear? . . .

SAVINA. (*Deeply discouraged*) Oh! . . . All right, I'll leave!

PAOLO. At once!

SAVINA. I'll leave, but . . .

PAOLO. Not another word, I won't listen to you!

SAVINA. . . .But . . . (*With clear sincerity in her voice*) Paolo, alone, without you, I cannot live . . . I don't want to live! You will have the liberation you desire, and very soon. (Paolo *turns and looks at her*) I prefer to kill myself, Paolo! . . . I will kill myself. (*She moves as though to throw herself into the lake*)

PAOLO. (*Seizing her hand*) No! . . .

(*A very long silence.* Savina's *face is all aglow. His anguish is obvious.*)

SAVINA. (*Softly*) Paolo!

PAOLO. (*Trying to recover himself*) No. I don't want you to go away now. Wait until this evening, as we had agreed! . . . This is what I meant! . . .

SAVINA. (*With great pity*) My poor friend . . .

PAOLO. (*In a stifled voice*) Leave me alone, please! . . .

SAVINA. I'll wait for you. (*She slowly moves away, shaking her head; as she reaches the threshold of the second door on the right, she turns again to look at him, then goes out. Paolo remains alone, takes a few steps; he is anguished and torn, then he falls into a chair, places his head in his hands. Unexpectedly the first door on the right opens and* Andrea *and* Giacomo *appear carrying four large lighted candlesticks, one in each hand; they walk slowly across the room and exit through the second door on the left.* Paolo *leaps to his feet as though he were terrified; then he remains there, stunned, looking after them.*)

ACT THREE

The same scene as the preceding acts. (The early hours of a sunny afternoon. The funeral is about to be held. Cirillo, Marco, Giorgio, Piero, Elisa, *and* Wanda *are in the living room along with many other men and women. The men are all in frock coats, top hats, and black gloves; the women are also dressed in black. The long tollings of a bell can be heard. Servants come and go busily. The guests are conversing, but so softly that one can only hear subdued and indistinct voices.)*

ELISA. *(Raising her voice)* It will be an impressive funeral! . . .

(Several voices try to silence her: "Sshh!")

CIRILLO. *(Pointing to the second door on the right, in a soft voice.)* Paolo is in there.

(And the conversation resumes its murmured and indistinct pattern. The women have handkerchiefs in their hands to dry a tear every now and then. The men are admirably grave. Someone is on the terrace looking down. Paolo *enters through the second door on the right, which he locks, putting the key in his pocket. He wears a light gray suit; he doesn't have a sad air at all. All gather around him and solemnly extend their condolences. He shakes hands in silence, then goes out through the second door on the left. Upon his exit, the voices become animated.)*

ELISA. Did you see poor Paolo's face?

WANDA. It's remorse!

CIRILLO. He is ruined , poor man!

PIERO. A corpse, even if only that of a woman, can be quite a burden in the life of a man! . . .

ELISA. He is so dazed that he didn't even think of wearing a black suit.

WANDA. We should tell him!

ELISA. *(To* Wanda) How does this dress suit me? I had it made in an awful hurry!

WANDA. It suits you very well! But I put on this little dress from last year!

CIRILLO. What impresses me is that Paolo shut himself up in his rooms last night and didn't come out until now!

WANDA. He must be in such torment!

MARTA. We must try to distract him! . . .

ELISA. But the maid, Teresa, who brought him the meals in his room, told me that he ate a lot . . . that he ate at least enough for two, especially this morning at breakfast!

MARCO. Good for him that he takes care of himself!

WANDA. Guess who I saw this morning?

ELISA. Who?

WANDA. Do you remember that couple . . . those two Americans . . . who were here last year, and every evening would walk along the lake singing?

ELISA. Oh! Are they here again? Such dear things!

WANDA. He came alone! She isn't here! . . .

ELISA. What could have happened? Perhaps they have broken up?

WANDA. Unbelievable! . . . She was so pretty!

ELISA. Oh, these men! . . . (*She sighs again, and looks at* Giorgio)

PAOLO. (*Enters again from the left. There is an immediate silence.*) Listen, my friends, will one of you do me the favor of going down stairs; people keep coming, and I have no intention of receiving them! . . .

MARCO. Yes, yes! Let's go down!

PAOLO. Thank you! . . . (*He opens the second door on the right, goes out, and locks it again.*)

CIRILLO. What's he doing locked in there?

ELISA. Poor Paolo! . . .

CIRILLO. (*Who is on the terrace*) Still more flowers pouring in! . . . (Marco, Piero, Wanda *and the other guests leave slowly, speaking in low voices, through the door on the left.*)

ELISA. (*Blocking* Giorgio's *way, imploring*) Giorgio! . . .

GIORGIO. Again?

ELISA. Giorgio! . . . It's impossible to break up like this . . .

GIORGIO. (*Annoyed*) Please get out of my way! I thought I'd made my position clear yesterday.

ELISA. I can't! I don't want to!

GIORGIO. I want it; and that's enough! . . . (*He shrugs his shoulders and goes out through the door on the left.* Elisa *makes a gesture of despair.*)

CIRILLO. (*Who returns from the terrace*) Elisa? What's happened to you?

ELISA. My friend! . . . My friend! . . .

CIRILLO. Well! . . . Henceforth her suffering is over! . . . Today we must sympathize with Paolo! . . . He had almost forced the crime upon himself! . . . And indeed it is tragic when we are forced to recognize that we have deceived ourselves in judging our feelings and ideas; and now he regrets this fatal error!

ELISA. Perhaps you're right! . . . What is the purpose of killing?

CIRILLO. (*After looking at her for a moment, ironically*) Exactly! . . . That's probably the only thing the two of us happen to agree on!

ELISA. You're wrong, Cirillo. I've always thought that a husband fully had the right to kill his wife if she betrayed him. I even felt that, beyond being right, it was beautiful!

CIRILLO. (*With a touch of bitter irony*) Ah! Are you reproaching me then? . . .

You're right! . . . If it is so, I have disappointed you . . . I have been a
bad husband! (*He laughs briefly.*)

ELISA. Why do you say this now?

CIRILLO. Or at least I have been a great egotist; I was more concerned with
pleasing myself than with pleasing you! (*He laughs again.*)

ELISA. Spare me these bitter words! . . . Can't you see that I'm suffering?

CIRILLO. For this?

ELISA. Please!

CIRILLO. For a grief I don't know about. It's very sad that you are telling me
now!

ELISA. My grief is myself, Cirillo!

CIRILLO. (*Surprised*) What?

ELISA. That is why I've asked you to weigh your words! . . . You who did not
kill me, don't now kill the possibility of a life together! . . .

CIRILLO. What do you mean?

ELISA. You doubt having understood? If it makes you feel good, well then,
you guessed right! . . .

CIRILLO. (*He slowly places a hand on her shoulder. After a silence, in a voice that betrays
some emotion.*) Elisa! . . .

ELISA. Ah, thank you, thank you! . . . I want to explain to you . . .

CIRILLO. Don't; if you are sincere, don't speak! It's better!

ELISA. I can't keep quiet! . . .

CIRILLO. Don't speak! . . . Just imagine that a long time ago we agreed to meet
here today! . . . We shake hands and continue our journey together!

ELISA. I need to open my heart to you . . . (Cirillo *makes a despairing gesture.*
Elisa *continues with emphasis*) I want to tell you all the torment of my
soul ever anxiously seeking a happiness that lay outside my life. Ah,
how bitterly I've paid for all my crazy illusions, for my mistakes! . . .

CIRILLO. Stop!

ELISA. Forgive me if I've made you suffer . . . but I also have suffered so
much, and the grief I gave you was also my own! . . . forgive me! . . .
(*She weeps.*)

CIRILLO. (*Sadly*) Calm down! Each of us lives as best he can! . . . If in this
moment you are sincere, the past doesn't matter any more!

ELISA. Forgive me! . . . Do you hold it against me?

WANDA. (*From the left, calls loudly*) Elisa! . . .

ELISA. I'm coming!

CIRILLO. Go, go! . . . You too are a poor creature! . . .

ELISA. (*Extracts a small mirror and a compact from her purse; after drying her eyes, she
powders her face coquettishly; then she puts everything back in the purse.*) I'm
greatly relieved! It seems that only today am I beginning really to live!
. . . You know how to forget, right?

CIRILLO. You are the one who must forget.

ELISA. Oh thank you, thank you.

CIRILLO. Go, they're waiting for you! Courage! (Elisa, *on the doorstep to the left, turns to look at* Cirillo, *then leaves.* Cirillo, *leaning against a piece of furniture, looks for some time at the door through which she has gone, then shakes his head and remains pensive.*)

PAOLO. (*Entering from the right*) Hi, there! What are you doing?

CIRILLO. (*Following a thought of his own*) Well . . . Who knows whether she is sincere or only in good faith!

PAOLO. Who?

CIRILLO. She, my wife! What a scene she made a little while ago!

PAOLO. One of the usual?

CIRILLO. If it were one of the usual you wouldn't see me so preoccupied, my friend. Unusual!

PAOLO. Namely?

CIRILLO. She spoke to me of feelings of penitence, weariness, disillusionment . . . of . . . of sentimental projects for the future! . . . It's serious! . . . Oh, well! . . .

PAOLO. Ah! Perhaps you were right!

CIRILLO. Well! Too much emphasis! We'll wait and see! Who knows? . . . (*Exits left*)

SAVINA. (*Opening the door on the right a little, she sticks her head out, calling in a low voice*) Paolo?

PAOLO. (*He turns around, frightened*) What do you want?

SAVINA. Is there anyone on the terrace?

PAOLO. No, but . . . (*Looks around fearfully*)

SAVINA. (*Enters; she's in a very elegant light-colored suit*) Still! . . .

PAOLO. Someone could come in through the other door at any moment!

SAVINA. I'm tired of being a prisoner in those rooms! I want so much to go about freely in my, our, house. I seem to have forgotten it, and I have it so much in my heart.

PAOLO. What are you saying?! . . . Think! . . . What if someone should see you?

SAVINA. Now, who cares?!

PAOLO. What? The situation is always the same.

SAVINA. It's only up to us to change it; and . . . we've already changed it!

PAOLO. It's not the same thing!

SAVINA. It's the only thing that has value! . . . What do all these people matter to you? . . . Why do you still think you have to subordinate your feelings, your life, your happiness to them? . . . What have they given you? Only grief! And a few words by way of charity!

PAOLO. Perhaps! . . . But our lives don't consist only of us!

SAVINA. But above all, it's up to us, if we love life!

PAOLO. That's just it. One has to be able to love it!

SAVINA. (*With infinite sweetness*) Paolo. We are both weak people convalescing from a deep sorrow . . . Realize that we must forget! . . . And only love can accomplish the great miracle of healing memories! . . . Why do you act this way?

PAOLO. It's stronger than I am . . .

SAVINA. That's not true! You love me! . . . And nothing is stronger than love!

PAOLO. I don't know! It's as though I've fallen back into a pit! Look, you triumph over me, over my life! . . .

SAVINA. It's not me, it's your love that triumphs!

PAOLO. Oh! But how can you be so sure of my love? Maybe you're deceiving yourself!

SAVINA. No, I'm not! Only through love have you been able to conquer yourself, only through love have you been able to free yourself from the enormous phantoms of social prejudice!

PAOLO. Maybe you're deceiving yourself!

SAVINA. And then the heart of a woman, of a woman who loves, Paolo, is a mirror of truth, like a page from the Gospel. And in my heart I feel mirrored all the frenzy of your love. No, I am not deceiving myself, Paolo!

PAOLO. Maybe you've been deceived. Perhaps your heart lies to you! Oh, you don't know all the torment that has been loosened within me this past night!

SAVINA. I knew that!

PAOLO. When I had you in my arms again! . . . When I felt again the ardent throbbing of your flesh! . . .

SAVINA. I was yours! . . .

PAOLO. When I saw you agonize under my passion! . . . I was seized by a destructive madness! . . . Within me I felt whirling all the deepest instincts, the hatred, the wild cruelties that lie dormant in our origins! I could have crushed you . . . I could have annihilated something in you forever, forever . . . It was the primitive beast leaping out to snatch back something taken from him with a childish snare, feeling his claws breaking against a thin veil woven in mystery! . . .Your memories, there is my despair! . . .

SAVINA. Paolo!

PAOLO. And then I had the sensation that I was lying in the depths of an abyss, all my limbs overcome, all will broken! . . .

SAVINA. You wept like a child last night!

PAOLO. From humiliation!

SAVINA. And you let me dry your tears! . . . You fell asleep to my comforting words like sighs of tenderness! . . . Without wanting to, you sought refuge in me in spite of the harm I had done you! . . . One cannot love more than that, Paolo! . . . That's why I have no doubts!

PAOLO. I feel nothing but my own anguish!

SAVINA. You love me! . . .

PAOLO. No, I don't love you! . . . Try to understand me! . . . I want to have you in absolute possession! Mine only! . . . And this, from now on . . .

SAVINA. Oh! If my sin has generated in you the necessity for this cruel love, I forgive myself! . . .

PAOLO. What?

SAVINA. Yes, because, before, your love was asleep at the bottom of your heart, you were ignoring it yourself. But today, now that you are all a cry of desire, today I feel truly loved! . . .

PAOLO. Be quiet, don't you see my torment?

SAVINA. Great passions stay alive, they nurture themselves on torment.

PAOLO. Be quiet, be quiet! . . .

SAVINA. We understand the supreme beauty of love only when we feel our souls break into sobs! . . .

PAOLO. You're cruel!

SAVINA. I love you because you love me!

PAOLO. You love me?! Ah!

SAVINA. I have loved only you!

PAOLO. Oh, this is it . . . But how can I be certain?

SAVINA. By feeling how I am all yours! . . .

PAOLO. All mine? Ah! . . . I seem to see on your skin the violent marks of the past!

SAVINA. You will forget!

PAOLO. How?

SAVINA. Because I have forgotten. Within me there is no memory of anything, anything! . . . Last night I gave myself to you serenely. This is the certainty that will make you find peace again! . . .

PAOLO. Are you sure? Your lips . . . your hair . . . (*In a muffled cry*) Ah! (*He seizes her, he strains her against his body, as if to assure his physical possession, he bends her under his grip. Then, after some time, he lets go of her and falls into an armchair.*)

SAVINA. If I were not here close to you! . . . If I were dead! . . . (Paolo *signals her to be quiet.*) Think of this if you want to understand your love! . . . Instead, I am near you, trembling, all entreating and submissive, anxious to please you, so that you might love me, so much, because without your love I would be a wretched, lost creature, finished, and I would be unable to do anything but weep, but weep, Paolo! . . . (*She is at his feet, and muffles her crying on his knees.*)

PAOLO. (*He caresses her hair, touched by emotion.*) Loving someone means suffering for him! . . . And I have suffered very, very much for you. I loved you and still love you so much! . . .

SAVINA. Paolo! . . .

PAOLO. So much! . . .

SAVINA. Forgive me!

PAOLO. No, don't talk like this now! . . . Let's think about the future! . . . Get up, dry your eyes! . . . It's past! . . .

SAVINA. (*Rising*) The future . . . You say! . . . As you wish! . . . With you! . . .

PAOLO. With me, yes! . . . Go over there now, I'm going down to see what's happening downstairs! . . . (*He accompanies her to the door on the right, she exits. He crosses the living room to go out through the door on the left.*)

LUCIANO. (*Enters from the rear. He is in a black frock coat and is carrying a top hat in his hand; in his other hand he has a bunch of violets. Seeing Paolo, he stops.*) You sent word that I shouldn't miss the funeral; that's why I'm here! . . .

(*Paolo looks at him coldly and exits through the door on the left. Luciano turns to watch him go.*)

SAVINA. (*Entering from the right*) Listen, Paolo! . . .

(*She sees Luciano and stops; she would like to turn back, but Luciano, at the sound of her voice, turns around and sees her. He gives a short muffled cry, and in a gesture of horror throws the hat and the bunch of violets in the air. Then, attempting to free himself from his anguish, he makes some mad and spasmodic movements. Wide-eyed, open-mouthed, entirely shaken by horrendous fear, he automatically takes a few steps backward, until he bumps against the piano and remains there as though he were nailed to it, his hands pressed against the keyboard, which at his every start emits harsh tunes. He is a man who has seen a corpse revived. Savina, who has watched Luciano in his surprise and terror, laughs ironically; then she takes a few steps toward a little table near her. Luciano makes another terrified gesture. She takes a newspaper, unfolds it, begins to read in a cold and ironic voice a passage from the harangue that Luciano had delivered in court. At intervals she turns her eyes away from the page, almost knowing by heart Luciano's words. He listens to her, as if beside himself, struck with horror.*)

SAVINA. "Well then, gentlemen of the jury, that woman who employed every cunning skill in order to keep her husband's trustful devotion, while she carried her lustful beauty into the feverish recesses of sin and vice, that woman deserves no compassion, no excuse; a greedy woman of perverse feelings, sick from betrayal, devoid of any decency and any moral sense!" . . . (*She slowly crumples the newspaper and tosses it at Luciano's feet, looking him straight in the face, mockingly!*) Beggar!

... (*A moment later she bursts into shrill laughter and turns her back on him.* Luciano *makes a great effort to control himself, moves away from the piano, which is still producing some sounds, runs away terrified toward the door on the left. But on the doorstep he meets* Paolo *who is returning.* Luciano *vacillates for a moment, then dashes out the back.*)

PAOLO. (*Enraged, he turns around to look at him, then in an excited voice, he says to* Savina) You met with that man?

SAVINA. Coming in I found him here.

PAOLO. And you spoke to him?

SAVINA. Didn't you see him? He seemed mad. I destroyed him with his own words, those of the defense! . . .

PAOLO. Ah! And now?

MARCO. (*Enters from the left, followed by* Cirillo *and* Piero. *Upon seeing* Savina *he jumps, remains for a moment still and confused.* Cirillo *and* Piero *are astonished from the shock. All three stand as though petrified.*) What?! . . .

CIRILLO. What?! . . .

PIERO. What?!

MARCO. What kind of a joke is this?

PAOLO. (*Calm and indifferent*) Well! . . .

MARCO. She's alive? . . .

PAOLO. Well! . . .

MARCO. And what about the corpse they are carrying away, whose body is that?!

PAOLO. Well! . . .

MARCO. (*To* Savina) And you . . . you! . . .

SAVINA. Well! . . .

PIERO. A voice from the other world! . . .

MARCO. Well! . . . Well! . . . What kind of answers are those?! . . . I'm asking you to explain . . .

PAOLO. Explain? Why? Explain what? Don't you have eyes? . . . Haven't you seen? That's it! . . .

(Cirillo *has sat down and with difficulty restrains his laughter.*)

MARCO. Oh! You think that's enough! Too easy to get away with that!

PAOLO. Excuse me, who are you? . . . After all, what business is it of yours? Rejoice that she is alive, and that's enough! . . .

MARCO. Oh, no!

SAVINA. (*Ironically*) Thanks! . . .

MARCO. This isn't the time to be funny! (*To* Paolo) Oh, do you think it's right to make fun of people in this way!

PAOLO. Do you want me to kill her in order to please you?

MARCO. Oh, you take it so lightly? . . .

PAOLO. You're beginning to annoy me!

MARCO. Oh yeah! . . .

PIERO. (*Touches* Savina *as if to make sure she's alive; he says to her in a low voice.*) I am very happy about this! . . . (*She stretches her hand to him and he wrings it*) You cannot deny it, she is still warm, and how! . . . (Savina *goes out slowly on the right.*)

MARCO. And you suppose they will let you make a mockery of the law?

PAOLO. Oh, you judges make just as much mockery of it, your Honor! . . .

MARCO. Very well! . . . But I warn you that this time you'll go to jail! . . .

PAOLO. What?! . . .

MARCO. Oh yes, my dear man, just so! . . . Simulation of a crime! . . . (*With an almost sarcastic joy and triumphant air*) Article 211 of the Penal Code, 211 . . . "Whoever reports to the judicial authorities, or to a public official having the duty to refer to the authorities themselves a crime which he knows was not committed, etc., etc . . . up to thirty months!" What do you say to that?

PAOLO. (*Very irritated*) I say . . . I say . . . But how is that possible? I killed her and they acquit me . . . I haven't killed her and they send me to jail? . . . Oh but it's absurd!! . . .

MARCO. Article 211! . . .

PIERO. Yes! . . . The Law . . . doesn't know law!

MARCO. Wait, wait! . . . Now that I think of it . . . that's not all!

PAOLO. Oh no?!

MARCO. Perjury! . . . do you understand? . . . Perjury! . . . You declared to a public official that your wife was dead; you identified, yesterday, as your dead wife the corpse that lies down there! . . . Article 279! . . . "Whoever falsely certifies to a public official, in a public act, his own or another person's identity or status, etc., etc., is punished by imprisonment from three months to one year; —pay attention!—from nine to thirty months, if it concerns records of Vital Statistics or Judicial Authority." Do you understand? . . .

PAOLO. It's fantastic!

MARCO. Thirty plus thirty, sixty months which, at the most, may be reduced to forty-five! . . . Are you satisfied? Take it as a joke! Take it as a joke! . . .

PAOLO. Aahh! I've had enough of this! . . . You can go to hell, you, the Law, the Penal Code, the Court, and everyone else . . . I don't give a damn!

MARCO. It won't be easy! . . . Crime subject to prosecution! You can be imprisoned immediately!

PAOLO. I don't give a damn!

PIERO. What a criminal!

MARCO. And what about the corpse? Whose body could it be? It will be necessary to reopen the case, to have an autopsy . . . Suicide or homicide? . . . This is the dilemma!

PAOLO. What do you intend to do now?

MARCO. Call off the funeral, and proceed . . .

PAOLO. Proceed to what? You're crazy. Now you'll let them carry that body away because I don't want it here in the house any longer; once it is at the cemetery, then you can do whatever you please with it! . . .

MARCO. I can't waste any time.

PAOLO. Are you afraid that I might run away from you? . . . And . . . be it understood, whatever comes, will come afterward, but now there will be no scandals in public . . . understand? Silence with everyone now, even with friends; there will be plenty of time for them to find out! . . . For now, let's not allow any foul snags in the solemnity of the funeral. Do we understand each other?

MARCO. All right, all right . . . I pity you! . . .

PAOLO. You are entirely free to do that!

MARCO. (*Exiting from the rear*) Who, then, can that corpse be?

PIERO. Oh! How amusing life is!

PAOLO. Ah, yes! . . . (*To* Cirillo) And you, what do you say?

CIRILLO. Me? I am making superhuman efforts to recover from this surprise! . . . (*He moves closer to him*) You were great! . . .

PAOLO. Do you think I was wrong?

CIRILLO. Wrong or right, it doesn't matter by now! I am very happy it turned out this way.

PAOLO. But now there will be a scandal!

CIRILLO. What do you care? . . . How many men who have killed their wives would be overjoyed to revive them, if only they could!

PAOLO. Just imagine how people will laugh!

CIRILLO. They'll grow tired of it!

PAOLO. It's always like that! . . . Even in the most tragic moments we are haunted by the ridiculous! . . .

CIRILLO. Yes indeed, in life the funniest, most grotesque happenings flare up along with the most frightful tragedies. From behind the smirk of the most obscene masks sometimes the most painful feelings cry out! . . . But we are not to blame if our happiness or our sorrow is not enough to fill even a single moment of our lives! . . .

PAOLO. So one must bear it?

CIRILLO. One must place oneself above our farces and our tragedies!

PAOLO. Be spectators of our own lives!

PIERO. Of course! . . . But what about Article 211 and Article 279? It's not easy also to be the spectator of the Penal Code!

CIRILLO. He was once, he can be again!

PAOLO. But how?! . . . I may be arrested at any moment, don't you see? . . . And I've had enough of jail! . . . Return there! . . . Oh, no! . . . Still . . . certainly it won't be Marco who spares me! . . . You heard him! . . . What shall I do?! . . .

CIRILLO. Run away! . . .

PAOLO. Where?

CIRILLO. Where?! . . . Far away! Take your Savina and run! . . .

PIERO. So many thieves save themselves that way, so many murderers! . . .

PAOLO. To flee! . . . Ah! . . . To be wanderers in the world, she and I, like two outlaws! . . .

CIRILLO. When people have money they run . . . as tourists! . . . A young couple on a pleasure trip!

PAOLO. This is what I am reduced to: I must keep hiding from the authorities! . . . Change my name, change my face, run from place to place, turn pale at the sight of every policeman! . . .

CIRILLO. It's an adventure!

PAOLO. And to have to hide our legitimate love!

CIRILLO. You lost a wife, but gained a lover! . . . What more do you want? . . .

ELISA. (*Entering from the left*) Well, what are you doing here? Are we going? And you, Paolo?

PAOLO. Oh, me? . . . No, I can't, it would upset me too much! . . .

ELISA. Poor fellow! Courage! . . . (*She walks close to* Piero) What a nice funeral! . . . When I die, will you remember to send me at least one flower?

PIERO. This will be impossible! . . . I will follow you to the grave!

ELISA. You make fun of everything! (*She sighs*) You don't understand the value of sentiments . . . (*She takes his arm.*) Why don't you ever come to visit me? . . . (Cirillo *watches her and makes a great gesture of hopelessness.*) Cirillo, come on! . . . good-bye, Paolo, and be brave . . . (*She exits from the door on the left.*)

CIRILLO. (*Falls into an armchair*) Again! . . .

SAVINA. (*Entering from the right*) Well, Paolo? . . .

PAOLO. (*Coming to life*) Oh! . . . Were you there? Did you hear? . . .

SAVINA. Yes . . .

CIRILLO. Savina, I was so surprised I couldn't find a single word to say! . . . But I am so happy that it turned out like this! . . . I'm rediscovering a good friend; and I am certain that now you can be happy!

SAVINA. Thank you! . . . But do you see what's happening now?! . . .

CIRILLO. If you love each other, nothing else matters! When you're together! . . . But to feel alone, instead . . . is sad! . . . And hope, hope only, is not always enough to fill our hours! . . . Tomorrow? . . . In a month? . . . In a year? Never? . . . Who knows?! . . . It's sad! . . . (*To* Paolo) Good-bye! . . . and see to it immediately, you don't have time to lose, run! . . .

And, above all, don't kill her again! . . . (*To* Savina) Good-bye, Signora; I'm going to your funeral! . . . (*He kisses her hand for a long time, touched by emotion. Then he slowly exits to the rear.*)

SAVINA. Good-bye, Cirillo! . . .

PAOLO. Well! . . . He too . . . Poor friend! . . .

SAVINA. Well, Paolo, have you decided anything?

PAOLO. Decided? There's not much to decide; we must flee, and right away . . . (*Growing more and more excited*) Flee, do you understand, like any two scoundrels! . . . There's no time to lose; before evening we must be away from here, far away, because that man, that representative of the law, will rush immediately to reveal everything! . . . We must hurry, hurry! . . . In jail? . . . They will not have that satisfaction! . . . Oh, no! . . . I don't want to account to anyone ever again in my life — not to society, friends, the law, nothing, enough. I want to become . . . (*Suddenly in the street sound the notes of Chopin's funeral march. Paolo, who had reached a high point of excitement, quickly falls silent and stands motionless to listen. Savina, who is near the terrace, turns her head slightly toward the street, and holding onto a drape, is overcome with acute anguish. Paolo, shouting as though he were hallucinating, stretches his arms toward the coffin that is going off into the distance*) Savina! . . .

SAVINA. (*She turns—with tears in her voice*) Paolo! . . . (*Both look at each other with anguished intensity. Then with a sudden rush, she takes a few steps stretching out her arms to Paolo in a supreme gesture of love.*)

PAOLO. (*Gathering her in his arms and holding her very, very close.*) Ah, you're here! . . . here! . . . here! . . . (*He kisses her hair with great tenderness. The notes of the funeral march die away.*)

NOTES

1. A picturesque tourist resort near Milan.
2. Tanagra is the name of a Greek town celebrated for its graceful figurines; by extension the meaning carries also to its people.
3. A Roman slave who led a revolt of gladiators (73 B.C.).
4. Italian monetary currency.
5. French emperor (1769–1821).
6. Playful literary reference to the work of the Italian patriot Silvio Pellico (1789–1854).

A Man Confronts Himself
Luigi Antonelli

Translated by
Michael Vena

Luciano de Garbines (Gregory), forty-five years old
Luciano de Garbines, twenty-five years old
Sonia
Dr. Climt
Rambaldo
Mrs. Speranza
Rosetta
First Guest
Second Guest
Third Guest
Fourth Guest
Servants
Oarsmen
Ballerinas, etc.

The action takes place on an island outside the bounds of geography.

ACT ONE

Garden path which rises sharply, towards the rear, to a magnificent mansion. Unreal landscape, marked with synthetic crudeness and characterized by violet-colored cypresses which give the scene a violent aspect and set the tone of a fairy tale nightmare. The right goes off to the sea. On the left, slightly downstage, two stone seats.

99

(Luciano enters from the right, along with two oarsmen. He looks around with a satisfied expression, breathes a sigh of relief, and then searches in vain for his purse in all of his pockets, without noticing that the oarsmen have disappeared. Instead, four servants in turquoise livery appear, standing stiffly in line, ready for his orders. He looks around surprised and embarrassed, still searching for his purse and the oarsmen.)

LUCIANO. *(To the servants)* I wanted to pay those two sailors from the boat.

FIRST SERVANT. They're at the island's service, Sir.

LUCIANO. At the island's service? I'm on an island? So we find out that this is an island! Oh well . . . Who knows where those two sailors from the boat ended up . . . Is that a hotel?

THIRD SERVANT. No, Sir.

FOURTH SERVANT. It's private property.

SECOND SERVANT. The whole island is private property. That mansion belongs to Dr. Climt.

LUCIANO. In that case could you kindly suggest a hotel nearby?

FIRST AND SECOND SERVANT. There are none.

THIRD SERVANT. The island is very small.

LUCIANO. So I could only be here as a guest of Dr. Climt? *(The four servants nod)* Either be a guest or leave? *(The servants remain impassive)* But I hope that you will do me the great favor of telling me the name of this enchanting island.

FOURTH SERVANT. We call it Dr. Climt's island.

LUCIANO. Without any other more geographically specific indication?

THE FOUR SERVANTS: No, sir.

LUCIANO. I see. Then do me the favor of announcing me to Dr. Climt. *(The servants bow and start to exit)* Wait a minute. To orient myself, I would like one piece of information. This Dr. Climt . . . what kind of doctor is he? Old? Young? English? Norwegian? Christian? Muslim? You don't even know this? Oh . . . on my word of honor let me tell you, being on a little island, this is real ignorance. There is nothing left for me but to beg to be announced to Dr. Climt. *(The servants bow and exit)* And frankly I don't understand why I came here without a suitcase. That could be at least a clue to a starting point . . . because it's certainly a fact that I'm arriving at this moment, but it's not equally a fact that I left.

(A very young woman, dressed in a violet robe, appears from behind a tree. As soon as Luciano sees her, he bows to her awkwardly surprised and confused.)

ROSETTA. Turn back! Don't try to see Dr. Climt!

LUCIANO. *(Startled)* Good heavens! Why?

ROSETTA. He is an evil man! He will harm you!

LUCIANO. An evil man? He'll harm me? How is this possible if I have done nothing to him, absolutely nothing? I haven't given him the very least help nor done the slightest favor! So why should he harm me? What about you, do you need help? Are you in any danger? Although I just got off the boat onto this island a few minutes ago, I'm full of good intentions! And if you, poor young lady, are defenseless, I am honored to tell you that I possess two strong arms which I put immediately at your service.

ROSETTA. *(Laughs loudly)*

LUCIANO. *(Disoriented)* I beg your pardon, but I don't see how that can possibly amuse you.

ROSETTA. What good are your strong arms if he is such a powerful man? He will do whatever he wants with you. If you have elastic skin, he'll have you embalmed.

LUCIANO. *(Disconcerted)* Let's not joke about this. He'll wait till I die and leave my written will.

ROSETTA. That's not necessary. You're not dead yet, but you already feel as if you're being held up by four moonbeams and carried away in the air by bats in a dream world. Once he gets a hold of you, sir, he'll embalm you.

LUCIANO. *(Same as above)* For what purpose. My skin is not worth much. If this man is a collector, however rare an animal he might think I am, I think he's exaggerating.

ROSETTA. On the other hand, do whatever you want. I thought it might be good to warn you, but I don't know your tastes.

LUCIANO. Ok, but I can assure you that my tastes aren't so extra-ordinary as to end up getting embalmed for the love of my skin. How long have you known Dr. Climt . . .?

ROSETTA. For more than a century.

LUCIANO. *(To himself)* I see. She's crazy! My God! Could this island be one big crazy asylum? Here you have to watch out not to contradict . . . *(To* Rosetta*)* Oh! A century! Hardly a century!

ROSETTA. More.

LUCIANO. Hardly more than a century!

ROSETTA. What do you mean hardly? Haven't you looked at my face yet?

LUCIANO. I have. I have. It's quite beautiful.

ROSETTA. Well then, do you understand now why I'm so blue? I am sentenced by Dr. Climt to stay here for eternity! He picked me from one of the ships that pass around the island at night, and since I was lamenting my youth, which would abandon me one day, he commanded that I would never be free of it . . .

LUCIANO. Of your youth? Lucky you!

ROSETTA. If you knew how sad this is! It's sad because my life no longer has any glamour! Could you love a statue? No one loves me. None of my friends can bear my going on forever. And here I am contemplating this unchanging light, this hour without shadows when the sun never sets!

LUCIANO. *(To himself)* What an odd kind of madness! *(To Rosetta)* And so your beauty is without melancholy!

ROSETTA. Like a salamander through the fire, I can go through time without my beauty deteriorating.

LUCIANO. What's your name?

ROSETTA. My name is Rosetta. My name is the only thing which seems to be growing a little old and which gives me the illusion of fading away. It's a small consolation, about as small as the amount of air moved by a dragonfly.

LUCIANO. Rosetta! Poor Rosetta! Tell me one thing. Who is this Dr. Climt?

ROSETTA. He's a handsome, cordial man, a terrible jokester. In his craze to study—and he can study as many years as he wants—he plays around with people like a boy with puppets. That's his secret. He's a terrible man, I'm telling you! He can do anything!

LUCIANO. I understand. I mean, I don't understand, but that's not important. Tell me rather . . . you don't know if this doctor, in his free time, might be the director . . . I don't know . . . of some sort of asylum . . . Not that there are any crazy people in this asylum, I didn't say that! Crazy people, not really, but . . . people who are a bit nervous . . .

ROSETTA. No. To look at him, he is simply a man like all the rest. If he were to do good he'd be like God. But then again, is it certain that God does good?

LUCIANO. *(Embarrassed)* Offhand I couldn't answer you. Give me eight days to think about it.

ROSETTA. Well, he's like a god who condescends . . . to invite you to dinner. But you won't have to fantasize too much about him because he's coming this way right now. Watch out! You should have fled! I warned you! Now I bid you goodbye. *(Exits)*

(Dr. Climt, a man about thirty-five years old. Very elegant. Impeccable. Courteous manners, but cold. Smooth shaven, very pale. Thick eyebrows. A penetrating glance.)

LUCIANO. *(Goes towards him teetering, with a smile that seems natural)* Dr. Climt? Luciano de Garbines, very pleased to meet you. I was becoming afraid of you, but now that I have seen you I feel less uneasy. Just a while ago, a beautiful crazy woman was speaking to me about you fearfully.

CLIMT. Rosetta! A truly beautiful woman. I saw her run off while I was coming. But why do you call her crazy?

LUCIANO. *(Disturbed)* Isn't she so?

CLIMT. Not on your life!

LUCIANO. *(Terrified)* But then . . . all of this is turning into something terrible! . . . Isn't a woman who has spoken in such terms crazy?

CLIMT. I don't know how she spoke. In any case . . . where do you think you are?

LUCIANO. On an island.

CLIMT. On an island where?

LUCIANO. In the world . . . Certainly we're in the world.

CLIMT. *(Coldly)* Which one?

LUCIANO. *(Stunned)* My god! If we're going that far . . . I can tell you that I have not traveled that much.

CLIMT. *(Looking at him attentively)* What's your name?

LUCIANO. Luciano de Garbines, a name with a long ending . . .

CLIMT. Age?

LUCIANO. Age . . . Well, in truth, I'm forty-six . . . But I'm used to cutting that down a bit by two years . . . Then you have to take into account that I look four years younger . . . So forty-six minus two is forty-four . . . Minus another four years which I should take off leaves forty.

CLIMT. Have you been married?

LUCIANO. Yes, unfortunately! But I was already a widower at twenty-six, following an earthly marital tragedy . . . And I have been a widower ever since. A few days ago, I think, I boarded a ship. Then another day—or night—a torpedo off the edge of a reef or some other similar kind of disaster sank the ship. I remember a big crash, and here there is a gap in my memory . . . a terrible gap . . . until I feel as if I'm waking up slowly . . . I sense that I am coming out of this awakening when I find myself stretched out in a boat propelled by two oarsmen. And here I am.

CLIMT. *(Smiling)* Oh! Your story makes no sense. Sit down, my good man.

LUCIANO. *(To himself, mortified)* My good man!

CLIMT. Your memory stops at the moment the ship was apparently torpedoed. But from that day a great deal of time has passed. Could you please tell me what time it is?

LUCIANO. *(Looking at his watch, stupefied)* It stopped.

CLIMT. Yes! . . . Stopped . . . for how many months?

LUCIANO. For how many months?

CLIMT. You have not wound your watch for two months, dear Luciano de Garbines. You! A meticulous, fastidious man, absent-minded and good-hearted . . . You must have forgotten much in the aftermath . . . So many things can happen in two months! From now on don't let anything astound you anymore.

LUCIANO. *(Turning around)* Indeed . . .

CLIMT. You could be already dead and brought to me after a long trip in my rescue boat . . . I could already have done an experiment on your corpse . . .

LUCIANO. *(Gasping)* You're joking!

CLIMT. I am speaking in a joking manner of probable things which are not worth the trouble of making worse with my tone of voice. Keep in mind, in any case, honorable sir, that every man finds the phenomena of his old age natural and likely. But this is a serious mistake. If one day by chance you landed on the planet Mars, you, having been born in Calcutta or Rome, would find so many things to be crazy or impossible, while the inhabitants of that planet—which I have never visited either—would be astonished by everything that normally goes on in Europe . . .

LUCIANO. That is true.

CLIMT. *(After a pause)* Were you a man of wit in your country?

LUCIANO. I always had a good sense of humor.

CLIMT. Then do me a favor and smile!

LUCIANO. I'm trying! I'm trying! But this mystery around me, aggravated by that terrible memory lapse, I'm afraid that it is making me melancholy. . . . Dr. Climt, I'm speaking to you frankly! If I didn't have this memory lapse, if I could tell you frankly what happened to me from the time I fell, maybe, into the sea until now . . . oh, I wouldn't hesitate in the least to consider this place an asylum of charming crazy people and you, Dr. Climt, the most conspicuous of them all. But since in the gears of my existence I have to admit that a screw came loose, I no longer have the capacity for sound judgment and I am at your mercy, dear, and, as of yet, not altogether agreeable Dr. Climt! I was a very good-natured man when in my life, twenty years ago, a tragedy occurred. This happens sometimes to happy people. So, to begin with, I let many years pass. Then I said to myself, "Let's take a trip! Let's go and look for a country or an island where no other people are living." I would have preferred a place without Dr. Climt, a troubling man, but since I have to bear with you without any way out apparently, be kind enough to tell me what time it is. I insist on having the right time; it seems to recharge me.

CLIMT. I'm sorry, but this also is a serious matter. On this island no one owns a watch. After having created the most perfect and most marvelous of them, here mankind woke up one morning without the need to know the time. *(He looks at him attentively)* Luciano de Garbines, what is this drama in your existence?

LUCIANO. A normal drama, nothing more than a newspaper story. You are not my friend, Dr. Climt, for this reason I don't see why I should reveal to you such an intimate part of my existence. You're taking advantage of me selfishly, knowing that maybe I am the comic protagonist of a little family drama.

CLIMT. You're wrong. Survivors of great tragedies have found peace on this island. Queens, poets, murderers of passion, men nostalgic for bygone eras, people driven by curiosity of the future, vagabonds who looked like kings, kings disguised as vagabonds, all those shipwreck survivors picked up by my men on the high seas have been reconciled to their dreams by Dr. Climt. I was once a poor man like you, Luciano de Garbines, assistant in a physiology laboratory. It was then that, studying the science of the masters on my own, I discovered the eternal secret of the destiny of man, and so I fled from my fellow man, because I understood that if I disclosed my secret, mankind would be unhappy. Had I put Death out of commission, my crime would have been enormous, a monstrosity... People would have bashed my brains in . . . For this reason I came here, where I was able to continue my studies . . . Usually scientific discoveries are handed down by aging generations. Young people are forced to study for a lifetime, from the beginning, to know as much about it as old people and maybe a bit more. But then death stops them and the task is handed over to young people of another generation which, through new errors, adds only a minute amount of new knowledge. As you can see, it's something that takes a long time. On the other hand, give youth to only one man, youth for a millennium, and you make a god out of him! But I am not a god. I would have told you. And then, if I were a god, you would not have been able to reach me. That beautiful woman to whom you spoke a little while ago was found floating on the high seas. She was nearly dead. It took me three hours to bring her back to consciousness. She begged me on her knees to give her eternal youth . . . Now she's tired of it. There is nothing I can do. I want my experiments to have some purpose: not to teach nor tame our fellow men—that's useless—but to say something wise about ourselves. Luciano de Garbines, did your wife cheat on you?

(Luciano *is stunned, does not know what to say. Then he makes a gesture with his hand as if to say "so-so.")*

CLIMT. Yes or no?

LUCIANO. My God . . . You're asking if she gave herself to another man besides her husband, you're asking if she sinned outside of the family unit . . . the answer is yes, Dr. Climt! Yes, I was the most cheated-on man on earth . . .

CLIMT. Did you have any suspicions?

LUCIANO. Naturally, I didn't have any. I always had, rather, a blind faith in the wretched woman that was my wife for two years. I believed everything she told me. And since she never told me that she had a lover, I was fully at peace. Also, she used to wear dark color negligees! . . . I thought you could place a lot of trust in women who wore dark color negligees . . . so I felt reassured, Dr. Climt! I don't know if you've ever heard about this in your country, but I was born in Italy, where sometimes entire cities are destroyed and buried by earthquakes. And this is how my story becomes a normal newspaper story. The earthquake revealed a horrible deceit. I was away. I had been away from home for about a month. . . . My house, buried by the earthquake, swept away my faithless wife together with her lover who, shocking to say, was my close friend. As you can see, this kind of story isn't unusual. It took an earthquake to open my eyes! The earth had to be ripped open and swallowed and slipped down for me to understand! And yet I swear to you that I would have preferred to know they were lovers, but alive, rather than finding them together as if they were still placidly sleeping under the cover which had buried them!—When I heard about the catastrophe, as I got on the train, I was out of my wits. I would call out loudly, desperately, "Sonia! Sonia! Sonia!"

CLIMT. *(Moving away)* Don't call her so loudly while you're touching my arm, because you might see her appear here, as if nothing. . . *(Laughs a bit diabolically)*

LUCIANO. *(After having looked at him with astonishment mixed with disbelief)* During the trip though, as it happens, I became resigned to the idea of finding her dead. I became resigned and I felt deeply shaken, in advance of my arrival. I could envision the pity of those present at the scene as they found my behavior to be exemplary. I could see myself digging with my hands among the ruins. I even thought, although I dispelled such thought with horror—but I thought about it!—that I would remarry. Those are things no one dares to confess, but as I loved, as I adored my Sonia, I thought stupidly, sacrilegiously, of some other woman, maybe a blonde who would love me for this tragedy. I also thought—and I dispelled this other thought with horror, but I thought about it—of the funeral, of the epitaph, and what can I tell you! That train ride was so darn long! On such a long ride, let me tell you, it takes the effort of a hero to reach the last station! So I got there somewhat prepared to find her dead . . . I wish I hadn't found her at all! My faith in her was so blind that when I discovered my friend's body next to hers, I yelled out, "Oh! Look! Rambaldo is here too!" Then I added right away, " To hell with Rambaldo! . . . Yea . . . To hell with him!"

CLIMT. And then?

LUCIANO. And then, after that proof of faithlessness, I had enough! I had to leave, I had to travel. I went around the world, many years went by, I was torpedoed . . . And in the end here I am. Yet I think of Sonia without the bitterness expected of a betrayed husband. Maybe I made mistakes as well. I could have protected her, but I didn't know that she was in danger; I could have comforted her, but I didn't realize she was unhappy . . . What did I know about her? Nothing! Nothing ever! I loved her like a silly boy, and before I could understand her she was dead. We men are big animals. Women should know that!

CLIMT. Oh, they know! They know!

LUCIANO. Dr. Climt! I have always thought of the boy who never dies within us. You can live a thousand years but that boy is always young.

CLIMT. That's true.

LUCIANO. I noticed him especially as I began to grow older. Do you know that I talk with him every day? . . . Maybe he is the one who takes me by the hand, and I say to him: this is the road we took to get to school . . . Here's the enclosed garden from which those songs came on summer evenings, when women were so mysterious and life had the same sharp fragrance of flowers as in our high school days . . . You understand now, Dr. Climt, the pain I am suffering from! Sometimes when I'm walking absentmindedly on the street in search of my youth, I find it going hastily toward the same old mistakes . . . And as I run after my youth, panting somewhat, with my eyes bulging and my heart pounding . . . "This way!" "No, that way!" "Be careful not to fall!" Frankly, there's no way to make my youth listen to my voice because youth doesn't give a damn, while I grow older like a real dummy.

CLIMT. Good. Now I want to know from you instead what you will do when in a little while from the other end of the street you see your youth coming towards you!

LUCIANO. *(Stunned, then disbelieving)* My youth? Dr. Climt! Aren't you exaggerating in making fun of me? If you are referring to my youth as I remember it in a dream, as an abstract image, I told you that I encounter it every day. . . All I need to do is walk through the streets I walked in my youth! I'm its traveling salesman and its acrobat! But if you mean to say, Dr. Climt, that around the corner from that street I shall meet a twenty-year-old young man whose name is Luciano de Garbines . . . and you introduce him to me and I shake his hand, and this young man is none other than myself . . . myself from twenty years ago . . . then, Dr. Climt, I suggest that you don't joke around . . .

I believe that you're a remarkable man, I believe that you're a thousand years old, I believe that your island is not part of geography, but you shouldn't take advantage of all those things which I pretend to believe in order to please you . . .

CLIMT. But you came on purpose!

LUCIANO. *(Even more stunned)* I came on purpose?

CLIMT. Of course! Since you've been talking about nothing else for half an hour . . . But, dear sir, people always come here for something that others consider abnormal . . . You've been talking to me about your youth for half an hour. Why? Because, maybe even subconsciously, you're waiting for this meeting with your self of twenty years ago. . . Since you already are well disposed towards him, I can hardly wait to put you to the test . . . Oh yes! . . . De Garbines . . . In a few minutes I will introduce you to a young man—a strange young man! It isn't at all an ordinary meeting . . . You'll shake his hand . . . Try to be good friends, and please don't frighten him by revealing who you are . . . He would think you were crazy! Meanwhile, I will have to introduce you under a different name . . . And also try to greet Sonia graciously, your sweet bride from twenty years ago.

LUCIANO. *(With distress)* Oh! But it's terrible! It's terrible!

CLIMT. And your close friend will be there too . . . the one you found under the ruins . . . Rambaldo . . .

LUCIANO. *(Yelling)* Oh no! Not him!

CLIMT. Why not?

LUCIANO. I would like him to stay under the ruins . . . You have to admit that I couldn't stand the presence of the man that did . . . what he did to me . . .

CLIMT. But he doesn't know who you are . . . And it's only right that, if a page of your youth comes back to life, all the people who were close to you should be there; those who loved you, those who bothered you, those who deceived you . . . And I will do more! For you I will do something I haven't yet done for anyone . . . If you succeed—be very careful—in redirecting your youth on the path of that wisdom which you acquired through experience; if you succeed in short in saving it from the error which precipitated it into tragedy, I will reestablish the perfect identity between you and your self of twenty years ago, and you will again have your wife forever. I will cancel the drama by reversing materially the course of time and, as a result, I will erase it from your memory. However, my friend, you must succeed!

LUCIANO. *(With a whisper)* This is terrible! This is terrible! And what about you, Dr. Climt, what do you want as a reward for what you're doing for me?

CLIMT. Oh, I certainly won't want your soul! Even if I were the devil, I would have the good taste not to repeat myself! For that reason it's unnecessary to look at my feet . . . You look at my feet trying to see something cloven . . . But if you prefer to believe that I am the devil, go right ahead! I know very well that people prefer to believe in the devil rather than in science. And my island is too hospitable to forbid anyone from having an opinion . . . *(Roused)* Let's go! Come on! Put on a nice face for the arriving guests! Never have more unusual people arrived on this island! Sonia! Luciano de Garbines! May the honors of Spring be bestowed upon youth which lives again on my land! Come to me, guests of the shining island! *(Clapping his hands)* Come to me!

(By virtue of this invocation given in a loud voice, the stage darkens and lights up quickly. It is at first the light of dawn which then changes into a burning blaze. In the instant of darkness the chime of silver bells is heard. Meanwhile, little by little two women wearing veils, almost incorporeal, appear indistinctly on the two sides of the stage. They are supporting long festoons of flowers, along which pass Sonia and Luciano, holding each other's hand, coming forward, smiling as at a party organized just for them. Mrs. Speranza and Rambaldo stay behind.)

YOUNG LUCIANO. *(Leading Sonia by the hand)* How beautiful this is! And what great kindness on your part, Sir!

CLIMT. May you be welcome!

SONIA. *(As if in a dream)* We didn't know this island. When he learned of your invitation, Luciano told me, "Maybe it's from that prince we met on the ship?" I said, "Yes, from that prince."

CLIMT. I wanted to organize a party, and I remembered you.

SONIA. *(Bowing for a long time, with coquettish grace)* Very kind.

CLIMT. Let me introduce a good friend of mine: Mario Gregory, millionaire, renowned scientist, bachelor, my guest.

(Gregory [Luciano], who has been until now as in a trance, responds to the bow of young Luciano. The two of them stay facing each other. The young man also appears perplexed, like someone who is undergoing an inexplicable magnetic attraction.)

CLIMT: *(Continuing his presentation)* The young Luciano De Garbines! Lady Sonia, his wife. *(Goes upstage, towards the other guests)*

SONIA. *(With a slight bow)* Delighted.

(Gregory nervously kisses her hand. Sonia takes Luciano by the hand and goes off towards the rest of the gathering which has stopped to chat with Dr. Climt. While going away, Sonia turns curiously to take a long look at Gregory.)

GREGORY: *(As if waking from a dream vision)* How beautiful she is! God, how beautiful! And I'm not too bad either! . . . Look at him over there! . . .

MRS. SPERANZA: *(Forty-five years old. Fat, white and pink. Gold glasses)* How beautiful! How beautiful! What an enchanted island!

GREGORY. *(To himself)* Where did I ever come across that ugly face?

SPERANZA. *(To herself, observing Gregory)* He must be one of the guests on the island.

GREGORY. *(Bowing slightly)* Madam . . .

SPERANZA. *(Bowing slightly)* Sir . . .

GREGORY. *(To himself)* Where did I ever come across that ugly face?

SPERANZA. Are you a guest on this island, too?

GREGORY. Yes, ma'am!

SPERANZA. How beautiful! How wonderful!

GREGORY. *(To himself)* I don't know what I'd pay to know where I saw that ugly face.

SPERANZA. Indeed I have a formidable appetite.

GREGORY. *(Smacking his forehead)* My mother-in-law!

CLIMT. *(Intervening in a hurry)* Mario Gregory, millionaire, renowned scientist, bachelor, my guest—Mrs. Speranza, mother of Lady Sonia. *(Turns on his heels and leaves)*

*(*Mrs. Speranza *and* Gregory *shake hands.* Gregory *does it with enthusiasm.)*

SPERANZA. Did you meet my daughter?

GREGORY. I have had the honor just now. Her husband was also introduced to me. And you are his mother-in-law?

SPERANZA. Yes, sir. I am his mother-in-law.

GREGORY. My compliments!

SPERANZA. Compliments. . . about what?

GREGORY. Compliments because you're the mother-in-law of that fine young man!

SPERANZA. You . . . knew him?

GREGORY. I have had the opportunity to observe him without meeting him, but he is undoubtedly one of those men who . . . when you see them . . . I don't know . . . you understand right away that there is something extraordinary about them!

SPERANZA. Yea? That pleases me! It's the first time I heard anyone praise my son in-law!

GREGORY. *(A bit disoriented)* Believe me I know my stuff . . . Oh! What a pleasure it is to see you here! I see you . . . I see you and it seems that I am twenty again . . . when my mother-in-law was alive and I used to walk at the side of my poor wife. Now I am alone, Mrs. Speranza, and I own three islands, bigger and more beautiful than this one . . .

SPERANZA. What! Three islands!

GREGORY. Yes! I started buying islands just to keep busy.

SPERANZA. Three islands! *(Sighs)* Oh, yea! You're a nice man. . . a man of the world, one can see . . .

GREGORY. You're very kind . . .

SPERANZA. Oh, yea! What a difference between you and my son in-law!

GREGORY. In what way?

SPERANZA. What do you mean, in what way! In every way . . .

GREGORY. What do you mean! Don't you love, don't you admire your son-in-law?

SPERANZA. Not me!

GREGORY. *(Surprised, indignant)* Why not? Why not?

SPERANZA. Why are you getting so worked up? What difference does it make to you?

GREGORY. To me? Nothing. I would have sworn the opposite, though.

SPERANZA. I am pretending for my daughter's sake. She's an angel of a daughter. I raised her on the income from translations.

GREGORY. From French and English . . . I suppose.

SPERANZA. What a discerning man. I translate for three supplements in the daily newspapers.

GREGORY. Dear Mrs. Speranza! I find you very kind!

SPERANZA. And so do I!

GREGORY. I like your sincerity!

SPERANZA. No, I don't like my son-in-law. If I have to be honest, quite the contrary . . .

GREGORY. Be honest, Mrs. Speranza! Be honest, indeed! *(To himself)* My God! What is she going to tell me?

SPERANZA. I can't stand him. On the other hand, my daughter used to say that as far as a husband goes, good or bad, one has to put up with him . . .

GREGORY. *(Annoyed)* Oh, yea? Would she say that? Poor Luciano . . . or rather, let's say, that imbecile of a Luciano . . .

SPERANZA. Be quiet! He can hear you!

GREGORY. *(Becoming more excited)* Yes indeed, Mrs. Speranza. You can't imagine how that pleases me . . . I can't stand the idea of a son-in-law so stupid as not to understand . . .

SPERANZA. *(Approaching him, she touches his elbow, looking at him intently)* Mr. Gregory! Maybe . . .

GREGORY. *(Confidentially)* What?

SPERANZA. *(Cunningly)* Mr. Gregory! I understand you! You saw Sonia, and . . .

GREGORY. And so?

SPERANZA. And she made a great impression on you . . .

GREGORY. *(At the height of amazement, but going along with the game and humoring her)* Yes . . . Mrs. Speranza . . . Yes! Yes! *(To himself)* Damn mother in-law!

SPERANZA. *(Lets out a big sigh)* Oh, I understand! There's a void in your adult life! Right? *(Laughs)* Did I guess right? *(They both laugh)*

GREGORY. Dear Mrs. Speranza! You're very kind! But what are you hoping for your daughter?

SPERANZA. *(Sentimental)* What am I hoping for? Oh, a mother's heart! What a mother's heart hopes for! Well, the marriage which she made is not ideal. . . But! In the more than two hundred novels which I have translated, not one single marriage has joined together happy spouses, except those who got married at the end of the book . . . And to say that I translated them with the best of meaning! . . . Yea, it's true, a mature man . . .

GREGORY. Wise . . .

SPERANZA. . . . who could be a father and a friend . . .

GREGORY. Three islands!

SPERANZA. Yes, that's good, three islands! But, meanwhile, what kind of security is that for a woman?

GREGORY. One to be with her husband, one to go off with her lover, and one to bring all three together!

SPERANZA. *(Prudishly)* My God! What are you saying!

GREGORY. *(Teeth clenched)* I'm joking, I'm joking, Mrs. Speranza. I could never imagine you to be like this! Such a practical, modern mind... so independent... Really, Mrs. Speranza, you embody for me the most delightful of surprises. I admire you! I admire you! *(In a confidential tone, hiding the agitation and the anger)* But could it be that your Sonia . . . so serious . . . so pure . . . so uncompromising?

SPERANZA. My daughter? Not on your life.

GREGORY. *(Perplexed)* A few little flings? . . .

SPERANZA. Other than that! Other than that! . . . That careless little head of hers . . . Oh, if I didn't stop her on time . . .

GREGORY. What a good mother! Because they had gone a little too far, right?

SPERANZA. Other than that! But fortunately it was a young man. . . a young man you could say she had grown up with.

GREGORY. Oh yea? And who was he? Who was he? You can tell me! I'm a cautious man . . .

SPERANZA. A certain Rambaldo . . . A young man! What's the matter?

GREGORY. Me? Nothing!

SPERANZA. Oh, childish games . . .

GREGORY. *(Smacking his palms and shaking them with rage)* Luciano De Garbines, of course, is completely in the dark.

SPERANZA. What do you want? First of all, he's a man to whom you can feed any story.

GREGORY. *(Barely containing himself)* Oh yea?! Oh yea?!

SPERANZA. And then, you don't go telling your husband about foolish things you've done . . .

GREGORY. It's obvious! It's obvious! Oh, that imbecile of a Luciano De Garbines! You can't imagine my joy at hearing the echo repeat my words when I say, "De Garbines, what an imbecile . . ." The echo sends the words back as if they were meant just for me, and I get a real personal satisfaction out of this . . .

SPERANZA. *(To herself, joining hands)* He's in love! *(With pleasure)* That assassin of my daughter! She will hardly have cast a glance on him and his goose is cooked.

GREGORY. *(Looking at her with comic terror)* God! What a mother-in-law she is when you see her up close!

SPERANZA. *(Seeing Sonia arrive together with Luciano and Rambaldo, goes towards her)* Oh! My daughter! My daughter!

LUCIANO. *(Holding Rambaldo by the arm and bringing him in front of Gregory)* With your permission, Gregory: Rambaldo, my friend.

RAMBALDO. *(With a slight bow, but cordially)* Delighted!

GREGORY. *(Very coldly, looking him from head to toe)* Pleased to meet you.

(Luciano approaches the group with his wife and mother-in-law; they are joined by Dr. Climt who every so often glances towards Gregory.)

GREGORY. *(After a pause, loosening up)* Of course! I am happy to shake your hand, Rambaldo, okay? Rambaldo! Don't you feel as if you've met me before in your life?

RAMBALDO. *(Shyly)* No! I don't think so! How can it be?

GREGORY. *(Shaking)* How can it be?

RAMBALDO. *(Awkwardly)* It doesn't seem to me, truthfully, that I have had anything in common with you.

GREGORY. *(Sneering)* Oh yea? And yet, my boy, we've had something in common!

RAMBALDO. *(Honestly)* Yea? What?

GREGORY. A wife!

RAMBALDO. *(Horrified)* But, sir!

GREGORY. Mine, of course.

RAMBALDO. *(Offended, stunned)* That's a joke!

GREGORY. No, sir. It's adultery.

RAMBALDO. *(Same as above)* Sir, it is a joke of the worst kind. (Turns on his heels and leaves)

SONIA. *(Seeing that Rambaldo is leaving)* Rambaldo!

(Rambaldo *stops and turns around.* Climt *goes away from the group, together with* Luciano.)

SONIA. *(To* Rambaldo*)* Take Mama on a tour of the island!
SPERANZA. *(Slowly, to* Sonia*)* I've landed millions for you!
SONIA. *(Bursting out laughing)* Oh yea? *(Laughs again)*

(Speranza *goes away with* Rambaldo, *but not before having cast an avid glance at* Gregory. Gregory *has followed* Rambaldo *with his eyes until he has seen him disappear, with his arms crossed, and with an insolent attitude. When he realizes that he has been left alone with* Sonia, *he gets emotional but tries to regain his composure, to look at ease.* Sonia *peeks at him flirtatiously.)*

GREGORY. Sonia . . . Sonia! Your mother talked to me about you.
SONIA. And to me about you . . .
GREGORY. Yea!
SONIA. She said to me, "You'll meet a strange type."
GREGORY. Nothing else?
SONIA. She said to me, "You'll meet a modern man, one of those who have lived a great deal." And by "lived" she meant close to women . . .
GREGORY. And you share that opinion?
SONIA. Yes, I do.
GREGORY. On what do you base it?
SONIA. On everything put together.
GREGORY. *(Gallantly)* Does everything put together suit you?
SONIA. What a question! It's not a question that a gentleman would ask.
GREGORY. Then I'll be quiet. You give the definition.
SONIA. My God! What do you want me to define? An expert . . . okay? We women notice instinctively when a man is professionally—that's what we say—attached to our sex, and so we approach him more frankly, like when you go to see an expert on paintings. What would a whole-sale salesman of eggs do with a Madonna by Perugino?
GREGORY. So, looking at me you realize . . .
SONIA. That you don't sell eggs.
GREGORY. *(Observing her with astonishment, after a pause)* Do you believe that I have had much luck?
SONIA. Maybe not. Maybe you loved them too much . . . Maybe you stayed too faithful to one of them . . .
GREGORY. To one that you remember in particular!
SONIA. Of all the women you like, it seems that you remember the one for whom you've suffered the most.
GREGORY. That might be true.

SONIA. So you must like me too?

GREGORY. Oh, God! . . . Of course!. . .

SONIA. Confess then that you already love me. *(Laughs)* Tell me kind things! This island is enchanting! I don't know where or when, but I have certainly dreamed about it . . . Oh! You breathe and you feel like you're in the air! Tell me kind things which might not be believable but which will please me all the same . . .

GREGORY. What a little flirt you are!

SONIA. A little. A little more than others. But not much more! And so Rambaldo won't like what we're doing!

GREGORY. *(Slightly annoyed)* Oh yea! Is that so? Rambaldo won't like this? Could this Rambaldo be the friend that follows in your footsteps? *(With a resounding voice)* So he's in love with you?

SONIA. *(Swooning)* Oh! How in love? How? Try to find a beast on this earth that's more in love! Well, it's a bit boring having him always at my side but, my God, when you're alone and bored, there's at least that zealous friend to whom you can say, "Rambaldo, the scissors." "Rambaldo, take Mommy to see the island!" He does everything. I make use of him for these things. He's a boy, after all! Now, looking at you closely, I find something of my husband in your expression, a more distant expression, though, like that of someone who has seen many countries.

GREGORY. The expression of someone who has loved you!

SONIA. In another life?

GREGORY. Maybe.

SONIA. *(Laughs)* Then tell me everything about a man in love! Tell me quickly before dusk deepens. I insist! Do it for dusk.

GREGORY. *(Frightened)* Well . . .

SONIA. *(Disturbed)* What?

GREGORY. *(Same as above)* Well . . .

SONIA. *(Same as above)* Well tell me!

GREGORY. *(Same as above)* Well, your husband . . .

SONIA. Damn it! You scared me! What do you want to know about my husband?

GREGORY. *(Same as above)* You don't love him!

SONIA. What a scare! I sure do!

GREGORY. Confess that you didn't marry him for love!

SONIA. *(Seriously, sharply)* Oh, no!

GREGORY. *(Tragically)* Oh! . . .

SONIA. What's so strange about that?

GREGORY. And why did you marry him?

SONIA. He told me that if I didn't he'd kill himself!

GREGORY. That's true. *(He smacks himself first on one and then on the other cheek)*
SONIA. What are you doing?
GREGORY. When something is true, I smack myself.
SONIA. My God! From now on I'll only tell you lies!
GREGORY. *(Pleasantly)* Flirt!
SONIA. Always lies!
GREGORY. Flirt!
SONIA. But why do you defend my husband? Mommy tells me that a man always acts like that when he has bad intentions towards the wife.
GREGORY. I don't have bad intentions!
SONIA. *(Flirtatiously)* You're wrong!
GREGORY. *(To himself, more and more stunned)* And this is my wife!
SONIA. You're wrong because it isn't kind to think of a young woman with too much respect. This offends the young woman.

(Gregory looks at her with his mouth open.)

SONIA. By this time Rambaldo would have already asked me to take a walk with him!
GREGORY. *(Angrily)* And would you have accepted?
SONIA. Who knows?
GREGORY. *(Same as above)* That false friend who shakes your husband's hand only to betray him at the propitious moment!
SONIA. You would do the same. I swear to it. My mother says that all men are the same.
GREGORY. *(With sadness)* Oh! Not me! I would not do the same!
SONIA. My God! What exemplary virtue! What would I do with a man so exemplary . . . to keep myself pure? *(Looks at him with brashness)*
GREGORY. I'm just amazed by one thing! It's shocking! You're twenty years old and you talk about enterprising men, about women who resist and women who don't—all things which customarily one learns much later . . . I bet your husband can't even surmise you have such erudition.
SONIA. He doesn't, and I am careful enough not to show my erudition. There is always something to gain being ignorant in front of your husband!
GREGORY. *(To himself)* And that's my wife!
SONIA. What about you! What about you? Haven't you made some heads turn with your display of good manners! So tell me, were there more blondes or brunettes?
GREGORY. Let's see . . .
SONIA. But what a strange idea to start collecting islands! . . . Are there at least some women?

GREGORY. *(Angrily)* Sure!

SONIA. And you must like someone more than the others.

GREGORY. *(Same as above)* They are all my lovers! When I carry one off, I bring her there, and good-bye!

SONIA. And then?

GREGORY. *(Same as above)* They stay there for breeding!

SONIA. Ah! Here he is! Here's the man of morals!

GREGORY. Now that you know my intentions, do you have the courage to take a walk with me?

SONIA. *(Merrily)* Of course! You intend to kidnap me?

GREGORY. Maybe! But will your husband allow it? Doesn't he want to come too?

SONIA. My husband is afraid of humidity. He wouldn't take a walk in the evening if I begged him on my knees.

GREGORY. That's true! *(Smacks himself)*

SONIA. What are you doing? Oh, I see! *(Laughs. Then, all of a sudden, seriously)* Did you really love a woman who looked like me? How long did you love her?

GREGORY. Two years.

SONIA. And then?

GREGORY. And then she died.

SONIA. Was she faithful to you?

GREGORY. *(Looking at her, with rage)* No.

SONIA. Then you hate her?

GREGORY. *(Touched)* No.

SONIA. *(Moved)* Really? Because she died?

GREGORY. *(More and more emotional, taking her hand)* Oh, Sonia! . . . *(Kisses her hand, with his head bowed so as not to show his emotion)*

SONIA. So are we going to take that walk?

GREGORY. *(Elated)* Yes! But on one condition!

SONIA. My God! What?

GREGORY. You must never be with that man!

SONIA. What man? Rambaldo?

GREGORY. Yes!

SONIA. How can I promise? I never know what's going to happen to me from one day to the next!

GREGORY. *(Grasping her, torn between desire and spite)* Coward!

SONIA. *(Trying to push him away, but not too much)* Oh, how you love me! You love me, too! How quickly you're moving! I can see that you're not a boy!

GREGORY. Coward! Coward!

SONIA. *(In his arms)* Yes, insult me! Call me a coward! I like it!

GREGORY. Evil woman! I'll kill you! I'll kill you!

SONIA. No . . . No . . . *(Pulls him towards her)*

GREGORY. *(Having kissed her furiously on her lips, he pulls away as if horrified)* How aweful! How aweful!

SONIA. Come on now! What's wrong with you?

GREGORY. I'm a beast! A beast! And with big horns!

SONIA. *(Boldly)* Oh, yea? Because it was your wife the one who . . . after two years . . .

GREGORY. *(With theatrical violence)* Yes, Sonia!

SONIA. Poor fellow! Then you shouldn't brag about it too much.

GREGORY. *(At the height of confusion)* Me?

SONIA. *(Walks in front of him)* Come, come, before the moon comes up!

(Gregory torn between yes and no, holding his head in his hands, all of a sudden turns around with a gesture as if to say, "Come what may, I'm following her!" And in fact he runs after his wife)

ACT TWO

Large veranda of a luxurious villa. Through the windows the sea reflects the moonlight. The veranda is a large roof top hall with gray doors edged in red and with windows all along the right. A rectangular mirror reaches to the floor. Visible to the right is a black and white striped curtain. On the left divans with their cushions reveal the same decorative motif. Only a few hours have elapsed since the conclusion of the first act.

(Seated around the sumptuous dinner table are four men in white tie and tails. The first guest is forty years old, the others younger. The fourth one is twenty-five years old. Rosetta is in the middle. The very merry get-together is coming to an end. As the curtain rises we hear the confused mingling of voices, all of them laughing and speaking at once. But when the first guest, goblet in hand, rises to speak, everyone becomes silent immediately.)

FIRST GUEST. Ladies and gentlemen! One could not imagine this dinner to be as jovial as it is because of the toast that we drink to death. And yet, it couldn't be any more jovial! Today our friend has taken leave—how shall we say?—of her eternity. As of today, through the efforts of Dr. Climt, she is again a creature just like us, subject to aging, withering and decay. As a result, her life has regained all its charm. Therefore, blessed be Death which will come to meet even her, for whom life from now on will look like a prize!

ALL: *(Raising their goblets)* Hear! Hear! Long may she live!

ROSETTA. *(Rising)* My friends, this evening I wanted to reunite my most exquisite lovers here . . .

THE GUESTS: *(Make a hint to rise and bow gaily)*

ROSETTA. . . . with the promise that I would reveal my secret. Now you know what that is! Taking leave of you this evening is that doll that was unbreakable in your hands. Instead, you have a small creature, mortal like all others, a creature who has the joy of resembling you in all the sadness of a life coming to an end . . . Well, then, doesn't it seem to you that today I am alive for the first time?

THE GUESTS. Long live Rosetta!

SECOND GUEST. One must acknowledge that this gift received from Dr. Climt is one worthy of the munificence which the island grants him.

ROSETTA. Gentlemen! Each one of us has his own terrible experience to undergo on this island. Each of our destinies is marked by a will that lies beyond this world. But this embalmed youthfulness which melts away in order to become a mortal creature is truly an undertaking worthy of Dr. Climt, of this gentleman for whom our admiration is always a form of hate.

THIRD GUEST. I love him for his impertinence.

SECOND GUEST. And I don't hate him because I'm too lazy!

FIRST GUEST. No! He is to be admired because he has been able to create an island which makes a marvelous fiction lying between immortality and farce.

(The guests laugh)

ROSETTA. So, I drink to my death!

THE GUESTS. Long live Rosetta! *(They rise, except* Rosetta *and the* Fourth Guest *who was seated on her right. The men assemble on the right, chatting among themselves)*

FOURTH GUEST. We'll no longer call you Salamandra! You'll be our Rosetta . . .

ROSETTA. *(Rising, followed by her companion)* Why do you look at me that way? Why did you look at me that way all evening?

FOURTH GUEST. I don't know . . . you seem new. . . you seem reborn . . . up to a few moments ago I admired you as a statue . . . now I look upon you as a woman . . .

ROSETTA. *(Radiant)* Finally! Finally! Tell me then that you feel closer to me! Oh, tell me that it's so! Tell me that you feel closer to me!

FOURTH GUEST. Yes, yes, Rosetta!

ROSETTA. It's the first time a man has spoken to me like that! I've waited so long for these words! I've given up a thousand lives to have a man say such things to me!

FOURTH GUEST. Squanderer!

ROSETTA. To make up for it I shall be miserly with my days . . . And I'll watch them glide by anxiously . . . What will my first affliction be? *(Clinging to him with childish terror)* Gray hair? Wrinkles? Now I feel that time is passing, passing . . . Will you love me? Hurry up and answer me because life is hurrying by! *(She clings to his arm)*

FOURTH GUEST. Tell me that I'll be the one to console you the first time you feel pain.

ROSETTA. Yes! Yes! And when you notice the first wrinkle on my face you will speak to me gently. . . and I will love you even if your words deepen my melancholy!

FOURTH GUEST. My dear! *(Both draw near the group)*

SECOND GUEST. On my way here I surprised a couple running along the shore. She was laughing, laughing like a crazy person . . . She looked very young.

ROSETTA. And he?

SECOND GUEST. I couldn't figure it out. His walking was rather heavy.

THIRD GUEST. Who were they?

FOURTH GUEST. Who knows!

THIRD GUEST. Who knows! This island is given over to mysteries.

SECOND GUEST. At a certain point it seemed they would hit one another! . . .

ROSETTA. *(Cheerfully)* Then they were lovers! *(All laugh as they leave from the right)*

(Arriving slowly from the opposite side are Sonia *and* Gregory. *He stops now and then and gesticulates oddly.* Sonia *looks at him with curiosity and impertinence. Then she sits down, turning her back.* Gregory *does the same. Embarrassing silence. Then* Sonia *turns quickly.)*

SONIA. Just what is the matter with you?

*(*Gregory, *beside himself, without turning around, starts to talk, then stops.)*

SONIA. One would say that you are going crazy. So very nice to me at first . . . I didn't want to give in to you . . . You begged me, implored me, you started to cry. In all honesty can you say that I wanted to . . . Yes or no? No! . . . Finally I allow myself to be deeply touched . . . because I swear that you made me feel sorry . . . so sorry . . . But when all's said and done you have to confess on your honor that I absolutely did not want to give in . . . and that I strenuously objected and defended myself. Yes! Yes! Don't shake your head! I put up a good fight! You're intent on saying no, but it's not my fault if you did not realize it. And then? When finally I believed that you desired nothing more of me . . . and I expected . . . almighty God . . . I won't say much but at least some gratitude, right then you jumped on me like a wild beast and wanted to strangle me! I don't understand your strange behavior. If that's the way you express gratitude I feel pity for all those unfortunate women who've had the sad luck to be nice to you . . . And if you're sick, get some treatment! Oh! I swear that you scared me to death! I believed you had gone crazy . . . your eyes changed from those of a tame dolphin to a pair of cannibal's eyes. And I don't know where the devil I've seen such eyes before! I ask if it was worth the trouble to fall into sin, wronging a husband like mine—so good, faithful, generous, intelligent, tender—with irreproachable sentiments and an exemplary nobility of soul . . .

(Gregory *gestures intensely in agreement, but utters a blend of angry and satisfied sounds that frighten* Sonia.)

SONIA. Oh, God! Don't make those eyes again! This man is crazy! *(Emits a loud shout)*
GREGORY. *(Jumping up)* Shut up, damn it!
SONIA. *(Somewhat reassured)* Oh, yes! Speak! Shout! Swear! Say whatever you want! Seeing you so silent made me feel suffocated!
GREGORY. *(Tight-lipped)* I don't know how I resisted the temptation to strangle you. You are right: it was exactly what I wanted to do!
SONIA. But why? Didn't you beg me to give in, didn't you?
GREGORY. Yes!
SONIA. And I readily consented.
GREGORY. Yes!
SONIA. Well, then?
GREGORY. You shouldn't have!
SONIA. Ah, no?
GREGORY. That consent is your crime!
SONIA. What crime?
GREGORY. Your disgraceful adultery?
SONIA. Oh, this is marvelous! But wasn't it you who pushed me to commit it?
GREGORY. Yes! And I hate myself for it! I could punch myself! I hate myself and I hate you!
SONIA. Woe to me! I give up trying to understand a man! But if anything this could be unpleasant for my husband. How should it concern you?
GREGORY. It's the same thing!
SONIA. What do you mean, the same thing?

GREGORY. Yes, it's the same. . . from a moral viewpoint!

SONIA. *(Stunned, almost filled with indignation)* Morals! Morals! Ah, well! You, you dare speak of morality? Come on? I judge you roughly on the basis of what you've told me about yourself and from that brief experience walking in the moonlight, you unmitigated pig!

(Gregory *looks at her stunned, not knowing whether to protest.)*

SONIA. Oh, yes! You be the judge. I shall remind you of the facts in brief. All right! You accompany me on the beach and put your arm around my waist. That didn't sit well with me, but you assure me, following our first hundred steps, that you will be like a brother to me. Then you tell me that the sound of the ocean is a sound that consoles, that addresses itself to all sad thoughts and deep anxieties. As if all this weren't enough, out comes the moon and we continue on. I laugh, jump and shout for joy . . . We've hardly gone two hundred steps when you rest your head sweetly on my shoulder, assuring me that you want to be a friend. Fine. But suddenly you ask me if I love my husband. I tell you that I do and enumerate his good qualities. *(Gregory nods vigorously in agreement)* and you seem pleased, so pleased as to seem that these qualities belonged to you. That struck me as being so dear of you, but then you kissed me right on my lips . . . I was about to take offense, but at that very instant the moon hid behind a cloud, and you said that the moon did so just for us, that it was charming on the part of the moon . . . And then you began with your strange talk. You tell me that my husband is possibly not my husband: that some day or evening I might meet up with a wiser, more knowledgeable, more indulgent soul mate of a husband, more experienced in life and more independent, on the beach, like you met me. I find it a bit strange that these fatal encounters have to occur at the shore rather than on a mountain or even a hill, but not to be contradictory, I agree with what you say because you're so delightful when you talk so oddly: but we've hardly gone four hundred steps when you force me to stop and swear to me that you will be my lover forever! Within four hundred steps, my clever one, you've come a long way! And now do me the favor of telling me why, after having compelled me to walk that far, including that large interval when we didn't walk at all, why you wanted to strangle me!

GREGORY. *(Deeply upset)* Yes! I want to strangle you! If during that moment when the moon was hiding behind the cloud you had given me a couple of hefty slaps, I would have knelt at your feet, I would have kissed your hand, I would have adored you!

SONIA. Then you failed to make yourself understood. My friend, if I had only known! At that moment I could have sworn you wanted something other than two hefty slaps!

GREGORY. *(With desperation)* And you tell me these terrible things without shame. You, Sonia, you! You make me so angry that I could annihilate you, pulverize you! You are the entire cause of my remorse! I hate you! I detest you!

SONIA. Ah! No, no. You're nothing but a madman! And now I understand!

GREGORY. *(Astonished)* What do you understand?

SONIA. Now I understand your wife.

GREGORY. Don't utter absurdities!

SONIA. Oh yea! Because with that bad temper of yours . . .

GREGORY. Madam!

SONIA. If she acted, as I presume, like an intelligent woman, I understand how she must have cheerfully avenged herself!

GREGORY. *(Beside himself)* Oh, really! Who gives you the right to . . .

SONIA. I would have done the same.

(Gregory hurls himself at her; she escapes, bursting out into a loud laugh. Left alone, he stops in the middle of the stage, scratches his chin and is lost in thought. Suddenly, noticing himself reflected in the large mirror against the wall, he thrusts out a fist as he watches himself with hate. Dr. Climt surprises him in that attitude.)

CLIMT. Well? What are you brooding about?

GREGORY. Dr. Climt! Dear Dr. Climt! I've ruined everything!

CLIMT. What the devil!

GREGORY. My wife, do you understand? She's playing the coquette with me! And she's a coquette in a way that she never was when she was my wife. I don't know . . . It's a matter of making one lose one's mind. She was never like that when she was with me . . . while that's the way she was with others! And she displays this attitude with the most unimaginable shamelessness. What's worse then is that as a husband I get angry but as a stranger I find her delightful! What a charming woman! What a magnificent lover! What finesse! What perversity! What refinement! But I would like to know why she has never been that way with me!

CLIMT. Come on . . . Don't get mawkish . . . Is there something else you dare not confess?

GREGORY. Yes!

CLIMT. Very serious?

GREGORY. Yes!

CLIMT. Irreparable?

GREGORY. Alas, yes! But to my way of thinking it's all the island's fault . . . Here one loses . . . I don't know how to say it . . . one loses the sense of the unattainable . . . Having cleared the obstacle of the human burden and of its traditional potential, everything is easy, everything is within reach . . . Just think, Dr. Climt! I never was unfaithful to my wife during the two years she was alive . . . Perhaps you don't know what it means not cheating on one's own wife . . .

CLIMT. Highly unusual as it may seem, I do understand perfectly what it means.

GREGORY. Well, I achieved this unusual thing without difficulty. I was loyal to my unfaithful wife for two years, as in an old English fable . . . Well, Dr. Climt . . .

CLIMT. Come on now! Don't think about it anymore. By now your good feelings are well known! Only a short while ago you said to me: my wife succumbed to temptation because I did not intervene on time . . . because I wasn't close enough to her . . . But if she could live again . . . Oh, I would be able to make a good person of her . . . And I am sure, my dear sir, that you are putting her back on the right track.

GREGORY. *(Shouting)* No, no, Dr. Climt, no!

CLIMT. *(Feigning astonishment)* No? What do you mean?

GREGORY. I mean that it's turned out just the reverse!

CLIMT. *(As above)* How come? That woman to whom you remained faithful . . .

GREGORY. I was unfaithful to her an hour ago! I was unfaithful . . . to her, with her!

CLIMT. *(Feigning incredulity)* It can't be.

GREGORY. What do you mean it can't be?

CLIMT. *(As above)* It can't be because I recall your good intentions. You felt the unfaithfulness so deeply that I cannot believe that, as soon as you encountered your self, you had the idea of doing your self such an ugly disservice!

GREGORY. *(Punching himself)* That's it! That's it!

CLIMT. *(As above)* Even not making a point of the fact that she didn't know who you were, still it was as if you were cuckolding yourself!

GREGORY. That's it! That's it! A horrible thing. A monstrous thing! My wife already said, without knowing to whom she was saying it, that I was an absolute pig. What do you say about that?

CLIMT. Oh, I'm not saying a thing. I'm enjoying myself. I'm your host, not your judge.

GREGORY. Because you don't want to humiliate me . . . But what a defeat! What a defeat! I wanted to begin anew . . . and begin right! . . . Oh, an hour ago that woman didn't know she was in her husband's arms.

CLIMT. She wouldn't have fitted into them so well!

GREGORY. Never, never was she so delicious! When I tell you, a completely different woman! . . . What a difference! What a difference! I wanted to strangle her!

CLIMT. Bravo! You blamed her, right!

GREGORY. Yes!

CLIMT. The injustice of men! But what more could that poor creature do? Not only has she accepted you as your husband of twenty years ago, but she accepts you, today, as a lover! What more can a poor woman do for the same man! . . . Your ego is flattered for having conquered her as a lover, but you would like her to have resisted you as a wife! You're hard to please!

GREGORY. Could I put up with her flirting with Rambaldo? I've told you the story of Rambaldo . . .

CLIMT. Yes, you said to me: Oh, I will guide her! I will separate her from that man! A nice way of distancing her from one sin by leading her into another!

GREGORY. But that man is ready to devour her with his eyes.

CLIMT. You are unfair, my dear Luciano—Gregory . . . You are unfair! If you can't resist becoming the lover of that woman—and you're her husband—how can you expect others to resist, who are, after all, just pursuing careers as males?

GREGORY. *(Open-mouthed)* The worst part is that I am helping her to prostitute herself . . . I have obliterated the sadness of a drama that had grown old with me. *(Becoming excited)* But at all costs, at all costs I must save that woman.

CLIMT. Still harboring some good resolutions?

GREGORY. Yes! Still! More than ever! Even if it means going to him . . . on my own . . . confronting him . . . telling him: "your wife is unfaithful to you! I know it's so! Therefore, save her!" I must prevent a catastrophe at any cost. I think that poor creature, fragile and bewildered, and badly advised by her mother, could be better off if someone . . . if her husband . . . if at least one of her many husbands could lend her support . . . In short I can't stand the idea of seeing her perish in the rubble, her unfaithfulness notwithstanding . . . Moreover I nurse a secret grudge . . . an intense resentment against that witch of a mother-in-law! Just think I considered that utterly mediocre translator of mediocre novels to be an ideal mother-in-law, an extraordinary mother-in-law, a rarity . . . that kind of monster. Nowadays she confides in me, and unable to imagine who I am, reveals herself to be that despicable procuress which she was. She even suggests that she would close an eye if I took her daughter away, and has the gall to speak ill of her son-in-law, calling him an insignificant man! Now you tell me if I am an insignificant man! Here she is . . . Look at her . . . approaching like a waddling goose.

CLIMT. And you make me forget my guests! . . . *(Edging away, he comes across Mrs. Speranza who bows deeply.)*

GREGORY: Here she is . . . here's the mother in-law!

(Mrs. Speranza *walks towards him, swaying her hips, all smiling.*)

GREGORY. *(Pointing a finger at her belly)* Faithless mother in-law! Cloying and immoral mother-in-law! (Mrs. Speranza *shrinks away somewhat, her eyes bulging in amazement*) You have gotten me involved in the most cruel deception! Having reared your daughter in a lousy way, you gave her to me in marriage, making me believe her to be a virgin of virgins, making me believe you to be the mother of the Virgin. . . . In short, you've gotten me into such a mess that I cannot resist the temptation of saying that you are the most charming and grossest piece of obscenity I've known in the last forty-six years down to this day . . . *(Modifies his tone, noticing her utter astonishment)* This is the way I would speak if you were my mother-in-law and I were Luciano De Garbines, your son-in-law. But since I am Mr. Gregory, bachelor and millionaire, I say to you: Dear Mrs. Speranza, God help you! Let's try to obtain some kind of divorce and give me your daughter because I am a very moral pig. Come and make merry on my islands! As a matter of fact, now that I think of it, I might put you on a separate island, with lots of sea around and in between . . . and without a boat with which to come and visit us . . . Otherwise I'd be cooked if another man, richer than I, turned up! Ah! I can no longer trust female translators. I'm joking, Mrs. Speranza! I'm joking! I've a terrible desire to fool around! Come now, a kiss on your forehead . . . There! It's enough of that! It seems I already regained a mother!

(Rambaldo, *looking inquisitive, having arrived at the moment of the embrace, stumbles in the very instant when* Gregory *is kissing his mother-in-law's forehead.* Gregory, *recoiling several paces in a tragic manner, looks ferociously at* Rambaldo *who gets very embarrassed.*—Mrs. Speranza *pauses a moment to look at the two men, then lifts her arms to heaven as if to say: "a massacre is about to take place here" and runs out to the left.*)

GREGORY. *(At a distance, with index finger pointing at him)* You seem to be and don't seem to be . . .
RAMBALDO. Rambaldo . . .
GREGORY. Rambaldo . . . Rambaldo . . . *(Looking him up and down)* What do you want?
RAMBALDO. Don't you recognize me?
GREGORY. *(As if searching his memory)* Ah, yes! It seems to me. . . you are the one . . . *(Seriously, hurriedly)* You're the fellow who is making a great

effort to go to bed with his friend's wife . . . Shush! *(Imposes silence and raises his voice)* I'm putting myself in my friend's shoes, for a moment only, and I tell you: "You are a dirty pig!" Just a moment . . . "Dirty pig" for the following reason: you pretend to be my friend. You follow me all over, even to the islands, and make an attempt against my wife's honor. You even become obnoxious . . ." Just a moment. Don't get worked up! He is still talking! . . . "You even have the cheek to take advantage of Dr. Climt's hospitality so as to improvise a marriage bed among the island's labyrinths. You are a false friend! You are a scoundrel! You are even a rogue!" He is still talking . . . Now I'll talk and say to you: how goes it, Rambaldo? How goes it? You want to know why, when we were introduced a few hours ago, I directed those strange words to you? Isn't that so? I actually told you that we've shared a wife . . . Oh, I have a bit of this fixation; don't mind it. Don't look at me with astonishment! . . . Really, between us, does it matter to me that you court the wife of a friend? Go right ahead! Want me to help you?

RAMBALDO. Listen, Gregory! I can't get used to your strange way of talking with me . . . unless you have your mind set to appear original, whatever the consequences!

GREGORY. It's only with you. Don't mind it. It's a kind of fixation, you're right! Everyone knows I'm sick . . . Aren't you aware of my misfortune? Oh, it's been in all the papers! One day a friend came to see me; actually he went directly to my house and made off with my wife. That's all.

RAMBALDO. *(Putting out his hand solicitously,* Gregory *puts his behind his back and looks at* Rambaldo's *as if it were an object of unusual rarity)* Oh, you poor thing! Listen, sir, I don't know how you can be so sure of a secret that I didn't even reveal to myself. On the other hand, this certainty of yours leads me to believe that it's useless for me to lie. . . . Besides, you are so original . . . let me tell you . . . that you can create a mess. Therefore, I'll tell you everything. You be the judge of my case. That woman . . .

GREGORY. Go ahead! Go ahead!

RAMBALDO. I knew that woman as a young girl. I also was a kid. Neither of us had thoughts of love, so that one day I became engaged while she was betrothed to the man who is today, unfortunately, her husband.

GREGORY. Let's go on.

RAMBALDO. We were in the country. As soon as she learned that I was engaged to another woman, she fell in love with me out of jealousy . . . and one night—we were in the country, sir—one night she came to visit me in my room!

GREGORY. *(Eyes bulging)* Eh?!

RAMBALDO. She came at night to visit me in my room.

GREGORY. I understand! You already told me! Well, then?

RAMBALDO. Well, sir, I treated her with respect.

GREGORY. *(Incredulous)* You? You?

RAMBALDO. Yessir!

GREGORY. Prove it to me.

RAMBALDO. By this simple fact: I did not love her! I reproached her gently. I made a joke of the situation and she left my room, the room of a gentleman . . .

GREGORY. Well done!

RAMBALDO. But that's not all!

GREGORY. There's more?

RAMBALDO. Yes . . . because you . . . isn't it so? . . . would almost praise me for my good deed, right? Well, no, sir! I regret, so very much regret not having made love to that woman. Had I committed a crime I would not have regretted it as much as I regret that good deed . . . She would have been mine, understand? But how could I foresee? Love came after the fact.

GREGORY. My dear chap, a quick decision is to made. You have to leave immediately.

RAMBALDO. Leave? Impossible! Under what pretext? You don't know Luciano (Gregory *gestures in protest)* No, you don't know him! If I leave under the pretext of a trip, he'll follow me. If I'm off to explore the polar regions, he'll come too, and drag his wife . . .

GREGORY. *(With sincere spontaneity)* But he's a beast!

RAMBALDO. *(In his ear)* An idiot!

GREGORY. *(Recoiling)* Thanks!

RAMBALDO. An idiot!

GREGORY. I understand!

RAMBALDO. *(Shaking him)* Wouldn't you say? Tell me! Tell me! Wouldn't you say? He's an idiot, isn't he? Why does he force me to follow her everywhere? I'm a coward. I don't dare tell him: "Look, I love your wife!" Instead I resigned myself to this torture.

GREGORY. Let me repeat that a quick decision is to be made. Soon, soon, soon!

RAMBALDO. For heaven's sake . . .

GREGORY. Because I am assuming that nothing irreparable has as yet occurred.

RAMBALDO. Ah, no!

GREGORY. Well, then, go away. Let me think things over. All for the good of everyone! Go, go . . .

RAMBALDO. Beware!

GREGORY. Go, go!

(Rambaldo leaves)

GREGORY. *(Pacing up and down the room)* All for the good of everyone . . . all for
the good of everyone . . . And now I shall tell the husband . . . Certainly, tell the husband. *(He stops suddenly, doubling his fists)* It's so difficult to talk to that man! He is so stubborn . . . that is . . . just a minute
. . . Stubborn, no! Just a minute! Stubborn is a man who has no doubts
about anything? Can he be called stubborn? Let's not overlook this
fact! Why shouldn't I talk to him frankly as one does to oneself? Would
I perhaps do something to wrong him? *(As if replying to the objections of
an invisible speaker)* Eh? Okay: I would have seduced his wife . . . But,
first of all, I had lost my head . . . And then, finally, his wife was also
my wife . . . Am I or am I not the husband? Old or young doesn't
matter . . . And what then? And then you were uttering nonsense.
(Changing tone and putting himself in the other's shoes) No! No! You are not
considering the fact that she thinks she's only the wife of the other
one . . . And it's precisely her awareness of belonging to him that you
should have respected as husband . . . That's where the deception
comes in. *(Changing places)* What deception? Just a moment, a moment, a moment. What deception? What deception?

*(While Gregory, replying and switching positions, debates and argues with himself
during this soliloquy, appear onstage, one behind the other, first peeking in their heads, then
inquisitively and on tiptoes, Luciano, Sonia, Mrs. Speranza, and Rambaldo.
Great is Gregory's surprise when he sees them all lined up, looking as if they were in the
presence of a madman.)*

GREGORY. Did you come to see a trained bear? Fine! Now I'll tell you the
story of the bear . . . This insane desire to taunt me that I read in your
eyes tickles me so much that I'll sit down right in the middle to make
it easier for you. *(Following his lead, all sit down at the same time.)* Well,
then! I'll begin by saying that it was a bear just like all the others . . . a
peaceful bear, moral, not philosophical as bears are usually thought
to be . . .

SPERANZA. In short, a down-to-earth animal! *(All the others protest, silencing her)*

GREGORY. Of course, Mrs. Speranza! A down-to-earth, but unimaginative, animal because one beautiful day he married a bear of the same type . . .
And it must be said that the marriage seemed to be a happy one—an
exemplary marriage rarely known in the city. No one came to the house.
Parties were rare. Only a black bear, who seemed to be a good fellow,
showed up frequently, and he was the only friend of the household . . .

(Sonia *coughs in a meaningful way.*)

GREGORY. Every now and then the three of us would raid a honeycomb . . .
But one day there was a tragedy. The wife, a bit sentimental by nature, got lost, failed to come home, and was awaited in vain all night.
The friend disappeared, also. The following morning . . . search where
he might . . . the poor husband seemed out of his mind. He began to
scour woods and mountains anxiously . . . Never before had one seen
a bear more exhausted in the pursuit of news. Finally, as a result of
searching, his eyes came upon a terrible scene. In the thickest part of
the woods lay the lifeless body of his wife, her throat cut into a trap.
And in the same trap, gripped by the identical snare, was the friend's
throat . . . End of the fable! *(Getting increasingly excited, standing up)* And
it is not without meaning for you because the characters don't change
just because they are transformed into beasts . . . and if I had a whip
I would crack it in front of you, up you go . . . Luciano De Garbines!
Are you a trusting husband? Look through roads and fields and you,
too, will encounter your snare! *(All rise together. Embarrassing silence)*

LUCIANO. *(Determination in his voice)* Leave me alone with this fellow. (Sonia,
Rambaldo *and* Mrs. Speranza *start to leave)*

SPERANZA. *(To her daughter)* What's the matter? What does it all mean?

SONIA. *(Doesn't answer, but looks mistrustfully towards* Gregory *and towards*
Rambaldo *who in turn eyes her questioningly. Then she speaks.)* If that man
thinks of playing a dirty trick on me he's making a big mistake! *(All
leave except* Luciano *and* Gregory)*

LUCIANO. Sir!

GREGORY. Yes, let's "sir" one another! It doesn't matter. Better this way! Sir,
I've told a little story that requires an explanation. Who knows why I
trouble myself with your affairs! No one knows. But it's a fact that I've
come to stick my nose into them! Shall we talk not like two beasts
ready to tear each other apart but rather like two men well disposed
to perform a good deed?

LUCIANO. *(Harshly)* I don't know you. In any case, I do not believe in your
good thought. I know that before me is a man who has, with absurd
insinuations, tried to cast a shadow of suspicion over my private life.
Anyhow, explain yourself!

GREGORY. You don't think that because of my age . . .

LUCIANO. *(As above)* You are neither my father, nor my brother, nor my friend.
I do not accept advice. I require an explanation.

GREGORY. *(Losing his patience)* All right, you presumptuous chap who raises
his voice on me, you must be told that it's necessary to keep an eye on
your wife!

LUCIANO. *(Threateningly)* Eh?

GREGORY. It's necessary to speak that way to a brat who wants to brutally confront a question which could have been handled with extreme care! The evidence? Perhaps I don't have any . . . Precise evidence? Overwhelming evidence? Not a bet. And so much the better for you! It means that you're still on time! *(Regretting his vehemence)* No . . . no . . . I didn't want to speak with you in those terms. My intention was to advise . . . to be a friend . . .

LUCIANO. *(With bitterness)* With you I'd rather be brutal! And . . . who might be the man who, in your opinion . . . There is only one man close to my wife. Is it on him that your delicate suspicions fall?

GREGORY. Calm yourself. There is a Rambaldo for every wife. I wanted to let you know so that you'd keep your eyes open for now. Since the moment will come when they need to be opened wide, and I'll tell you when, keep this to yourself and play dumb.

LUCIANO. *(Mockingly)* You love me so extraordinarily?

GREGORY. It's your youth I love. Your genuine expectations for the future. I had a love like yours, too, but for lack of vigilance it all collapsed.

LUCIANO. What collapsed?

GREGORY. The roofs of the houses collapsed; the dream collapsed and I was left searching twenty years through the ruins without being able to retrieve her innocence!

LUCIANO. *(Less distrustful)* Who knows what mystery lurks in you as you're facing me!

GREGORY. You're right. It's too terrible an omen for the two of us to be facing each other!

LUCIANO. *(Searching his face)* I sense a certain cowardliness between us. I don't know where it lies.

GREGORY. Maybe right in the middle!

LUCIANO. What's the charge for your services?

GREGORY. Not a thing.

LUCIANO. Could you shake my hand with the same sincerity that I can?

GREGORY. Our hands are on a par.

(They shake hands, perplexed with one another. Then Gregory *turns spiritedly towards the rear.)*

LUCIANO. What are you looking at?

GREGORY. Nothing. I was thinking that if I were Hamlet armed with a spear and I pierced that tapestry, actually that curtain, while shouting "a mouse," "a mouse," I would be sure to strike your wife right in the chest!

LUCIANO. *(Raises the curtain, pleased to show* Gregory *that he is deceiving himself)* You see? There is no one. You exaggerate your obligation to see deception everywhere!

GREGORY. She's not there? This shows that she was there, and that the mouse will reappear elsewhere . . . as a matter of fact . . . here she is!

*(*Sonia *enters with a march step, then halts in the middle of the stage, quite agitated.)*

GREGORY. Didn't I tell you? *(Then, turning to* Sonia*)* Has milady heard anything?

SONIA. *(Very irritated)* As a matter of fact, I heard everything! But you may refrain from addressing me! I wish to speak to my husband! *(The two men make the identical gesture, as if to say: "Here I am!" and simultaneously begin to step forward.* Gregory *changes his mind in time.)*

LUCIANO. Sonia! You certainly want to comment on the words just uttered by this gentleman in you husband's presence. If what you are about to say serves to clear up any misunderstanding, I want him to be present. Either he has committed a vile deed, for which I'll demand an explanation, or, there's a misunderstanding, and he will not fail to apologize to you.

SONIA. All right. So much the worse! This gentleman wants to open your eyes? He wants to save your honor? Just listen to how much he cares. It will suffice to tell you in minute detail how he behaved during our stroll along the seashore, a stroll I thought I was taking in the company of a gentleman! . . .

GREGORY. *(Very upset)* But what has that got to do with it? Just a minute! She must be crazy!

LUCIANO. Let her speak!

SONIA. When one meets a man of that age . . . introduced by Dr. Climt as being a gentleman . . . who could possibly suspect that, under such darkened surface of a doltish moralizer, there lingered an out-and-out libertine?

GREGORY. This is sheer madness!

LUCIANO. *(Irritated)* Be quiet! Let her continue.

SONIA. We were walking along, innocently chatting about this and that when this gentleman begins to flirt . . . "Hold on, Gregory," I say to him, "it's the first time that a man has taken this odd attitude with me!" He makes excuses and turns the matter into a joke . . . We continue on for a hundred steps and it's the same story . . . The gentleman begins to be angry with Rambaldo! The gentleman goes into a fit of jealousy! Understand? A fit of jealousy! Why? On account of that dear boy who, in our house, is like a brother! It's sheer madness!

GREGORY. It's incredible! I can't permit her to go on this way! On my word of honor, it's madness . . . allow me . . . allow me to explain before the lady continues, because I object to the meaning she attributed to my words . . . Just a moment! Just a moment! *(Prevailing over the other voices)* How can we all talk at the same time?

SONIA. *(To* Luciano*)* And he started out by saying: "I am jealous of him! I cannot bear seeing him at your side! I will do all I can to prevent him continuing as your husband's friend . . ." *(To* Gregory*)* Explanation? There's little to explain! It's useless to try to twist meanings! And there's more, more, more!

LUCIANO. *(To* Gregory*)* Don't interrupt! Let her talk! I insist that you keep silent and let her talk! That's enough! I don't want to know anything! There's nothing to consent to, nothing to explain! Meanwhile we know that you dared to use improper language in referring to our friends . . . What right did you have to do that?

SONIA. This man who claimed to be your friend and who for four hundred steps was absolutely indecent, has finally shed his mask, revealing clearly his real intentions! . . .

GREGORY and LUCIANO. *(Together)* Oh!

SONIA. But there came an instant when I forgot the respect due his age just as he overlooked the respect due a woman, and I landed two resounding slaps! *(To* Gregory, *hurriedly)* Would you like to have them? Here you go!

GREGORY. *(With farcical resignation)* Ah, no! There's nothing to be done! As a rule, a wife dupes one husband at a time. This one dupes two at the same time!

LUCIANO. *(Overcome with anger, takes several steps towards* Gregory, *and is lightly restrained by* Sonia*)* And now, leave! Go away! I don't know if I can prevent myself from treating you as the most vile of rogues!

GREGORY. Who me?

LUCIANO. Yes, you! Go away! I even made the stupid mistake of believing your offers of friendship!

GREGORY. But you're not aware, you wretch, that it's precisely you who arouses great pity in me!

LUCIANO. On the other hand, I harshly hate you! I hate you! You're the first man for whom I feel hate! I hate you with all my strength, and I say this with all the rebelliousness of my twenty years! You're the first man I hate because you are the first who dared cast an evil shadow over my life! I don't know why I don't manhandle you! Probably because you have transmitted some of your cowardice to me. But go away! Go away!

GREGORY. On the other hand, I'm still saying to you: "Save her! Save her while there is still time!"

LUCIANO. Don't insult her! Beware! Don't insult her! Go away!

GREGORY. And save yourself as well, if you can! It's a friend speaking to you.

LUCIANO. *(Mockingly)* What!?

GREGORY. . . . just as if he were speaking to himself!

LUCIANO. *(Erupting, with hate)* You are the worst of my enemies!

GREGORY. Me?

LUCIANO. *(Furious)* Of course! Of course!

GREGORY. *(Ashen with anger)* You're blaspheming! Beware!

LUCIANO. *(Grabbing a chair and threatening him)* And I tell you: go away!

GREGORY. Beware, I tell you! *(Tries to grab him by the chest, more to persuade him to be reasonable than to maltreat him)*

LUCIANO. *(Freeing himself and pushing the other angrily out the door)* Go away! Go away!

(One senses, rather than the bitterness of two adversaries, the hatred of two irreconcilable enemies. Luciano angrily repeats his "Go away" while brandishing the chair up high. Sonia, in the middle of the stage, watches the scene calmly, hand at her waist.)

ACT THREE

Pathway of a park divided by a hedgerow taller than a man's height. This hedgerow divides the stage lengthwise in two parts. On the right are tall plants. On the left a rose bed whose branches are so arranged to form a green chamber of which a wall, the one on the right, is part of the hedgerow. In the middle of this green chamber is a small, round stone table.

(Mrs. Speranza wanders about in the green room gathering roses and arranging them in a bunch. Sonia arrives from the right. Mrs. Speranza does not notice her. Sonia shakes her head as she watches her mother. Then she coughs in order to be heard.)

SPERANZA. *(Embarrassed)* Oh! You're here? You know, I was gathering roses.

SONIA. I can see that!

SPERANZA. I don't understand why you are making those eyes. You know that roses were always my passion. Your father got to know me that way.

SONIA. Good heavens, mom!

SPERANZA. Does it bother you?

SONIA. No, mom. It doesn't bother me that you gather roses. But you are here for another reason. Come on. You're gathering roses while you wait for a man . . . a man who, among other things, has not asked you on a date! But you, knowing that you will see him pass by here, you can't pass up the opportunity to block his path by picking roses. It is your literature, mom. Your literature translated into garlands! For heaven's sake, this Gregory has bewitched you. As far as you are con-

cerned, he is perfect in every way. You'd certainly love to have seen
him as my husband!

SPERANZA. *(With her eyes toward the heavens and her arms raised)* Oh! A husband
like him! Too much joy for a mother!

SONIA. And you forget, naturally, you forget that he has tried to get me in
trouble by inventing some stupid things. Mom! Mom! Mom! Where
is your dignity! Where is your self-respect! What will become of you
in life? At your age, mom!

SPERANZA. Eh! You keep pounding on this age stuff. An age like any other.

SONIA. It's not true. An age that shouldn't permit you to neglect your rub-
bing, your chamomile . . . Did you take it today, your usual cup? No?
You see? *(Mrs. Speranza seems very mortified)* See how you are? Instead
of acting seriously, instead of being serious-minded, you get interested in Mr. Gregory . . . The ideal man, for you! And then you complain you have a bad digestion.

SPERANZA. Do you want me to leave? Do you need to be alone?

SONIA. Absolutely not! Among other things, I have decided not to worry
anymore about anyone, except my husband!

SPERANZA. Since . . . when?

SONIA. This morning, looking out of the window, I said to myself: what a
beautiful day! Then I thought: who knows how nice it must be to love
your husband and not be bothered by what other men say! Believe
me, mom, it's good for the heart!

SPERANZA. I can see you have good feelings. Where is your husband?

SONIA. What can you make out, about my husband? He's busy following
Mr. Gregory's every step. He's become his police watch dog. Now he's
probably tailing him: how did it come to this?

SPERANZA. Jealousy?

SONIA. Who knows? I don't! But I don't think so. I believe it's this island that
goes to our head. It seems . . . I don't know . . . that I am lighter, more
transparent . . . It's a lightness, I feel, that makes me say what I think
without fear . . . even lies, you see, even lies burst out in such easy-
going form that they come out before I can even think about them . . .
Now I understand also your lightness, mom.

SPERANZA. Let me tell you, my daughter, no night goes by that I don't dream
about flying.

SONIA. See? See, mom? This is real lightness!

SPERANZA. I don't know how I set my legs, I don't know how I move my
hands, but yet they are there in the air!

SONIA. I can visualize that!

SPERANZA. Some day, my child, you will no longer find me.

SONIA. Mother dear! *(Throws her a kiss)* Now we are in agreement over Gregory. Some indifference from both of us would be more opportune. Rambaldo is a good kid.

SPERANZA. Be careful! He'll get you involved.

SONIA. But he's a kid! I consider him a kid. What are you looking at?

SPERANZA. Your husband is walking with a letter in his hand . . . with something he is observing attentively. Did you perhaps leave a letter around?

SONIA. I never write letters, mom.

SPERANZA. Great system. Nevertheless he's looking at a letter.

SONIA. Don't you see? He put it back in his pocket as soon as Rambaldo approached him. Now they are talking to each other.

SPERANZA. Let's go away?

SONIA. They saw us. They are coming over.

LUCIANO. *(From inside)* Sonia! Mother!

SONIA and SPERANZA. Luciano!

*(*Luciano *enters from the right followed by* Rambaldo.*)*

LUCIANO. Sonia! Mother . . . you come too, Rambaldo. Now that you are all here, I want to do just the opposite of what I had planned: that is to share with you an extraordinary happening I wanted to keep secret . . . You know what happened between me and Gregory . . .

SONIA and SPERANZA. Oh, yes . . .

LUCIANO. I had a violent encounter with him.

SONIA, SPERANZA and RAMBALDO. Oh, yes. Well then?

LUCIANO. Well . . . I don't know . . . There was something mysterious about his behavior. It did not seem natural to me that such a jolly man, who in so many respects still acted like a boy, would have a fixation for the wives of others. I must confess from that day on I have had, in turn, my own fixation. I followed him like his shadow! I felt attracted to a man I did not love . . . I felt attracted to a certain undefinable something . . . And I trailed all his moves, not to catch something in his life that might concern me . . . not that! But to see what kind of a man he is, how he lives, and what is the mystery surrounding him. Two hours ago he was sitting on a stone bench right in front of the fountain of the villa. He was bent on watching something that I couldn't exactly make out. I was, though hidden by a hedgerow, extremely close to him. At a certain point Dr. Climt's voice calls him. He suddenly gets up and goes away. I get closer and find this portrait on the bench.

SPERANZA. This is my daughter!

SONIA. My portrait? Oh, no. . . it's not mine!

RAMBALDO. In fact it is Sonia's portrait.

SONIA. But I never had this portrait. It is a woman dressed in an old-fashioned style.

LUCIANO. In fact! That's right! If it didn't seem to be yellowed from time and if the dress was not old style, you would say it's a portrait of my wife.

RAMBALDO. *(To* Luciano*)* What do you think of this?

LUCIANO. Since this isn't a portrait of my wife, it obviously belongs to a woman who resembles her in a unique way: the puzzle is all here! She resembled her so much that when Gregory saw my wife in flesh and blood, a ghost came back to life before his eyes, he saw it once again walk through the world. This thing cannot be explained otherwise, and this way it is explained very well. I understand today many of his obscure words, his excitement, maybe his madness! Don't be surprised then if I want to get close to that man again. Perhaps I won't ever be his friend, but the temptation is too strong. I feel a kind of attraction that pushes me toward his footsteps. I can't resist! It's stronger than I am.

SONIA. It won't be too difficult for you to find him. It's him, it seems, who seeks to come your way. *(She points to* Gregory *who is coming from the left)*

LUCIANO. Well then, leave me alone! I want to speak to him! I will tell you the results of our conversation later.

*(*Sonia, Rambaldo *and* Mrs. Speranza *go away to the right, turning their head behind from* Gregory's *side who is about to enter. But* Sonia *stays behind. She takes a few steps keeping close to the hedgerow and disappears among the trees.)*

*(*Gregory *is approaching with caution. He pretends not to notice* Luciano *but his desire to address him is visible.)*

LUCIANO. Mr. Gregory!

GREGORY. Eh?

LUCIANO. Mr. Gregory! I said, Mr. Gregory! Am I allowed to shake your hand?

GREGORY. What do you mean? Don't you still want to stone, murder, and eat me in salad?

LUCIANO. No! Rather I feel like telling you some nice things!

GREGORY. Oh! Well! It's a bit too much! On my word of honor it's a bit too much!

LUCIANO. Yeah. For example, excuse me for being somewhat violent, that day . . .

GREGORY. You were in your right, at the moment you considered me your enemy.

LUCIANO. But you are not really? My enemy . . .

GREGORY. Depending on which point the question is considered.

LUCIANO. Come on, be sincere with me. You are less young, therefore wiser and more experienced . . . Is there something in your past which brings you close to me?

GREGORY. What's gotten into you? Why are you talking like that?

LUCIANO. You really don't want to tell me anything? Not even if I gave you back something that you've lost?

GREGORY. Oh, yeah! You are exactly the one who could give me back what I've lost! But it's useless insisting on it . . . You have such a bad temper! Who allowed you be born with such a temper?

LUCIANO. Didn't you misplace a small portrait an hour ago?

GREGORY. A portrait?

LUCIANO. This one.

GREGORY. *(Very surprised)* Give it here? It's mine. Who has . . .?

LUCIANO. In the garden. I found it on a bench.

GREGORY. It's true. *(He quickly puts it in his pocket)* I did not realize I had misplaced it.

LUCIANO. Oh! Don't hide it so quickly! Let's look at it together instead! You loved a woman who strangely resembled mine.

GREGORY. *(Staring at him)* Resembled. . . Oh, yea!

LUCIANO. Don't be suspicious! Since I am coming to your help . . . since I am beginning to understand everything . . . and to justify your anxiety, your excitement . . . Looking at this portrait, I don't know . . . I immediately felt the need to ask for your forgiveness . . . Maybe there is a dramatic sadness in your existence that, by strange chance, is tied to mine . . . Isn't it true? Isn't it true? And I unconsciously struck my little resentment, my brutal suspicion, my stupid jealousy against that sadness . . . Now, if you talk to me, we can overcome this disagreement, and maybe become friends . . . Look: this faded distant picture, and yet present in your memory, is for me like a dream . . . Something that goes beyond the petty present reality . . . Memory and dream aren't basically the same thing? Come on! You still don't trust me? Bravely open your soul completely.

GREGORY. Yeah . . . yeah! This woman that I loved twenty years ago resembles so much your wife . . . resembles her so miraculously, that if I were able, closing my eyes, to relive those times, she would be the same!

LUCIANO. See? I was not mistaken. Only listen, but without getting annoyed because, my God . . . you also have a bad temper—your fault lies in believing that this strange physical resemblance should establish, let's say, a moral identity with the woman that I have the honor of having as my wife. Pardon me. You made me understand that in the two years of your marriage you were not very happy.

GREGORY. Just the opposite, I was most happy!

LUCIANO. Most happy?

GREGORY. I was most happy during the two years she was living!

LUCIANO. Poor thing, she couldn't continue after death!

GREGORY. But in fact it's her death, the irony of her death which destroyed everything! It was precisely her death which revealed to me her betrayal.

LUCIANO. *(Holds out his hand as if to ask forgiveness for having brought up a painful subject)* Ah, Mr. Gregory!

GREGORY. No, don't sympathize with me that much! Or maybe you should sympathize with me . . . Yea, go right ahead . . . Let's sympathize with each other! . . . Oh well, my dream is precisely what I want to defend this time, at any cost!

LUCIANO. *(Looks at him surprised)* Your dream?

GREGORY. *(Getting excited, his face convulsed)* At any cost! Yes! It's for this reason that I want to open your eyes!

LUCIANO. *(Frightened)* Oh, God! This man is really crazy!

GREGORY. You look at me with that contrite pity with which one observes a mad person! Okay, I agree to be a mad man. I agree to be crazy until we have established if I am crazy warning you about the danger you run, or you're crazy for not listening to me . . . because she is not betraying you yet . . . Okay! But precisely because that creature can be saved, I insist upon this thankless task. If she were to die—you understand? Any reserve on my part would be criminal, and any reluctance on your part would be unforgivable!

LUCIANO. Go on! Go on!

GREGORY. In no more than half an hour, notice that I am precise, Sonia and Rambaldo will meet right here.

LUCIANO. *(Looks at him surprised)* Here? To do what?

GREGORY. Certainly not to reason about the immortality of the soul. The soul is immortal, but they don't care about it!

LUCIANO. Naturally, you believe that this meeting will take place for sure?

GREGORY. I'm certain.

LUCIANO. When, did you say?

GREGORY. In about half an hour, when the oboe gives the signal that the party in the country is about to begin. Do you know there will be a party in the country?

LUCIANO. Yes.

GREGORY. Well then, the oboe has been given the privilege, I don't know why, to serve as signal, a thing that one would not suspect in an instrument so simple and of healthy traditions.

LUCIANO. *(To himself)* What if this man weren't crazy!

GREGORY. As you can see, the destiny of musical instruments has changed! Cats pet the violin on rooftops when they are hysterical. The coronet is even object of gossip in a good house. The bass, which appeared so serious, hides a sneering and cynical spirit. The accordion has a poison for every tongue, and woe to give it breath! There remained the poor oboe for the parties in the country, sigh of authentic shepherds and still in good stead for a certain undefinable simplicity which came from the valleys. Now you see that even the oboe is used for equivocal purposes.

LUCIANO. *(Annoyed)* Well then, I will wait for the sound of the oboe in order to run here. But if . . .

GREGORY. If it's not going to be, the crazy one is me. And I authorize you to place my head in warm water. In exchange, if I lose my wit, you'll regain your honor. Doesn't it sound like an interesting game?

LUCIANO. *(Turning his back to him without looking any longer)* Okay. Good-bye. But what if this man were not crazy? *(Leaves on the right)*

GREGORY. *(Spreading his arms like a man who has completed the most thankless task)* It couldn't be helped! It couldn't be helped! There was no other way with that stubborn man! *(He sets off toward the rear on the left)*

SONIA. *(Coming out of her hiding place, which is from the right, running in short steps behind* Gregory *who doesn't notice anything, she gives him a low bow, threatening him in a soft voice)* I'll give you the oboe! *(Disappears on the right)*

CLIMT. *(Coming from the left with* Rosetta, *he meets* Gregory*)* What's the matter, my friend, that you are so rattled? You don't seem to be at ease on this island.

GREGORY. *(Looks at him in silence, as if he were at a loss; then taking control of himself)* Here we are. When I see you, Dr. Climt, everything changes! I swallow the bitter pill and I even enjoy making a fool of myself! You should know I am still unable to persuade that man that his wife deceives him! I knew it would take a great effort because we have known each other for a long time but never would I have believed that I had to fight with such a person. Then when I think that ultimately it's a question of persuading myself, I wonder and say is it possible to be more beastly than that. Now I will drag that man to a decisive test. And if I fail? Will they go away? Will they vanish?

CLIMT. Of course. How can you expect me to keep you together, given your incompatibility of character? You would end up taking each other's eyes out, you and him!

GREGORY. Dr. Climt! When I am gone, in turn, from this island, will I be able to tell what I have seen?

CLIMT. Ah! When your boat passes again over the last concentric waves that leave from this island, you will fall into a kind of drowsiness like between wakefulness and sleep. Then, once out, your little wheel, which has been enchanted, will begin to function again, and you will not believe at all that you were on the island of Dr. Climt. Even if, with an extraordinary effort, you remember what happened to you, you'll think

that you dreamed it. That's why this island is unknown. At most someone can think to have seen it in a dream. Nevertheless, cheer up. Human life is but a small adventure in time and space. And man shouldn't
think of stopping at his small cemetery! You need to live in the meantime! Live! Stopping at the past, as you're doing, is like taking care of
a cemetery.

GREGORY. Ah! Your words make the world larger! But I still hope to snatch
my woman away from her tiny destiny.

CLIMT. Do you see Rosetta here? As you know, this creature for having been
loved so much, and indeed she is still loved madly, has renounced to
live her eternal years! Now that she has caught a disease and feels
next to the end, do you know what she came to ask me? To let her live
a few days longer. You understand? A few days longer, the one who
was tired of eternity! And do you know why? Because there is a man
who despairs at her bedside!

(Rosetta *has been silent throughout the scene and is moved by* Dr. Climt's *words which
she heard attentively; she is broken-hearted and now sobs mildly, hiding between her
hands an extremely pale face.*)

GREGORY. Ah! Rosetta! What wisdom in your sorrow!

CLIMT. Let's go, the party is about to begin.

GREGORY. And also my last game, Dr. Climt, will be undertaken shortly. (*All
three leave from the right*)

SONIA. (*From the left, followed by* Rambaldo, *enters cautiously, looking warily around*)
Come here quickly!

RAMBALDO. But, for heaven's sake, Sonia, what are you looking at? What do
you have to tell me?

SONIA. (*Motions him to be quiet*) Shsss! First of all call me Lady Sonia: bear in
mind that in this town every leaf on a tree is a listening ear. What do
you want me to tell you? That's the way the island is. Especially on
this stretch of the pathway, where you set foot, I am Lady Sonia to an
unbelievable degree.

RAMBALDO. But . . .

SONIA. You still don't give the impression that you understand enough! Therefore, hold your breath and listen carefully to what I tell you.

RAMBALDO. How you treat me!

SONIA. I treat you in a great hurry. Listen, we were supposed to meet each
other here in fifteen minutes . . .

RAMBALDO. But no longer now?

SONIA. Yes, still, my friend. Still! More than ever! But, plans have changed.
Luciano knows about our meeting.

RAMBALDO. *(Scared)* Luciano?

SONIA. Gregory told him

(Rambaldo *makes a gesture of anger.*)

SONIA. You speak loud, and he evidently spies on us. That's what happens speaking loudly. And they will come and listen from behind the hedgerow.

RAMBALDO. Behind that hedgerow?

SONIA. Don't keep repeating my words! Yes, behind that hedgerow.

RAMBALDO. Then wouldn't it be better if we called it off?

SONIA. Not at all! All the more reason, to meet just the same. Only, we have to keep in mind that my husband is a short distance from us. Do you understand? What we say doesn't matter. It's important to bear in mind whose ears are listening.

RAMBALDO. I understand.

SONIA. Are you sure you understand very well, Rambaldo?

RAMBALDO. Are you real sure that . . .

SONIA. Let's not lose ourselves in useless chatting. I'm very sure.

RAMBALDO. Then I shouldn't complain that you mistreat me!

SONIA. Men's ego! You don't understand the importance of this moment! I was about to fall into a trap and lose everything. By sheer miracle— then you tell me that it isn't good to eavesdrop behind doors! Then you tell me that one shouldn't listen behind the trees!—Things will be arranged instead so I can build a good reputation for myself. But this man does not understand the importance of this moment!

RAMBALDO. Because you're logical! You reason, you create, you undo, you redo! While I am reduced, on your account, to serve as the plaything of events, waiting for the right time to go to the dogs . . .

SONIA. *(Affectionately)* Don't say that. Your reputation is also on the line towards my husband! What would have become of you if, while at the meeting we were supposed to have, he had surprised you while you were saying nice things to me? And you do say nice things!

RAMBALDO. I would have said: it was my turn. What every man says when he loses a game and knows, quietly, that he is even setting himself up to be murdered.

SONIA. Really? You love me that much?

(Rambaldo *looks at her with intensity and passion.*)

SONIA. Do you know why I am like this with you? Who knows! Maybe . . . because you don't lie to me enough! Maybe, you see that in me there is something irretrievably rotten!

RAMBALDO. No, no . . . but I would like to know why Gregory is so interested in the two of us!

SONIA. He is crazy!

RAMBALDO. He is not crazy!

SONIA. And if he isn't, so much the worse for him. He will appear as such in a little while. And so he will be totally discredited. *(The sound of an oboe can be heard from afar)*

SONIA. Leave! Leave! Run out but get back here in a few minutes! Remember that I am Lady Sonia, and you are a good friend, who is talking to me wisely about good things.

RAMBALDO. *(Kissing passionately her hand)* Yes, yes . . . *(He leaves in a hurry)*

SONIA. I am warning you! A real good conversation . . .

(Rambaldo leaves on the left)

SONIA. *(Is about to pick some roses when she sees the ones left on the table by her mother)* My God! My mother's roses! I reproached her so much for those roses and just to think that they are the same ones! . . . *(One can hear again the sound of the oboe)*

SONIA. Again the oboe . . . a sigh of authentic shepherds . . . And here is my husband arriving on tiptoes accompanied by that unspeakable Gregory . . . *(She laughs, starts picking roses and singing softly)*

GREGORY. *(He arrives leading Luciano by the hand and every so often makes a gesture to him to keep quiet. He already has a supportive look around him, ready to affectionately console Luciano)* Look! She is there!

LUCIANO. *(With despair)* She is there! . . . Sonia . . . *(With anger)* It's definitely her!

GREGORY. *(With a comforting gesture)* Cheer up! *(He holds out his hand. Luciano holds it reluctantly)*

LUCIANO. She even dares to sing! *(Taking heart again)* Ah! She is calm and serene as if she were doing the most natural thing in the world!. . . No, no . . . I don't believe she is guilty! I'd rather think the devil bewitched her or this scene was created in hell, rather than believe that my Sonia may be picking roses and singing while waiting for another man!

GREGORY. I would like it to be so, my friend. But here comes Rambaldo.

LUCIANO. *(With bitterness)* Ah, in fact! There he is! I swear that, if she's deceiving me, I will give her away to you for a dollar!

(Gregory covers Luciano's mouth with one hand as if to force him not to talk nonsense.)

SONIA. Hello, Rambaldo! *(Rambaldo respectfully kisses her hand)* Thank you for coming. I cannot offer you a chair. I'll offer you a rose.

RAMBALDO. Thank you.

*(*Sonia *places a rose in his buttonhole,* Gregory *turns to* Luciano *to comfort him, but finds no other way besides holding energetically his hand.)*

SONIA. Well then, dear Rambaldo, thank you again if you chose, rather than walk through this beautiful island, to come to my place. Think again of the risks! Think if my husband might remotely imagine what we are doing!

LUCIANO. Shameless!

*(*Gregory *without turning toward* Luciano *holds out his hand.* Luciano, *annoyed, makes a gesture as if to send him to the devil.)*

RAMBALDO. You know, madam, with what great devotion. . .

SONIA. *(With stern ladylike look)* I know . . . I know . . . and I am not here to express my regret for the way it has been tried, by a person who hardly knows you and does not appreciate you at all, to give a disloyal and sinful intention to the brotherly friendship that you have for me and my husband . . .

*(*Gregory *and* Luciano *look at each other perplexed, with silent and reciprocal questioning.)*

RAMBALDO. If of my devotion I were now called to give further testimony, I would consider myself, madam, the most fortunate of mortals.

SONIA. That's exactly it, my friend. My husband runs a great risk.

RAMBALDO. Luciano?

SONIA. Yes! You know how good he is, how spontaneous, how easy to convince and to get along with.

RAMBALDO. It's his good faith, his righteousness, his sincerity that at times force him to . . .

SONIA. Yes, but he exaggerates.

RAMBALDO. No, he doesn't . . .

SONIA. Yes, he exaggerates I tell you. He exaggerates in righteousness.

*(*Gregory *and* Luciano *meanwhile hold out and shake their hands.)*

SONIA. So now, you see, he started getting interested in that Gregory, the one who even dared to bring a grave offense to my honor. You say: "But he is crazy!" And that's fine. But don't forget that he, albeit in an absurd manner, dared think maliciously about an innocent walk along the seashore: a walk which, if I had been more prudent and my husband more suspicious, I wouldn't have taken nor my husband allowed . . .

GREGORY. *(Between his teeth)* What nerve!

SONIA. And that's fine. Nothing serious up to this point. My husband is not jealous. My husband trusts me! I am certain that if he were told tomorrow: "Your wife has a date with a man: go and catch her," I am certain that my husband would respond with scorn to an insinuation of that sort, and would go off for a walk in a different direction!

(Luciano moved, humiliated, nods silent approval, while Gregory looks at him with an expression of pity.)

SONIA. But it is not about this. The serious matter is that Gregory is not just, as my husband believes, a man simply to feel sorry for. Gregory is unfortunately a rascal.

(Luciano holds, embarrassed but happy, his hand out to Gregory who, in turn, refuses to shake it and tells him to go to hell.)

RAMBALDO. Frankly, I must tell you, madam, I had the same suspicion!

GREGORY. *(Between his teeth)* Scoundrel!

SONIA. I don't deny he had some disappointments. That's well known. If his wife, my God! I blush having to speak about certain things! If his wife did not keep him good company and in the two short years they were married even found time to betray him and derange his mind to such a point that the poor wretch still feels the effects even after twenty years, still it's not right that such derangement should disturb our own peace! I don't deny he had some disappointments. But that my husband too should end up in a madhouse, on account of this mad man, just cannot be! And you, dear Rambaldo, being the great friend that you are, you have to definitely help me.

RAMBALDO. Tell me how, and it will be done.

SONIA. You must speak to my husband. Oh! He listens to you! He would listen to me as well . . . but . . . my God . . . there is like a shadow between us now . . . And if I tell him to watch out Gregory, maybe he might think I am doing it for revenge . . . You, on the other hand, have freedom of judgment. My husband has all the confidence in you that you deserve!

RAMBALDO. Thank you! Then we'll establish exactly what I must say to him besides what I think.

SONIA. Fine! But, my dear friend, do you realize that I kept you standing and prisoner for a long time now? As I have compassion for you, I propose that we think about our plan while on a walk along the pathway. Do you want to?

RAMBALDO. I am at your service.

SONIA. Fine. I will get, in the meantime, my roses and we'll go. . . And if we meet my husband we'll be forced to change conversation so that he won't be able to hear a thing.

RAMBALDO. While we conspire for his own good!

SONIA. Exactly for that! Ah! How strange life is! Listen! I happen to think that a good wife must always say things that could be listened to with satisfaction by a husband! Always! But this is the first time, you see, that I would prefer not to be heard . . .

(Luciano throws her some silent kisses from his fingertips.)

SONIA. Give me your arm, my friend, and let's go and continue our conversation on the pathway.

RAMBALDO. *(Quietly)* I will cover you with kisses!

SONIA. *(Quietly)* Quiet, for God's sake! *(Loud)* Let's go, my friend . . .

(Luciano advances toward front stage, continuing to throw kisses from his fingers to Sonia who is getting farther away.)

GREGORY. *(Furious)* Now, you should go and listen to what they are saying.

LUCIANO. *(Irritated, looking at him from top to bottom)* Ah, Enough! Enough! That's enough now! *(Then, thinking it over, he collects himself and smiles)* Not at all! I am a big fool! I thank you, sir. I thank you for having pushed me to listen to this conversation. I thank you because, by sheer coincidence, you have offered the best demonstration to reassure me, definitely reassure me of the one thing about which, frankly, I was sure even before and I won't forgive myself for having doubted it even for a moment . . . I mean, sir, the purity, the innocence, the nobility of my wife!

GREGORY. *(As above)* I repeat you should go and listen to what the two of them are saying now!

LUCIANO. I feel sorry for you! I am at a loss for words! And I would love to use some kinder words because I regard all your actions confined to the drama of your life. And that deserves something more than indulgence!

GREGORY. I don't know what to do with your indulgence. It's pushing that woman toward disaster. That woman is going to her death. I beseech you: rush to save her! Snatch her away from that man's arm! It is not just from betrayal that you must snatch her! From death, death, death!

LUCIANO. But it's madness!

GREGORY. It's not madness. I am ready to never see her again. But she must be saved, and to save her one must believe in her guilt! Go there because I am no longer speaking to you for me! She is the one who must avoid her grave! Poor creature more unfortunate than guilty, or, even if guilty, punished more cruelly than her guilt deserves, poor creature, she believes she can find refuge in a house in this world, while the house falls and buries her, and you will remove in vain with your hands each and every stone, and death will seem such a frightening thing that it will destroy both your anger and any compassion. You will want to remove in vain your past, and then you'll feel guilty for not having spied long enough, for not having saved her when she could have been still yours! Go, go, run to her if you don't want that even your dream be buried! Snatch her forcefully away from that man who, if you don't, will take her away.

LUCIANO. Oh! But even if I wanted to take into consideration the strange things that you say, if I even wanted to find some concrete reason to accept this dismal outlook of yours, I would have to begin by forgetting what we have seen and heard in this place a few minutes ago! You first should not believe your eyes when they see and your ears when they listen!

GREGORY. Lies! Lies!

LUCIANO. Meantime I am sick and tired. If yours is a fixation, it's already by itself something too sad for me to make a mockery of it. Therefore it's best that I leave the island immediately. In a few minutes I will be gone . . . You will no longer see me, and maybe you'll be more relaxed. Goodbye! Goodbye!

GREGORY. Wretched! What do you expect me to do for you to believe me? Do you want to die from sorrow? Do you still need to put your hands on me as if I were you worst ferocious enemy? Well then, be it!

LUCIANO. What do you mean?

GREGORY. *(Overwhelmed by a terrible outrage)* I want to tell you that, since there is no way out, I want to tell you that I am a living proof that your wife is betraying you. It's inside of me! Not only is it in me because I exist and I am talking to you—a miracle you cannot understand—but I myself have the sure proof of what I am stating . . . And I beg you not to force me to give it to you.

LUCIANO. Force you? I asked nothing of you! In fact: you say you have the proof? Well, keep it. I don't want to know.

GREGORY. Ah! You don't want to know? You don't want to know?

LUCIANO. No!

GREGORY. *(Staring him with hatred)* You kill it!

LUCIANO. Goodbye, my poor friend, I am leaving. We won't talk about it any more.

GREGORY. *(Blocking his path)* You kill it. But it shouldn't be! At the price of feeling your hands strangle me!

LUCIANO. Not even in a dream! On the contrary, I extend my hand to bid you goodbye.

GREGORY. *(Getting even more irritated)* Wretched, prepare yourself for the most atrocious torture: and if you have blood in your veins, take revenge on me, but then run to save her. You should know that that woman, your woman, was mine! She was mine on the night we walked along the seashore. She gave in to me, your woman! Are you convinced now? Are you?

LUCIANO. *(Flings himself against Gregory, inflamed with anger. But then he restrains. Looks upon him as a madman. Shakes his head, smiles, gets a hold of himself)* No . . . poor thing, no!

GREGORY. You don't believe me? Ah? You don't believe me because I am a madman! You're right! You can leave! It's all over! There is no other escape! Ah, ah! . . . I am a madman. I am a madman! *(Gives a horse-laugh as if really being overcome by a fit of folly)*

(Luciano is moved. He stoops his head in dismay. Then he goes boldly toward rear stage)

GREGORY. *(Seeing him leave, raises his arms desperately and calls him back with a clear and loud voice)* Luciano!

(Luciano from rear stage stops and turns his head, waiting.)

GREGORY. Since you're leaving, and I won't see you again, listen to the last word of a madman. Do you know who I am?

LUCIANO. A poor wretch.

GREGORY. May be. But you know that you and I are the same thing!

LUCIANO. Ah! No! Let's not play games! I am a respectable person! *(He leaves)*

GREGORY. Ah, ah, ah, ah! . . . Ah, ah, ah, ah, ah! . . . *(A horrible laugh repeated twice upsets him while he is standing still, facing the audience. Then, as if knocked down by his own crisis, he falls to the ground. And his mocking horselaugh turns into a desperate sob.)*

(As he begins to sob the curtain falls.)

The Bird of Paradise
Enrico Cavacchioli

Translated by
Michael Vena

CAST

Anna Corelli
Donatella
Ina Ronzi
Ms. Camagni
First Ballerina
Second Ballerina
A Maid
Him
Giovanni Ardeo
Mimotte
A Doctor
His Highness
Mecenate
Preparator (Taxidermist)
First Conventioner
Second Conventioner
Third Conventioner
A Butler

This stage setting is centered around HIM.

HIM. An unreal, philosophical, abstract character. An old centenarian. His body lives on. His spirit has a life beyond. His head is cadaverous. But his behavior is still youthful, impeccable, very elegant. The tone of his voice—ironic, sharp, pleasing—is made of contrasts: slow and deep, or thin and unevenly high pitched. He is a braggart, a mocker, a demon. Only in the third act does he reach a tragic pitch, but after having reached the highest intensity he falls back on his impassive and arrogant mask.

ACT ONE

The study of Giovanni Ardeo, *cold, dark, gloomy. Around the walls are wide glass cases containing books and specimens of ornithological collections. A sense of cold sullenness permeates the entire room, weighing like a note of musical gravity. A writing desk. A window on the right overlooking the garden. In the rear, also from the right, one has access to the Gallery of the Museum of Natural History, which can be perceived and recognized through its wide glass cases and the large windows decked with white curtains. On the left, in the rear, the entrance door that also leads to the gallery, and the door that leads to* Giovanni Ardeo's *apartment. A spring afternoon. Five o'clock.*

MECENATE. *(Has flung open the left door and has stopped to let someone through. He is a small man, lean and wiry. He speaks and gesticulates with a trace of irritating Neapolitan dialect).* Gentlemen, come this way in the meantime. The director will not be long.

(The conventioners enter one by one, looking around. As they enter they stop in front of Mecenate *as if to ask him to explain something)*

MECENATE. Usually by now he would already have been in his office for a while, to sign things. But today is the first day of spring. And there is also all this chirping of swallows. Look. *(Points to the garden window).* Please sit down. *(He arranges the chairs)* If I were to meet him in the halls of the museum on his way back, whom should I announce?

CONVENTIONERS. *(Give their names, one by one)*
Professor Soffici
Luraschi
Mr. Griffini, Esq.

MECENATE. *(Looking at the last one, carefully, from behind his spectacles).* Griffini? Griffini? Let's see . . . In Naples! . . . At your service . . . Twenty years ago . . .

THIRD CONVENTIONER. Mecenate?! . . . But surely. You haven't changed at all. Surely . . . How is life treating you? *(And he clasps his hand with enthusiasm)* What a good fellow you are!

(First conventioner sits down: his colleague looks about with curiosity, looks out of the window and turns around)

MECENATE. How do you think it treats me, Professor? Sixty years, you know? One can't help becoming a grouch. We need to forgive ourselves if our eyesight doesn't hold up and our appetite increases. What do you expect? We are always sour, gouty, and starving.

THIRD CONVENTIONER. *(Addressing the rest)* Distinguished colleagues, with your permission. *(Introducing* Mecenate*)* He is an old friend I used to work with. He was with me in Naples.

MECENATE. Anatomical Preparator. Yessir. And today I enjoy the fruit of thirty years' hard work . . . As you can see! . . .

FIRST CONVENTIONER. But you will get along very well with Ardeo! They tell me he is exceptionally good-hearted. And he is a very fine scientist.

MECENATE. Regarding his scientific qualities, oh gosh! He is a famous stuffer of birds. There is no question about it. As for his goodness . . . he is . . . truly exceptional . . .

SECOND CONVENTIONER. But what kind of man is he?

MECENATE. Don't you know him?

THIRD CONVENTIONER. We were colleagues in Rome, and he was a strange character, stuffed behind the display of his eyeglasses. I have only one memory of him: he spoke softly and did not articulate clearly. He would cough and blow his nose under his hat. He almost spat on himself, and expected to be left alone to sneeze . . .

SECOND CONVENTIONER. Gentlemen! We have come to pay homage to an exhibition of science, of our science, are we going to start by defaming it!?

MECENATE. It always happens that way, Professor. Don't worry about it. The best is yet to come.

FIRST CONVENTIONER. How ?

THIRD CONVENTIONER. He got married. *(To* Mecenate*)* Is his wife still alive?

MECENATE. If only he hadn't married her! Doesn't he know? Even at the Ministry they know . . .

SECOND CONVENTIONER. Why? Is he unhappy? Betrayed?

MECENATE. *(With an air of mystery)* Separated. One year after marriage . . .

THIRD CONVENTIONER. Children?

MECENATE. One girl . . . if you stay, you'll see her.

SECOND CONVENTIONER. What about her mother?

MECENATE. Today is her day. She comes to visit her daughter once a week.

THIRD CONVENTIONER. How old is the girl?

MECENATE. Eighteen. She is a beautiful girl. She has been here for a while, but can hardly stay on! . . . She has a great longing for freedom! . . .

SECOND CONVENTIONER. The mother's influence.

MECENATE. Naturally. Mind you that whenever she comes she is escorted by a new lover, to place him right under her husband's nose.

THIRD CONVENTIONER. And he?

MECENATE. Impassive.

SECOND CONVENTIONER. It's quite a spectacle then!

MECENATE. A real spectacle. He watches her from behind his eyeglasses without saying a word. An hour goes by. The visit is over. Just like the parlor of a convent. The professor takes out his watch. He checks it. She understands but does not move. The professor blows his nose. He says slowly: "It's time for dinner." And Madame decides to go away, swaying as if she were about to collapse and pretending to cry like a turkey. Disgusting, with all due respect to these gentlemen! Truly disgusting.

SECOND CONVENTIONER. What about Giovanni Ardeo?

MECENATE. He's somewhat scared but remains impassive as ever. That man's ability to bear the weight of certain decorations is extraordinary! *(makes the sign of the cuckold's horns)*

(The conventioners laugh, beginning to feel ill at ease, impatient, and even annoyed by the persistent Neapolitan gab of Mecenate.)

THIRD CONVENTIONER. All right, my friend. Now go and announce us to the professor.

MECENATE. With your permission . . . *(Exits from the door on the right)*

(The conventioners are left by themselves. They look at each other)

FIRST CONVENTIONER. What a mosquito!

(They continue to examine the room they're in, with a gossipy curiosity, as if they wanted to weigh everything in it)

SECOND CONVENTIONER. *(Suddenly)* I would love to see this woman!

THIRD CONVENTIONER. Oh, God! She must be like the others.

SECOND CONVENTIONER. A nonclassifiable type . . .

THIRD CONVENTIONER. As you find them and detect them by the smell. You can imagine her.

FIRST CONVENTIONER. Oh, no! You need to judge women from their dainty shoes up to their hairstyles to get a precise idea about them. In the same way you measure fish from head to tail . . . Who said that?

THIRD CONVENTIONER. Yes, indeed, your typical literary leftovers.

(At this point the voice of Giovanni Ardeo *is heard in the distance. And* Mecenate's *voice responding to him)*

ARDEO. Where are they? Where are they?

MECENATE. In your study, Professor. A surprise.

ARDEO. *(Appears through the door that leads to the Museum Gallery and comes toward the* three conventioners*)* What a miracle, indeed! *(He shakes hands with the* third conventioner*)* How are you! It's a great pleasure to see you again. In Milan for the convention, obviously?

THIRD CONVENTIONER. Yes, my dear fellow. And we didn't want to miss the opportunity to come and shake your hand. After so many years! The proceedings of our convention begin tomorrow. So, it was right and proper for us to come and pay homage to you . . .

ARDEO. You have been very kind. I don't deserve that much. I am really confused.

THIRD CONVENTIONER. *(Introducing him)* Professor Soffici.

ARDEO. Delighted to meet you.

THIRD CONVENTIONER. Professor Luraschi . . .

ARDEO. I know well who you are. Very honored. *(To the others and to him)* Make yourselves at home. *(They sit down, while* Ardeo *remains on his feet in front of them)*

THIRD CONVENTIONER. And so? How much time . . . ?

ARDEO. . . . . has gone by, exactly. Many people have changed. Many things have happened. A tide that ebbs and flows . . .

SECOND CONVENTIONER. Life. In fact, our life. One vegetates in a town that is the last in the universe. Family, worries, illnesses. We grow old among the pages of our notebooks, teaching a few brats who will never feel obliged, I won't say, to be grateful, but even the more decent duty to respect . . .

FIRST CONVENTIONER. Oh, my dear professor! That's how it is, exactly.

ARDEO. Do you have children?

FIRST CONVENTIONER. Unfortunately. And when they see me intent on my studies on the vivisection of mayflies, they laugh!

ARDEO. *(To the* second conventioner*)* And you? A large family?

SECOND CONVENTIONER. And a model one! A perfect wife. There are few so perfect that they can keep a husband from regretting once a day having a wife and considering anyone who doesn't a happy man. I am extremely happy in this.

THIRD CONVENTIONER: *(Disingenuously)* How about you, dear Ardeo?

ARDEO. *(Stares at him almost mistrustfully. Then he shrugs his shoulders and enunciates slowly)* My existence is no mystery to anyone. I have been living with my daughter for a short time. That's all. My wife? I can tell you about it, since everyone in our circle either has talked or is talking about us. And I come across as a man of wit, putting up a front that is both my indictment and my self-defense. Since you also certainly know something about it . . .

THIRD CONVENTIONER: I assure you . . .

ARDEO. No need. I tell you myself. You have seen the great scientist, that sort of intelligent puppet that dazzles idiots from afar.

THIRD CONVENTIONER. You are the poet of butterflies . . .

ARDEO. Precisely. Butterflies have let their pollen fall mercifully on the little man who has studied them. And my little glory belongs totally to them. *(Pauses, then proceeds slowly)* My wife had humiliated and buried me to the point that no one in the world talked about me anymore. I am wrong in saying "in the world." But you understand. I am speaking of my world. And it is not insignificant. Was I still alive? Wasn't I living? In the family, I was expected to set an example of timid silence and perfect submission. Disregarding the fact that I could not procreate, she was the husband, I was the wife. We spent entire months in the same house without running the risk of meeting each other. Until one day . . . *(He stops again)* she left me, loaded with debts and ridicule, and with a torment I was unable to conceal, feeling as if she had split me in two!

THIRD CONVENTIONER. We didn't come here to reopen your wound . . . In the life of a man like you, deeds are what really count . . .

ARDEO. That's why I poured all my suffering and embarrassment into my work. And it saved me. Locked in my study, doing research with the microscope for hours and months, it seemed that whatever touched me was no more than a distant vibration . . .

SECOND CONVENTIONER. It is the strength of superior people . . .

ARDEO. No. Anyone would have acted like me. It's the instinct of self-preservation, the selfishness of one's own cowardice. And at certain times, sinking as far as you can into the depth of your own soul constitutes the only possible happiness. I ended up being happy with the solitude that grew out of my suffering, like a tree in the desert that thinks it's the only one enjoying that gust of wind which rises every evening from the hot sand, bringing a fragrance of oasis and spring water.

SECOND CONVENTIONER. Poetry that resurfaces through glass.

ARDEO. Like the sun in wintertime. I apologize for speaking to you in these terms. It's an act of chivalry toward myself, which I am inflicting on you . . . *(Pauses)* So, you will be presenting a report?

THIRD CONVENTIONER. Nothing much, really. It's my old thesis expanded to
    include some very recent research. Nothing more.
SECOND CONVENTIONER. But it's time to stop taking up your time, our visit
    threatens to become a hearing.
ARDEO. Are you saying that because I acted both as a public prosecutor and
    as a lawyer?
SECOND CONVENTIONER. God forbid . . . I wouldn't dare . . . *(They rise . . . get
    ready to leave)*
ARDEO. See you tomorrow. *(Handshakes, etc)*
FIRST CONVENTIONER. We came through here, I think?!
ARDEO. Yes.

*(Donatella appears at this point. She is like an apparition of spring, albeit modestly
dressed, with the simplicity of a schoolgirl)*

DONATELLA. May I come in, Dad?
ARDEO. Come in, Donatella.

(Donatella enters)

ARDEO. And here is a live masterpiece: my daughter.
SECOND CONVENTIONER. The image of youth!
ARDEO. All that remains to me of grace and serenity.
THIRD CONVENTIONER. We are very honored, young lady.

(Donatella bows but remains aloof, silent)

FIRST CONVENTIONER. And sorry to be on our way out!
ARDEO. Goobye then, dear friends. *(Calling)* Mecenate!

(Mecenate appears)

ARDEO. See the gentlemen to the door.

*(Mecenate stands still beside the door to allow the three guests who are leaving to pass
through. Then he vanishes behind them. After they have left, Donatella bursts out laughing)*

DONATELLA. Who are those mummies, Dad?
ARDEO. Three great devils. Professors like me.
DONATELLA. Maybe. But how silly they are! The first one is so stuffed with
    science, up to his nose, that he seems ready to explode . . . the second
    one . . . the big one . . . what's his name?

ARDEO. Griffini.

DONATELLA. Probably it is Griffini . . . Imagine him teaching me!? . . . He is a kind of cattle merchant, and that has nothing at all to do with the chair of natural history . . . The third ?

ARDEO. *(Interrupting her)* And what about your father then? What kind of merchant is he?

DONATELLA. Oh, you're my dad. And my dad is not in question. He's my dad. A great wizard. Everyone says so. Even that bad mouth Mecenate says so!

ARDEO. Which means that it's true, since truth personified has spoken! . . .

DONATELLA. Sure. *(Silence)* Dad!

ARDEO. Donatella!

DONATELLA. Do you know what day it is?

ARDEO. Yes, why?

DONATELLA. Mom is supposed to come.

ARDEO. That's right. Mom is supposed to come. Your mom . . .

DONATELLA. What a tone of voice!

ARDEO. *(Repenting)* What tone do you want me to use, my dear daughter?

DONATELLA. You are almost sorry. Tell the truth. Aren't you sorry?

ARDEO. Oh, let's not put my intentions on trial at this point!

DONATELLA. You also appear to be in a bad mood. Are you bored? What's the matter?

ARDEO. My baby! . . .

DONATELLA. Yes, yes, I can tell . . .

ARDEO. I am telling you no . . .

DONATELLA. Yes, of course. Mecenate told me.

ARDEO. This too sprang from that well of knowledge?

DONATELLA. There's an unmistakable sign!

ARDEO. What's that?

DONATELLA. That tuft of hair in the middle of your forehead. When it gets ruffled a storm is in the air! Look at yourself! *(Looks around her)* My God, there isn't even a mirror in here!

ARDEO. Come on, don't be silly . . . Why do you want a mirror in here? Aren't you convinced yet that you're beautiful enough! *(He pauses while* Donatella *makes faces)* Tell me, are you very happy to see your mother?

DONATELLA. Certainly.

ARDEO. How happy?

DONATELLA. Why so many questions?

ARDEO. You're right. She's your mother . . . and I am not young, elegant, and decorative enough, while she is a fragrance of grace and love.

DONATELLA. Dad!

ARDEO. You always think of her and wait for her with a touch of melancholy. Strange! You're her daughter, and she is the creature of your dream!

DONATELLA. Are you upset with me for this, dad?

ARDEO. No . . . I am just saying.

DONATELLA. You don't remember anymore how she laughs! How musical it is!

ARDEO. So she teaches you to have regrets? . . . and to tolerate me . . .

DONATELLA. *(Caresses him like a child)* Quiet! Quiet! Quiet!

ARDEO. Do you miss something here, Donatella?

DONATELLA. What are you saying?

ARDEO. Do you have any unfulfilled desires? Tell me. Everything I can do for you, you know, I will . . . everything within my power. *(Suddenly a secret thought makes him blush)* But if you too!? It would be my deepest disappointment. I adore you also for this, and I consider you straight-forward and good. You wouldn't want to hurt me . . .

DONATELLA. My dad . . . my dad . . . This is the first time you've talked to me like this.

ARDEO. You must excuse me. It was stronger than me. I didn't really want to. But I am a little man, all thumbs and a heavy hand . . . these glass cases and the armchair of my library have almost mummified me . . .

DONATELLA. What big secrets this handsome and wicked father is confiding to me tonight!

ARDEO. He opens up to you his grieving heart, like a sudden spring, and you descend in it without surprise.

DONATELLA. Dad . . .

ARDEO. And you look at it with all the new curiosity of your adolescence.

DONATELLA. I have seen a lot of things.

ARDEO. Have you?

DONATELLA. The secret passion that you don't want to admit! The torment that turns your hair gray . . .

ARDEO. Oh, Donatella!

DONATELLA. . . . and makes harsher the memory that hurts you.

ARDEO. I swear to you, my girl. That particular wound does not bleed any-more.

DONATELLA. *(Maliciously)* Really?

ARDEO. It took all my will to heal it, and I am healed.

DONATELLA. You speak about it in such a heart-broken voice.

ARDEO. Say, rather, with fear. I am anchored on the old rock of my wisdom, and I no longer fear being submerged, if you don't abandon me . . . *(In a whisper)* for her . . .

DONATELLA. *(Throws her arms around his neck and kisses him again).* My jealous father! . . . My jealous father! . . .

MECENATE. *(Enters again)* Mr. Director, the anatomical preparator . . . Do I let him in now? Or shall I tell him to come back tomorrow?

ARDEO. Did he bring the specimen?

MECENATE. Yes.

ARDEO. Let him in then . . .

MECENATE. Around here, you never run the risk of wasting time! *(Leaves)*

DONATELLA. What a character! Can I stay? Do I disturb you, Dad? I 'll keep out of the way and won't say a word. Here in the window seat. And as soon as I see Mom coming, I'll run! O.K.?

ARDEO. Do as you please.

MECENATE. *(Reenters leading the new person)* Here's the preparator! It's five-thirty!

ARDEO. I understand. You can go.

PREPARATOR. Here I am, Professor. And here is the specimen . . . *(He presents a beautiful bird of paradise, stuffed; like a divine gift)*

ARDEO. Let's see! Let's see! *(Takes the specimen from his hands, with impatient curiosity)*

PREPARATOR. A rare, magnificent thing that required minute care . . . It's so fragile . . .

ARDEO. Truly wonderful!

DONATELLA. Can I see it too?

ARDEO. Of course! Here it is the complete category—difillodi, forini, manucodi . . .

DONATELLA. A bird of paradise! How nice it would look on Mom's hair!

ARDEO. That too. But you are not familiar, my little one, with the legend originated by this delicate creature centuries ago! And there is a whole stock of literature on the legend. Fable, fantasy, prejudice!

MECENATE. Here comes the lecture! Professor, may our friend leave?

ARDEO. What kind of behavior is this, Mecenate?! Keep your place and leave me in peace!

DONATELLA. Tell me, Daddy!

ARDEO. For a long time people believed that it had no feet . . . But then, the physiological secret was revealed . . . A trifle! The natives of New Guinea sent birds of paradise to Europe, prepared that way . . .

DONATELLA. Better without feet than without a head!

ARDEO. And so they created a variation on the fable. People had thought about the strangeness of this "paradise" condemned from its origin never to alight and always to fly . . . myth of eternal restlessness. There are those who saw it or thought they saw it perch on branches to rest, hanging from the precious beard of its expensive plumage . . . while others claimed that having no other element than air, it had to sleep, mate, and hatch, while flying . . .

MECENATE. *(Pointedly)* And to eat, Professor? . . .

ARDEO. The Muslims said that it lived exclusively on dew and the scent of flowers.

DONATELLA. How beautiful!

ARDEO. So that, the exquisite elegance of modern dress, having come down from the blue depths of the heavens, nourished on ambrosia, in order to arrive at the bold, easy manners of muddy streets or parlors or theaters, had to appear almost like a miracle of nature, created on purpose for the finest femininity . . .

MECENATE. *(To the* preparator*)* But isn't all this also written in some book?

DONATELLA. Mecenate, stop grumbling! You're unbearable!

ARDEO. In truth, of the whole pack of lies so lightly assembled about this creature, the only accurate fact is that it lives isolated and haughty. And under the blows of hurricanes, whipped by rain and tossed by wind, it rises in a vertical course and darts out of the inclement zone toward the calmer regions of the skies: above the storm. And it goes looking for its . . . paradise . . .

DONATELLA. But all that is beautiful!

*(*Mecenate *gestures at the* preparator *as if to invite him to leave.)*

PREPARATOR. So, Professor, are you happy with my work?

ARDEO. Very happy. *(Sets the stuffed specimen on his writing desk)*

PREPARATOR. Then I thank you. The other preparations are in formalin. They will be ready next week.

MECENATE. So, we take a bow and leave.

PREPARATOR. With your permission . . . Good evening . . .

ARDEO. Good evening.

MECENATE. Finally! *(They exit)*

ARDEO. How long the days have gotten! The sun is still on the trees.

DONATELLA. *(Suddenly)* Dad, why don't we leave?

ARDEO. Where do you want to go?

DONATELLA. Away. I don't know where. What if we were to go and make the acquaintance of those illustrious savages of New Guinea who cut the feet off birds of paradise? . . .

ARDEO. That time will come, no question about it! We'll pack our bags and go through mountains and forests . . .

DONATELLA. Not through mountains and forests! That's ridiculous nowadays. To large hotels? You bet! Where you meet so many good people! Theaters, cafés, tennis . . .

ARDEO. Where you won't breathe this vast fragrance of the earth, this healthy smell of fertility and plenty, which the sun brings as a blessing of its splendor! . . .

DONATELLA. *(Impatient, stamps her foot on the ground)* Dad . . . Mom is late! . . . I am going to meet her! Do you mind?

ARDEO. Indeed, it's almost the hour. And that old grumbler Mecenate is getting impatient, measuring for the thousandth time, as he has done for twenty years, the length of the halls! Go ahead.

DONATELLA. Goodbye, Dad . . .

ARDEO. Meanwhile let's put our new guest in a safe spot! My poor friend! One's better off in a glass case, believe me. The world is an ugly sponge that must soak up the tears of too many people!

(Anna comes in, escorted by Him holding a big bunch of flowers. Him follows her carrying lots of packages: a mute and obliging character)

ANNA. May I?

ARDEO. Come in. It's your house. *(He is cold, measured, impeccable)*

ANNA. Thank you. What a curious feeling! *(To Him)* My friend, you may put down the packages. *(To Ardeo)* Donatella?

ARDEO. I'll have someone call her. She is well.

ANNA. *(To Him)* I forgot to introduce you. Excuse me. *(To Ardeo)* He is a friend . . .

(He bows, Ardeo reciprocates with a slight movement of his head)

ANNA. Now you can go and wait for me in the coach. Watch the clock. Go for a ride and come back.

(Him bows again and goes away)

ARDEO. *(Ironically)* Your latest conquest?

ANNA. Why? Do you care?

ARDEO. Oh, just to make conversation . . .

ANNA. My poor Giovanni! . . . It's strange. But deep down I love you so much. Don't be astonished by my frankness. I return here to your house with a feeling that wrenches my soul, with part remorse and part shame. You feel sorry for me, don't you? *(Ardeo smiles sadly)*

ANNA. We were too different and didn't understand each other. What a pity!

ARDEO. But you quickly found your way. And it was natural . . .

ANNA. Now it's too late to blame me. If you presume I'm happy . . . well, I'm not . . . I still don't know anything about life. Everyday I open my eyes wider, but am still unable to find my bearings. And with each disillusionment, my stubborn heart seems to regain its youth in the spirit of contradiction. Do you consider me bad for this?

ARDEO. No, you're not bad.

ANNA. Thank you. Confidentially, I find you gentle and serene like that old little boy of before. Come on, give me your hand. You haven't shaken my hand yet. We are two friends now. There. Don't give me that suspicious look.

ARDEO. Next time come by yourself. It's pointless to make your escort climb all the way up here. The stairs are long and steep . . .

ANNA. Oh, my escort! For goodness' sake! He is my aspiring porter because he finds pleasure in following me for an hour. That's all.

ARDEO. If you don't want to do so for me, do it for my daughter and for the respect you don't have for yourself.

ANNA. All right. Next time I'll do so. But do you know what I think? How crazy?! I come here everytime with my heart beating as if I were fifteen years old and meeting you for the first time. I come with remorse . . . I caused you pain. In my life I have always had the sensation of walking on tiptoe so as not to disturb anyone.

ARDEO. Such tact!

ANNA. And I often say to myself: enough of this nonsense! You have squandered your soul and your money, and have the same devouring anxiety that racks your mind! Let's go! A jump in the blue without falling again!

ARDEO. Why do you think I should care? I feel no nostalgia anymore, fortunately.

ANNA. Who knows? One evening you told me: "When I've lost you, what beautiful woman could fall in love with me? That's why you are my youth." That sentence, at times, buzzes in my soul!

ARDEO. It was the truth. But you didn't have to recall it!

ANNA. Perhaps. Not everything is dead inside. Make allowances for the good memories. And don't be my enemy in front of our daughter. Let's talk here, calmly, now. And I foresee, as usual, that when she is here, we'll snap at each other like two beasts. The feelings of parenthood have divided instead of reuniting us.

ARDEO. *(Raises his head)* Oh, what a woman! What a woman!

VOICE of DONATELLA. Mom! Where did you come from?

ANNA. Baby, I am right here. How are you?

DONATELLA. And you, Mom? How are you? Flowers for me? *(She embraces her, takes the bunch of flowers from her)* What a sweet perfume you wear, Mommy!

ANNA. You silly little dear!

DONATELLA. And what is this? *(She points with girlish joy to each one of the packages Him has left.)*

ANNA. The fondants that you like.

DONATELLA. Oh, thank you. And this?

ANNA. Guess.

DONATELLA. The gold chain . . .

ANNA. Of course. I kept my promise . . . *(Opens the box)* with a medal.

DONATELLA. *(With a little cry)* Saint George!

ANNA. Are you happy? I'll put it on your neck. *(Places the chain around Donatella's neck, fastens it)* There you are!

DONATELLA. But over this dress . . .

ANNA. We'll take care of that too! . . .

DONATELLA. Mommy, you're so good to me!

ANNA. We'll take care of all your wishes, all your whims, all the dear vagaries of your moods . . . *(Opening the other packages, she hands them to the girl)* Here is some perfume, a turtleshell comb, and the nail polisher. Here: embroidered handkerchiefs.

DONATELLA. How can I thank you?

ANNA. With another kiss. You still haven't told me how you are!

DONATELLA. How do I look to you?

ANNA. Oh, feminine coquettishness! You're a bit pale . . .

DONATELLA. And you more beautiful than ever, mama.

ANNA. What a lie! *(Turning toward Ardeo, who is seated at his desk and not moved, his head hanging down, as if he were absent)* Is she studying?

ARDEO. Yes, she is studying.

ANNA. *(To Donatella)* Maybe that wears you out a bit, doesn't it? . . . You need to look at yourself in the mirror every once in a while . . . Otherwise those beautiful eyes become big, much too big! . . . Who taught you to comb your hair like that?

DONATELLA. Maria . . .

ANNA. Bad taste! You need to tell her to change styles. These golden locks are too tight. Tell her to leave them loose. For goodness' sake! And a curl here, in the middle of your forehead, wouldn't look bad! . . .

DONATELLA. *(As if excusing herself)* Dad doesn't like that . . .

ANNA. Dad doesn't know about these things. And any woman has an obligation toward herself . . .

DONATELLA. Oh . . .

ANNA. Not to give up her own vanity . . .

ARDEO. Madam! I've kept quiet up to now. But these are not lessons to give my daughter.

ANNA. Bravo! Ideas to educate mummies, not women!

ARDEO. Oh, no! Here, fortunately, people don't think like you! We breathe a different air!

ANNA. But there is a stuffy odor in here . . . And the day when this air becomes too stale, it will be unbearable!

ARDEO. What do you mean?

ANNA. That youth demands its right to live! We all demanded that!

ARDEO. Those who did not feel responsible for their own obligations!

ANNA. Life is a more practical school!

ARDEO. In which experts drown!

ANNA. Good luck to them! It's worse for the weak ones!

ARDEO. *(Almost with anguish)* Haven't you learned anything at all?!

ANNA. I told you already. What can I do about it if, when I come here, after five minutes I feel overcome by an elusive sensation of malaise, a vague discomfort. How to explain . . . it's the feeling of being plunged into a cemetery where there is an effort to trap my daughter. First you, then the law: you're responsible for it!

ARDEO. But it's a cemetery of honest people where you don't meet harlots and unscrupulous dandies.

ANNA. Your honesty is based on ignorance.

ARDEO. And I'm proud of it, if your learning is acquired in bad faith.

ANNA. Learning! You've got it all bottled up, you've got it all stuffed in those four carcasses garnished with feathers!

ARDEO. Oh, Anna! How can you say that? You enter the realm of beauty, coming here.

ANNA. I never realized that! So much so that I ran away from it.

ARDEO. Life stopped here in its very best attitudes and its most diverse manifestations . . .

ANNA. *(Ironically)* Are you really sure?

ARDEO. Yes, from the moment we caught it in its shapes, colors, changes: a mixture of dream, harmony, suggestion, snatching from death everything that could survive it!

ANNA. I would love to see this surviving harmony!

ARDEO. Look around you! *(Little by little he becomes animated, his appearance seems to change)* It's all there, in a relentless, daily, binding act that cannot be erased. It's a gleam of romance on the surface of a running stream. It's a reflection of light, feathers, wings, softness; an alternating of songs, issuing from the throats of birds that seem still to preserve the warmth of flying. A sort of primitive force, greed, violence, instinct; from the gesture of the massive troglodyte to the imperceptible vibration of a cell!

ANNA. *(Has continued to say no, shaking her head impatiently)* Immobility!

ARDEO. *(Continuing her thought)* . . . that has set the supreme limits of beauty in an endless range! . . . . Look around you again! Examine closely this cemetery of which, in your opinion, I am the useless undertaker! It's a spring of eternal youth, which is teeming with life, as long as one understands the word that reveals and the spirit that creates . . . And it is right here that Donatella, still not open or disturbed like the bud of a flower awaiting its sunbeam, prepares for life without longings.

ANNA. That is the word. Our daughter is nothing if not tremulous with longings! I see myself as a child in her . . .

ARDEO. Oh, no . . .

ANNA. . . . from a thousand trifles, from a thousand details that escape only you! And I think that she is going to wither away with you, as I feared, in a corner of the country! . . .

ARDEO. I forbid you! I forbid you to speak like that!

ANNA. Amid the tame sulkiness of the usual family quadrupeds, and the consolation of a gramophone record that shrieks on Sundays its irritating charge to the well meaning people of the town or at the pharmacy . . .

ARDEO. Not everybody was born in a big city or cares for its giddiness !

ANNA. And so, when one has a thirst for living, the four broken-down glass cases in which your beauty is nested is more or less the same as that shadowy corner in which I lived through my adolescence . . . and outside of which there is fever, fever if you will!

ARDEO. Stop! Stop!

ANNA. No! There is agony if you need agony! There are people who move about at their pleasure. And there is shouting love, rending passion, palpable luxury.

ARDEO. *(Faces her threateningly, as if to attack and silence her)* You're talking like the woman you are! . . .

DONATELLA. *(Restrains her father, throwing her arms around his neck)* Dad, dad! Stop it!

ANNA. Let him insult me now! I couldn't help yelling at him: life is outside, outside, in the sun, in the dust, in the dirt; in love and hatred! . . '.

ARDEO. Your daughter hears you and judges you!

ANNA. I will take her away with me, God willing, before you kill her with this ridiculous obsession of your short-sightedness.

DONATELLA. *(Still restraining her father)* Dad . . .

ANNA. I will take her with me! *(To Donatella)* Come, Donatella!

ARDEO. Don't you dare! *(To Donatella)* And don't you listen to such nonsense unworthy of you!

ANNA. If not today, someday she'll be the one who will run away to my house.

ARDEO. *(To Donatella)* Go over there, go over there . . .

DONATELLA. *(Bursting into tears)* I don't want to! I don't want to!

ARDEO. *(Breaking away from her)* I told you to go over there!

DONATELLA. *(Throws her mother an imploring look, gathers up her flowers, shaking)* Since you order me . . .

ANNA. I will follow her.

ARDEO. *(Comes between Donatella, who has left and Anna, who wants to follow her, on the threshold)* You are in my house.

ANNA. It's true, I am in your house. It doesn't matter. It's useless to continue with repulsive scenes. I know very well how I'll snatch my daughter away from you.

ARDEO. You wretch!

ANNA. Didn't I ask you not to be my enemy in front of her? You wanted this. Donatella is eighteen. She can freely choose now because I am holding out my arms to her . . .

ARDEO. It's the height of absurdity. You tried to fly but fell on your wounded wing . . . Take care of yourself!

ANNA. What does it matter? The flight was headed toward the sun!

MECENATE. *(Has appeared at the door, listening to the last words of the argument)* Professor, the bell rang. There is nobody. The gallery is closed already. *(Pointedly)* Do you need anything?

ARDEO. *(Curtly)* No. What time is it?

MECENATE. It's time for dinner . . .

ARDEO. *(Takes out his watch, looks at it calmly, unmoved)* Already? So late? *(To Anna)* If you like, you may leave with him.

MECENATE. This way, Madam.

Act Two

The hotel where Anna lives. Through large windows a parlor overlooking a gloomy garden. The right side of the room is full of armchairs, screens, and mess. It is like a peaceful oasis, surrounded by soft light, while from the open doors the noise of a thousand voices drifts inside. There is dancing, games. A small orchestra thrums discreetly.

(As the curtain rises, Ms.Camagni, Ina Ronzi, and the first and second ballerina enter, followed by Him, who draws them all along at his pleasure like a living, floating wave)

CAMAGNI. So, you must be Mr. "Opportunist?"

HIM. At your service, my dove.

INA RONZI. Here's someone who believes in always being on time.

HIM. You're wrong. Precisely because I am "Mr. Opportunist" I always arrive at the most inopportune moment. And when I really should be there, I never am.

FIRST BALLERINA. You've become an expert?

HIM. Naturally.

FIRST BALLERINA. Is that your profession? . . .

HIM. Sure. I crisscross life like the threads of a skein, till the skein becomes tangled . . . I don't rush impulsively because I have no ideals to defend. I have no remorse because I have no virtue to follow. I don't swear because I don't believe. All I do is produce life.

INA RONZI. Oh God, how complicated!

HIM. It doesn't seem so to me.

CAMAGNI. Well then, will you tell us something pleasantly heretical, in this paradise of rational people?

SECOND BALLERINA. Who can we gossip about?

HIM. About those who are absent, we're not in the dock.

INA RONZI. About Anna Ardeo?

HIM. Why not? There's a type, by God. The most intelligent and yet the stupidest of girls. She would give her life for a tear! Ready to believe anyone and with an objectivity that's downright repulsive! That's why she's the protagonist of the most delightful live novel that I've ever produced. For those who don't know it, I have a weakness for literature in action. It's just that I hate newsprint.

CAMAGNI. We understand. And where do you keep your library?

HIM. In the bathroom.

CAMAGNI. Excellent idea. In fact, all Italian literature is purgative.

SECOND BALLERINA. Let's take advantage of this moment of rest, before Anna Ardeo joins us.

HIM. The matter is very simple and you understand what led up to it. Let me then proceed in some orderly fashion. I told that old guinea hen, pulling the number one thread: take your child back with you! Donatella, the delight of our soul! She looked at me. You want her to wither like a leaf of verbena between two pages of a toxicology manual? . . . And she answered me, "You are right . . . Tomorrow I'll go and take her away no matter what."

CAMAGNI. Oh, then it's you giving the encouragement?

HIM. But of course, my dove! Two days later Donatella was here, still a schoolgirl, still green as a green plum. And then began her finishing course, which didn't last very long. Six months! Well then, I spoke again in confidence to the old guinea hen. Don't be shortsighted, I told her! Look and look carefully around you. You are almost at the end of your flight, and you never wanted anyone to suffer for you. Therefore everyone is in debt to you. And because money never cost you anything, you've spent it in abundance. You are a fine lady! For this reason you have created the most unlikely complications: men who tried to commit suicide on account of your beautiful eyes but then preferred, after thinking it over carefully, to gaze at the eyes of any other ordinary girl. Women mad with jealousy who learned to hate you, and ended up asking you for a loan. You are a fine lady! . . .

FIRST BALLERINA. Oh, my God, let's get back to dancing. What you say is so boring. His Highness is probably looking for me . . .

INA RONZI. I know that you despise thinkers: you've got no brains. Don't pay any attention to her, sir.

HIM. As you wish . . . Finally, after so many detours of love, pain, passion, tenderness, disillusion, and grief, you squat on one cornerstone of your life. Mimotte!

CAMAGNI. What a nice person!

HIM. I know that . . . *(continuing)* Mimotte! Open your eyes as you never have! First, he was immoral, in theory and in practice. Now that he's made himself rich off you, he will become a moralist in theory and preach holiness and correct behavior. He will become as chaste as a turtledove. It doesn't matter. He will aspire to marriage. And, naturally, he will want to have a family. He is entitled to it. One must always form a family on a solid basis! But to prove that his theory can conflict with his practice, he will reward you by taking away what is most dear to you: your daughter.

SECOND BALLERINA. You believe that?

HIM. I don't believe it. I know it. Facts lead to answers. And I'm waiting with resignation for what is bound to happen.

CAMAGNI. Do you want a cigarette, you devil?! I like this juggler's act.

HIM. You like it? Here's a cigarette for you . . . Quick! Who smokes? We must burn like hell.

INA RONZI. Thank you. We'll order ice cream.

HIM. *(Continuing)* And here is thread number two. I said to Donatella "You're eighteen years old, my child. It's time to choose a boyfriend with care! There is one . . ."

CAMAGNI. No! . . .

HIM. Wait! . . . Mimotte . . . Mimotte . . . the beautiful Mimotte . . . the paradisiacal Mimotte . . .

CAMAGNI. Him? That fellow?! . . .

HIM. The ideal, a pearl among men. He grew rich at the expense of others, therefore he'll be a spendthrift. He has lived like a nabob and like a hobo. Therefore he knows the various tastes and the various alcoholic gradations of existence. He has squeezed from life all that there was to squeeze. It could be, then, that he desires nothing else. And is it the portent of fidelity? Take it as it is!

INA RONZI. But it's monstrous! He's her mother's lover!

HIM. It's precisely for this reason that the combination excites me. You have the skeptic who denies everything, even his own spirit, and becomes the victim of his own thoughts . . . He who denies pleasure becomes a Stoic. He who denies pain becomes an Epicurean. I don't deny. I affirm. And I wait with a sense of fatalism for what is bound to happen.

FIRST BALLERINA. Ah, you and your sense of fatalism! Stop it, since none of us believes in fate!

CAMAGNI. Is that all?

HIM. No. There's still more. I said to Mimotte, and here is thread number three: pluck this graceful flower! It's yours, because her mother belongs to you! She is too old for you. Donatella is so young . . .

CAMAGNI. Cynic!

HIM. Anna is fading away . . . while this gem appears on the vast horizon of your adventure. One represents your past as a man without a present and without a future.

INA RONZI. God, what a calamity!

HIM. The other can be your real future. One was your misery, your shame, your shackle . . .

CAMAGNI. What a lucky man!

HIM. *(Without losing his poise)* Donatella is freedom. And if her mother destroyed your appetite as a young restless beast in the days of a false sentimental captivity, she can drink with you all that you gained then . . . And I wait . . .

INA RONZI. . . . with a sense of fatalism for what is bound to happen.

HIM. Exactly.

SECOND BALLERINA. By now we know the refrain.

CAMAGNI. You are indeed a live novel! And is that all?

*(*His Highness *appears on the threshold. He is a tall, thin, clean-shaven man with white hair and a fresh rosy complexion)*

HIS HIGHNESS. May I? I am looking for . . . my wife.

FIRST BALLERINA. Your arm, Your Highness. *(They leave together)*

HIM. There's the ideal couple . . .

CAMAGNI. . . . when they are at the gambling table.

HIM. Will you shut up, loudmouth? We are almost at the end. I said to the naturalist . . . and here is thread number four that intertwines with the other three.

INA RONZI. The father?

HIM. Yes, the father: what a gentleman you are! Serious, modest, balanced! Honesty in a skirt! And your wife, your fine wife is all this! And your daughter, your fine daughter is all this! And the lovers of your wife, the respectable lovers of your wife are something else! Open your eyes, you too, for God's sake! Is it worthwhile to teach comparative zoology, if you aren't yet familiar with all this livestock? I know, this upsets your stomach! But you won't raise your voice for this! And I wait . . .

EVERYONE ALMOST, IN UNISON: . . . with a sense of fatalism for what is bound to happen . . . Oh! Oh! Oh! How funny!

INA RONZI. Is that all?

HIM. Of course.

SECOND BALLERINA. We can go then. But first tell us. Why did you do all this? Is it a fraud or the truth?

HIM. The truth, my dear. The truth. I do this, basically, for love of mankind. Of course. *(He gets up. Now he is like a lecturer in front of a small audience of three women)* With what I know, I enjoy creating what I don't see, foreseeing what will happen, with mathematical exactitude. And all to simplify life and reduce it to the lowest common denominator of sentimental expression . . . Because there is no truth other than the one we make!

CAMAGNI. And so I, my good prophet? . . .

HIM. You will fall into Mimotte's arms before tomorrow, because the fruit is already ripe and sweet-smelling . . .

CAMAGNI. Imbecile!

INA RONZI. Me?

HIM. You'll get up later than usual, sniffing better than before that sweet cocaine that darkens your eyes; without courage and without cowardice, waiting for the lion in your old trap-hole . . .

INA RONZI. *(Outraged)* Oh!

CAMAGNI. How can you say such things?

HIM. Like this. It's a suggestion of the Unknowable. You think I'm talking to you. But that isn't true. You translate a suggestion of the spirit into a reality. You give me a body, an appearance, an outfit, and a voice. I think but I don't exist, the answers I give to your objections are formulated from your own fantasy. I don't exist either for you or for others. If I were in a theater and were reciting a play, I wouldn't exist even for the public, other than as a simple abstraction. And I could allow myself both the wisest and the craziest things. Shooting the moon with a revolver or walking like a bat. Poisoning you with phosphoric fumes or letting you die of diabetes from the extreme sweetness of my words. If we have embarked on a conversation that seems logical, it is because you have attuned your statements and contradictions to a topic that appears harmonious. That's why I shall also enunciate to this other most reverend public *(Enter Anna, His Highness, the First Ballerina and some guests)* the last discovery, consecrated by my revered umbilical wisdom . . .

ANNA. What's this? Mr. Preacher, our guests demand their ballerinas. And it's not right for you to monopolize them. It's scandalous.

HIM. *(To the others)* You see? We're coming right away! *(He starts walking, then stops at the door)* Why are there still tragedies of jealousy? Because we give fidelity a tragic importance. And this, truly, is an inconceivable weakness in those inferior animals . . . that we are! Good night . . . *(Leaves hastily)*

A GUEST: But who was that?

HIS HIGHNESS. He must be a theosophist giving lessons . . .

CAMAGNI. Is it his way of taking leave? And what about this tango? This tango? *(The sound of the small orchestra is audible, muffled in the distance)* Who will follow me?

EVERYONE. All of us! *(And they get ready to leave)*

ANNA. Even you, Your Highness?

HIS HIGHNESS. No, I'm staying. It's suffocating in there.

ANNA. Come in, then.

HIS HIGHNESS. *(Ringing a bell, he sits down)* We're alone. Aren't you afraid?

ANNA. Of you? No.

HIS HIGHNESS. That's flattering. *(A butler comes to the door)* Open the door a little. There is a heavy smell of virtue here. It's oppressive. *(The butler obeys)*

BUTLER. Anything else, Your Highness?

HIS HIGHNESS. You may leave.

(The butler leaves)

ANNA. Even in your kingdom the odor of virtue is annoying?

HIS HIGHNESS. Once, yes. But ever since I gave my legislators a free hand, virtue has wandered out of bounds. And it has never returned. The public, as a result, has given me permission to pursue it.

ANNA. At the gambling tables?

HIS HIGHNESS. There, too.

ANNA. In the alcoves of Western ladies?

HIS HIGHNESS. Where it can be found.

ANNA. Everywhere?

HIS HIGHNESS. Everywhere.

ANNA. And you have never been left unemployed?

HIS HIGHNESS. I have an invaluable secretary who directs my inquiries and every so often sends his report to the National Treasury.

ANNA. But, excuse me; where is your kingdom? . . .

HIS HIGHNESS. Oh, far, far away! . . . beyond the Nile.

ANNA. You belong to a superior race: Arabian! Aren't you going back there?

HIS HIGHNESS. I am a dethroned prince . . . in exile . . . We're at war.

ANNA. Oh, my poor friend. You must get bored! . . .

HIS HIGHNESS. You're mistaken. I adore this equivocal petty bourgeoisie of yours, in its carnival mask, so diverse and multicolored. It has a most delightful flavor of embittered rabble.

ANNA. It's a new world to you.

HIS HIGHNESS. Indeed. Where one meets a purchasing agent for the state who still has dirty, muddy fingernails from his days of poverty but has rewarded his industrious hands with many diamonds of innumerable grades! All women are his. He could buy a kingdom along with its ruler. But he is so kind. And he fattened himself on human blood, like a greedy vampire, starving his fellow creatures, sabotaging his competitors, leading a life of hatred and fraud, while we, the real kings of the comedy, stroll Europe taking our hats off to them morning and night.

ANNA. You created these people while the public was agonizing!

HIS HIGHNESS. A necessary evil.

ANNA. What about their women? You corrupted them from the workshop to the royal palace!

HIS HIGHNESS. Could be. In my town women are kept locked inside. Here they betrayed both their husbands who were on the battlefront and their lovers who were shirking their military duties . . . But you . . .

ANNA. How do I fit in?

HIS HIGHNESS. Excuse me if I forgot to tell you before. Tonight you are exquisite, more exquisite than ever. And it's not worth, looking into your eyes, to talk about useless melancholy . . . Do you want half of my lost kingdom?

ANNA. Why not? But what do you ask in exchange?

HIS HIGHNESS. A token of love.

ANNA. I'm sorry. But you've run up against the virtue you were pursuing. I've never had more than one lover at a time, and I still give, as our preacher said a moment ago, a tragic importance to fidelity. I'm desperately faithful to my friend. It's an illness.

HIS HIGHNESS. My secretary told me, suggesting a cure. But I wanted to convince myself. You are such a delicate exception. Malésch, I ask your forgiveness . . .

ANNA. For goodness's sake, Your Highness.

HIS HIGHNESS. Let's go and see our merchants . . . they dance like bears.

DONATELLA. *(Enters)* Mommy . . .

HIS HIGHNESS. She should call you sister.

ANNA. Come in, dear . . .

HIS HIGHNESS. *Léltk saída ia bent.*

DONATELLA. Good evening, Your Highness.

ANNA. You look tired! You should go upstairs. It's already late . . .

DONATELLA. As you wish, mommy. But will you come up to kiss me before I fall asleep?

ANNA. Of course, go along, my darling.

HIS HIGHNESS. May all the stars of heaven watch over your sleep.

DONATELLA. Thank you. Good night. *(Leaves)*

HIS HIGHNESS. What an exquisite creature!

ANNA. You think so?

HIS HIGHNESS. *Uat el aini el nebi!*

ANNA. Marry her!

HIS HIGHNESS. Anna, my good friend, two hundred sad wives await me in my country . . .

ANNA. Ah! That's true! I had forgotten. And who was left to watch over the purity of the harem?

(They start toward the exit)

HIS HIGHNESS. The eunuchs of the family. Please. *(He lets her precede him)*

(They leave. For a moment the stage is empty. The small band still plays softly. Then from the two doors, almost together Mimotte *and* Camagni *come onstage.)*

MIMOTTE. *(Stopping with surprise)* Oh! You're looking for your fan!

CAMAGNI. Actually . . . no . . .

MIMOTTE. Your gloves?

CAMAGNI. No.

MIMOTTE. Well then, you're dazed by the music, smoke, and whiskey. And you've beaten a retreat into the parlor of lost sighs.

CAMAGNI. You call it that?

MIMOTTE. Everyone does. And certainly you knew you would find me here.

CAMAGNI. How presumptuous!

MIMOTTE. Just as I was sure you would come . . .

CAMAGNI. It's fate . . . As if you were the best-loved, the most madly loved man! . . .

MIMOTTE. Precisely . . .

CAMAGNI. Oh, your presumption is irritating!

MIMOTTE. Like all truth.

CAMAGNI. The truth irritates only ugly women.

MIMOTTE. Ugly ones and beautiful ones! They are flowers too soft, too vulnerable, too fragile, not to bow down before the burning altar of an irresistible god.

CAMAGNI. That is to say, before you?

MIMOTTE. *(Shamelessly)* Yes, me. This is what I came here to talk to you about. And I was absolutely sure that I wouldn't waste a single word.

CAMAGNI. Well then, hurry up. What do you want to tell me?

MIMOTTE. How nervous you are!

CAMAGNI. You think I am a woman like all the rest?

MIMOTTE. Yes.

CAMAGNI. Thanks. Like those who couldn't resist you for more than five minutes?

MIMOTTE. Yes.

CAMAGNI. Well then you're wrong.

MIMOTTE. I don't think so.

CAMAGNI. *(More emphatically)* You're wrong!

MIMOTTE. There's no need to shout. You are not Susanna. I don't represent the three old men in the Bible, and I didn't surprise you nude or bathing. Because then I would have behaved differently . . .

CAMAGNI. In what way?

MIMOTTE. Without warning, imprisoning the blue shudder of your skin in a caress . . .

CAMAGNI. Is that your technique?

MIMOTTE. Among others.

CAMAGNI. You do this to all women?

MIMOTTE. Possibly.

CAMAGNI. You know, you are a curious type!

MIMOTTE. When my mother had the good sense to conceive me, she was already counting on your far-fetched and posthumous assessment. She was not mistaken. But I am also a man of genius and that's why I am a scoundrel. That's why you like me . . . yes . . . yes . . . exactly for this! And because, for me, life has no value anymore, from the moment I killed off theory, scruples, and feelings.

CAMAGNI. That too?

MIMOTTE. Almost always.

CAMAGNI. Lucky you!

MIMOTTE. Do you envy me?

CAMAGNI. A tiny bit, yes. But not too much. For I know that, deep down, this is a pose. You're sharp like a razor and hard like a rock, by way of reasoning.

MIMOTTE. No, by instinct. Looking a woman directly in the face, I know already that she must fall . . . It's a matter already settled under any circumstance . . .

CAMAGNI. Presumptuous!

MIMOTTE. For a very primitive reason: I don't recognize any obstacles. I am bold, strong, proud, and young. I'm not afraid of anything because, basically, my life is only a risk and I've gotten used to fearing and controlling that risk.

CAMAGNI. And what if someday, sure of your infallibility, you were to burn the wings of that imprudent dragonfly?

MIMOTTE. *(Tries to take* Camagni's *hands as if to draw her to him)* Your hands.

CAMAGNI. Why are you looking at me like that?

MIMOTTE. Listen to me carefully . . .

CAMAGNI. No, you don't have the eyes of a man in love!

MIMOTTE. Who says so? What do you know, my dear Don Quixote, of romantic interludes at one thousand francs each? Do you think that if it happened to me, and it could happen, to leave a piece of my soul, body, heart, at a turning point of my existence, I would be humiliated? . . .

CAMAGNI. Perhaps.

MIMOTTE. In that case I would begin anew, with the greedy patience of builders! . . . Ready to destroy myself and others, at the first sign of weakness . . .

CAMAGNI. What a scoundrel!

MIMOTTE. One must have the courage to judge oneself so as not to fall from the clouds before the judgment of spectators. Am I a scoundrel? What do I care? It's for my pleasure.

CAMAGNI. You, selfish!

MIMOTTE. There is no selfish scoundrel who doesn't drown, sometimes, in the sour milk of his romanticism! And you, my little lady, half respectable and half about to commit your first sin, are searching precisely for me, the confessor who will give you absolution for your very moral intentions! . . . And you tremble . . . waiting for me to start kissing the bare skin of your little hands.

CAMAGNI. *(Draws back her hands)*

MIMOTTE. It's useless. I'll do it later and at my pleasure . . .

CAMAGNI. No.

MIMOTTE. But first I must warn you that I can find a reason for everything. Always. I weigh people and things, making adjustments, preparing life as I see fit, ready to be the first to laugh at it, ready to trample even myself, if that course can be to my advantage—a bit of a poet, an actor, the arbiter of my smiles and tears . . .

CAMAGNI. What an impressive display of doctrine for a little creature like me!

MIMOTTE. It's the typically Latin formula of my cynicism. But it stops here, and it reopens with a complication of joy that you didn't believe. Because tonight, while I wait for you, and you are left for a moment in doubt whether to knock on the door of my room, and you will make your intimate toilette with careful attention, and meditate on the overbearing strangeness of your new adventure, I will have created the most lyrical poem of the day on the subject of the carnal bases of your desire.

CAMAGNI. *(Almost scanning the syllables)* Do-na-tel-la . . .

MIMOTTE. *(Shouting)* Who told you!? . . .

CAMAGNI. Your shout.

MIMOTTE. What a fool I am! Oh well, what does it matter? You'll still think of Mimotte!

CAMAGNI. Nonsense!

MIMOTTE. And he will recite the strophes of his song to some other woman.

CAMAGNI. No . . . No. . . No . . .

MIMOTTE. *(He takes her face into his hands with a sudden gesture, his eyes gazing into hers)* And he will sigh at another woman like a boy of twenty . . .

CAMAGNI. Let go of me . . . Let go of me.

MIMOTTE. . . . trembling for her with passion, anxiety, sadness; nightingale of love in a blooming forest, flute of May on a moonlit night . . .

CAMAGNI. Mimotte!

MIMOTTE. . . . until his habit of vice and the cruelty of his selfishness recapture him and make of him what this thin band of silk makes of your body, which imprisons, leaving him a rapid heartbeat . . . as rapid as yours! . . .

CAMAGNI. *(Freeing herself)* You'll wait for me in vain.

MIMOTTE. I'm too sure . . . There is a clock in the nearby church that rings the hours. They still serve a purpose, those church clocks. Count and wait for two o'clock. It's the height of romanticism. Knock discreetly . . . Goodbye . . .

CAMAGNI. *(Angrily)* Scoundrel!

MIMOTTE. I knew it! . . . *(He makes a friendly gesture of goodbye, very proper, while Him appears at the door)*

HIM. *(To Camagni)* Did I guess right!? . . .

CAMAGNI. *(Regaining her poise)* Ah, the prophet!

HIM. Well?

CAMAGNI. Not yet.

MIMOTTE. *(To Camagni)* Watch out for this man. He wants to be called "Mr. Opportunist" . . . That's his goal . . .

HIM. Please . . . I'm not a man . . .

CAMAGNI. You're not a man?

HIM. By no means. A shadow.

MIMOTTE. Have you abolished your sex?

HIM. I never had it.

CAMAGNI. How do you live?

HIM. I enter, I exit, I vanish. No one wants me, but when I come back, every one of you feels me, in that mild thrill that excites your heart. I hate both truth and lies.

CAMAGNI. Are we going back to definitions?

HIM. I am theory for all and method for no one . . .

MIMOTTE. But what did you come for?

HIM. I represent the four stages of the cadaverous putrefaction of feelings. I stand before you, and you see me sometimes at the green stage, sometimes at the gaseous or skeletal stage, at the mercy of the eight light migrations of insects that will wear out someday, God willing, even your own honorable carcasses. And immediately I rise again to the infantile stage, like a dream-image: nightmare, delirium, hallucination, airy traces of hashish, blue smoke of opium, oceanic infiltration of morphine . . .

MIMOTTE. Let's go, swindler! Are you really waiting for midnight for your revelations and the outline of your horoscope?

HIM. Prophecies are a chemical distillation of logic: anti-logic. Add up the actions of men and, naturally, sum up the homogeneous quantities . . . You will have some absolute revelations. You only exist, therefore, as feelings shown in synthesis. Flesh doesn't count. Only your appetites count, unchained in this night party of life, superimposed one over the other.

CAMAGNI. *(Suddenly)* Goodbye, shadow . . . *(Leaving)*

HIM. Leave on time. *(Pointing to a door)* This way, my dove, if you fear encounters. *(He escorts her)*

MIMOTTE. What do you mean?

HIM. *(With a mysterious air)* You'll see. Anna is looking for you. She knows everything. She's here . . .

(Pause)

MIMOTTE. Where?

HIM. Here. *(*Mimotte *looks around nervously)*

MIMOTTE. What kind of joke is this?

HIM. *(In a loud voice)* Come forward!

*(*Anna *appears)*

HIM. What did I tell you?! . . .

MIMOTTE. You teach people to listen behind doors?

ANNA. What? Who listens behind doors?

MIMOTTE. I asked you: what kind of joke is this?

HIM. Calm yourself, my friend. *(To Anna)* He claims that you were listening behind the door and that I went along with you in this. Nothing is more false and more foolish, right?

ANNA. In fact . . .

HIM. Sir, I already told you that prophecies are a distillation of logic . . . That's why I give you complete freedom, so you can exchange all the bad words possible with your girlfriend, as is fitting among ladies and gentlemen.

ANNA. Stay. You can listen, too, to what I have to say.

HIM. It's useless. I know point by point. I could write and verify them later. I'll come back at the right moment . . . with your permission . . . *(Leaves rapidly)*

MIMOTTE. And now?

ANNA. You'll explain.

MIMOTTE. I have nothing to explain to you, my dear.

ANNA. You'll explain, I tell you. I have been spying on you all night.

MIMOTTE. And did you need a witness?

ANNA. I'm tired, Mimotte.

MIMOTTE. Of me?

ANNA. Of suffering.

MIMOTTE. Postpone this precious confession to a better time, would you?

ANNA. Oh, no, you won't escape me.

MIMOTTE. Come on! Come on! It would be too ridiculous for us to be caught in this attitude. Please . . .

ANNA. I don't care about anything or anyone.

MIMOTTE. *(Ironically)* The line, Anna! One must never lose it. It is the architecture of personal dignity.

ANNA. Mimotte, stop joking!

MIMOTTE. *(Sneering)* A man who has learned to dance the Halli-Hukk can certainly permit himself this agility.

ANNA. *(Angrily)* You'll force me to do something stupid! *(Pause)* Don't you know what to do with me anymore?

MIMOTTE. But is this the right moment?! We will talk about it tomorrow morning. Be reasonable . . . it's more elegant. *(Lights a cigarette)*

ANNA. Miserable me! Having to wring my hands in such despair!

MIMOTTE. Oh, come on. Don't exaggerate.

ANNA. Then take responsibility for your actions, and let's look each other in the eye.

MIMOTTE. So be it, since you stand firm in your resolve.

ANNA. I know you for what you are and what you are worth. No one knows you better than I do. I'm not afraid.

MIMOTTE. Good.

ANNA. I had the illusion of having created a phantom of love, and I don't intend to throw my life away for nothing. So listen well. And speak as directly as I do. What do you want to do?

MIMOTTE. Do you know that you're surprising!? And that I don't understand you!?

ANNA. Oh go on, you understand me very well! Not for nothing have I allowed myself the luxury to have a man of your stamp as a lover!

MIMOTTE. I've always considered you a lady . . . but the way you're talking to me tonight! . . .

ANNA. When one loves as I do, there is no more distinction between a queen and a maid. And since I feel you want to be free of me . . . we have to settle the bill first.

MIMOTTE. Have you received confidential information from a trusted friend? So be it. I want to be free. Yes. Your games humiliate and degrade me . . .

ANNA. You never talked that way before.

MIMOTTE. And I was wrong. I accepted your help? That's fine. And so? Did you acquire the rights to my life and my intelligence?

ANNA. Mimotte!

MIMOTTE. Did you think that I would be tied forever to the vice that wears you out?

ANNA. Oh, no! Why do you talk like that? Why?

MIMOTTE. You wanted it. I made myself the thickest mask and I'm tearing it off. My face is cheap. My soul is soaked with blood and mud. I am an adventurer without a future!

(Anna *makes a gesture imploring him to stop*)

MIMOTTE. But your money is worth less than I am, and will not give you love, or the appearance of love. You thought you held in your fragile fist, who knows? The most perfect joy . . . Oh, how foolish of you!

ANNA. Yes, how foolish!

MIMOTTE. . . . . and in truth you'll only be left with a little cynicism, the sour powder of sin, which will make the sky in which you boast of soaring more open.

ANNA. You've destroyed everything that was close to you!

MIMOTTE. What can you do? That's how it is.

ANNA. And for a new phantom that arouses your desire, you squeeze to the last spasm the tears of a woman who loves you!

MIMOTTE. It grieves me. It's sad. It's inhuman. But that's how it is.

ANNA. And you think I will leave you quietly, after what has been between us?

MIMOTTE. If you have good sense.

ANNA. After what I've done for you? Oh, no! It would be stupid! You'd be the first to laugh behind my back!

MIMOTTE. After all, what have you done that I've not reciprocated with an hour of illusion?

ANNA. I gave you a soul that you didn't have!

MIMOTTE. Oh, a soul!

ANNA. You were a vagabond, without home or homeland, an unprincipled and heartless wanderer. You mustn't forget that.

MIMOTTE. Words!

ANNA. I gathered you up as one gathers a cry of youth, with a pity that was even motherly! My body was conquered by the knowledge that you were alone, useless to yourself and to others, and I believed in your boyish look, your frightened eyes that seemed to beg for rest and stability. I said before . . .

MIMOTTE. Come, come . . . These are just beautiful words. And beautiful phrases are not enough!

ANNA. And they weren't enough! Especially for you! Deep in my desire for good, you always tried to throw a punch of falsity. You even corrupted my tenderness, you traded it, you bartered it! I wanted to see you above everyone, above everything. Be able to say: finally, a complete happiness has risen from my love, and I created this happiness myself, even if at the cost of the greatest sacrifice! You're a man, understand? And you owe it to me! My entire life's dream has exploded. Earlier deceptions don't count. Bad moves, sentimental swindles, pointless disgust have served for something! . . . *(Silence)* But what frightens me is that you are listening to me resigned, and you don't even have a scrap of decency left to answer me anything.

MIMOTTE. What should I say to you?

ANNA. Why did you make me believe that illusion was reality? Your crime is not in having made fun of me, it is in having undone all the good I could be capable of! *(More silence)* But answer me! Tell me that I'm not living in a dream! God! I feel like slapping myself, to persuade myself that, indeed, you and I, here, tonight, are throwing away two years of life, the thing seems so impossible.

MIMOTTE. Listen, Anna, let's stop it. I've been brutal. I should have prepared you, not attacked you. But you asked for it.

ANNA. Me? Me? It's true then? Is it true? Then I would like to at least meet her, the woman who snatches you from my living heart! And shout at her that I hate her . . .

MIMOTTE. If you knew how close she is to you and how much I love her!

ANNA. *(In a stifled voice)* You love her! You miserable man! Don't say anymore! Don't say anymore. I don't want to know!

MIMOTTE. You can't hate her!

ANNA. *(With a desperate crescendo: she closes her eyes)* I don't want to! I don't want to! *(She backs up to the wall, as* Him *appears, arm in arm with the two ballerinas of before)*

HIM. Are you done?

MIMOTTE. Go to hell!

HIM. You're not strong in diplomacy. *(To* Anna*)* Anna, my good friend! Prepare for the final sprint, after which the meeting is adjourned. Let's go. Is it worth to be so sad? Look at the faces of these two fresh young girls who are endangering my late virility! Want to come with us? Afterward, we'll go up together. And I'll keep you company for an hour so that you'll fall asleep faster. Would you like me to give you my arm? Come on, my sweetest seductresses! We'll go back that way. Will you have the kindness to precede us?. Come, Anna.

(Anna again lifts her face full of tears; she starts to leave and is trembling)

HIM. But not like this. I don't want to see you like this. Your powder puff? *(From her pocketbook he takes out a gold compact and hands her the powder puff. She looks in the small mirror and powders herself)* And your lips? *(She takes a red lipstick and colors her lips.)* And here are the salts . . . like this. A line of blood. You seem wounded . . .

ANNA. Yes. To death.

HIM. Take my arm, then?

(Everyone exits. Only Mimotte *is left alone, while the music of a desperate final galoppe can be heard. He stretches out in an armchair, smoking contentedly, till the music stops and a* Butler *enters the living room)*

BUTLER. Sir, are you going to stay here much longer?

MIMOTTE. I don't know. But you can turn off the lights if you want. Leave only the big lamp.

BUTLER. *(He bows. One by one he shuts off the chandelier, the side lamps)* I'll leave the hall light on for when you want to go upstairs.

MIMOTTE. What time is it?

BUTLER. It's almost two o'clock.

MIMOTTE. Has everyone retired?

BUTLER. Yes, sir. Only in the yellow sitting room some people are still playing cards.

MIMOTTE. Who's in there?

BUTLER. His Highness and his entourage. The ladies have retired to their rooms.

MIMOTTE. Good.

BUTLER. Good night . . . *(Leaves)*

MIMOTTE. *(Looks at his watch, arranges his hair, throws away his cigarette, gets up, paces back and forth)* What a day, Mimotte! We have a right to be tired, you and I. And it's not over yet . . .

(From the outside door a faint, rustling noise is heard. He is startled. He brings the two entrance doors together, flings the glass door wide open. A beam of bright moonlight invades the room. He turns off the last lamp that was left on. Looks outside. Calls in a soft voice)

Donatella!

(The room is semidark. There is total silence. And suddenly, from the garden, Donatella *appears behind the glass , her hair loose)*

DONATELLA. It's me, Donatella.

MIMOTTE. My little one, my adored one! . . .

DONATELLA. I came! You see?

MIMOTTE. Like a frightened sparrow in a squall.

DONATELLA. I crossed the silent hallways, holding my breath, as if someone were chasing me. And the garden was full of monstrous shadows. The wind whipped the rain of the fountain in my hair!

MIMOTTE. And here you are in a crown of pearls.

DONATELLA. To be your little queen . . .

MIMOTTE. All blonde and trembling.

DONATELLA. If Mom were to see me!?

MIMOTTE. Did you leave her upstairs?

DONATELLA. I heard her come in.

MIMOTTE. Will she look for you?

DONATELLA. She never does at this hour.

MIMOTTE. Come here, then. Sit here . . . near me . . . Let's open this interlude of paradise . . . Let's open this window of bliss . . . Let's breathe this fragrance of forbidden youth . . . Tonight happiness lives in this corner of the house . . . And it's you, it's you who brings it like a wonderful gift . . . I needed it so much!

DONATELLA. I'm in a daze . . . Your voice enchants me and scares me . . .

MIMOTTE. All our youth shakes in my voice. Listen? You hear? It's like a pilgrimage in a dream . . . You walk, walk, walk . . . The road is long and without end . . . without stars, without moon . . . It seems almost like being carried away by a long wave that pushes us along . . . We finally arrive . . . And there divine beauty awaits us. Who is it?

DONATELLA. Me.

MIMOTTE. Who are you?

DONATELLA. Donatella.

MIMOTTE. Who is Donatella?

DONATELLA. A woman who loves you . . .

MIMOTTE. Swear it.

DONATELLA. I swear.

MIMOTTE. On what?

DONATELLA. On this instant of passing happiness.

MIMOTTE. Stop it.

DONATELLA. How?

MIMOTTE. On our lips . . . like this . . .

DONATELLA. No . . . not now. *(She pulls back)* First tell me . . . Tell me . . .

MIMOTTE. Are you afraid?

DONATELLA. A little, yes.

MIMOTTE. And there is the poem of a little sentimental folk singer, drunk on the blue through which he passed, who still has a terror of the night from which he descends and brings with it the damp smell of a tempest, and shakes like a child, kneeling in front of the child that you are.

DONATELLA. Kneeling?

MIMOTTE. Like this.

DONATELLA. Get up, get up, Mimotte!

MIMOTTE. Allow me to forget about myself for a moment . You take my soul prisoner! And I am so happy to be closed in the magic circle that unites us! I am a man without past and without love. My life is born again here, at your feet. And only if you want, only if you want, Donatella, my life will be different.

DONATELLA. How, my love?

MIMOTTE. With you, with you, with you! . . .

DONATELLA. Surely I want to! We'll tell Mother . . . She asks your advice about everything . . . We'll go to her, holding hands . . . Mommy, we love each other so much! . . . Mommy, your child is no longer entirely yours! . . . An ugly man, you see, wants to take her away from you . . .

MIMOTTE. Yes, Yes, I'll take you away.

DONATELLA. When?

MIMOTTE. Right away. As soon as you want. Tomorrow?

DONATELLA. Tomorrow. What a dream!

MIMOTTE. Do you like it?

DONATELLA. Like a song of joy in the bright sunshine.

MIMOTTE. Then close your eyes. And say with me, together with me . . .

DONATELLA. Yes . . .

MIMOTTE. I love you!

DONATELLA. I love you!

MIMOTTE. I am your burning passion.

DONATELLA. Be . . .

MIMOTTE. The fever that caresses you . . .

DONATELLA. Be . . .

(A shadow moves behind the glass door, as if searching: Anna*)*

MIMOTTE. My hands graze you like a rain of roses . . .
DONATELLA. Be . . .
MIMOTTE. Your lips give themselves to me!
DONATELLA. Be . . .
MIMOTTE. My little Madonna! My little Madonna! My little Madonna! . . .
    (But a short, stifled cry comes through the door, which suddenly opens. Mimotte
    falls apart like a thief caught in the act) Who is it? *(No one answers)*
DONATELLA. *(Runs to the door and draws back in shock with a painful cry)* It's Mother,
    Mimotte! . . . *(Runs from the right)*

*(*Anna, *motionless in the opening of the door, stares at* Mimotte. *She is about to pounce
on him.* Mimotte *on one side, as if waiting, is stiff, haughty, implacable.* Anna, *a long
pause, a tragic silence. Then all her strength deserts her. She collapses on the threshold,
bent over in her pain)*

ACT THREE

In Anna's *bedroom, a delightful room of intimacy, luxury, refinement. One side of the
alcove, half-enclosed by a large velvet curtain.*

(As the curtain rises, Him *is standing discreetly on the threshold)*

HIM. If you need anything, call me. Goodbye.

*(*Donatella *is buried in an armchair, her face between her hands, and* Anna *is next to
her, half-kneeling. One can detect physical pain in her as well as moral suffering.* Him
nods good-bye and leaves.)

ANNA. Donatella! Raise your head, come on. I'm your mother. I don't want
    you to act like that.

*(*Donatella *sobs more copiously. She is totally shaken by convulsions)*

ANNA. No. No. See how strong I am? And I'm suffering like you because I
    never guessed. I could bang my head against the wall! Listen to me,
    my poor little girl. You must calm down . . . Come , come , this sweet
    little face wet with tears! Look at me! Look at me! *(Helps her to raise her
    head, as she caresses her)* Later Daddy will come to pick you up . . .
DONATELLA. I won't go!

ANNA. It's necessary. You'll forgive me. And this resentment of yours you won't talk about will seem inhuman to you, as it seems to me now. You will see that your mother is a poor wretched woman without peace, and her suffering will seem overwhelming to you . . . And the unrelenting torment of her life will appear to you as the nightmare of your entire existence led recklessly, from the moment you are able to judge it.

(Donatella *makes a gesture of disagreement. She can't talk.*)

ANNA. How could I have destroyed your happiness, my child?
DONATELLA. One word was enough . . .
ANNA. Oh, at your age you can begin to live again whenever you wish! For us, men have voices without echo. One can rebuild happiness.

(Donatella *makes a gesture of denial*)

ANNA. Then your daddy will make you forget this moment of sorrow.
DONATELLA. I won't go ! I won't go !
ANNA. On the contrary, you'll be reasonable. And I will make any sacrifices for you, I will give up anything. All right? What wouldn't I do for my baby? . . . But you here, Donatella? In the shadow of this cruelty that for a second has divided us and made us enemies? It's not possible . . . both of us need to be calm.
DONATELLA. *(In a stifled voice)* You want to send me away so you can be with him . . . I won't go because I love him . . .
ANNA. That's what frightens me! You love him! But you didn't think about my love. Didn't you ever have eyes? Ears? What dream have you been living in till now, my child? Oh, this base competition of ours for the same man is outside of life, outside of morality, outside of any law! Well then, call! Ask! If you didn't see before, ask the first person who comes through this door! And even if it will torture my heart, from humiliation and embarrassment, it won't matter. At every turn of life, I would find him in front of me like a specter of my sorrow. My life was filled with his smile and his falsehood. And I loved him like the best part of myself . . . What a confession I'm making to you!
DONATELLA. Without defending me!
ANNA. Don't kill my pity, so that I may still feel like a woman suffering the humiliation of an insult. Suffer with me. Stroke my wound softly, as I stroke yours. Be sweet! Why don't you want to hear that I'm not your enemy, not even a woman who's defending her love? I wish I weren't even bemoaning my affliction, so that I could be closer to you!
DONATELLA. I don't have any more courage. I woke up so suddenly!

ANNA. My child!

DONATELLA. I couldn't guess. You, my mother? My mother, an enemy?

ANNA. No! No! No! Rather hold my heart between my teeth so as not to scream! And then to turn back, to confront the illusions that have been lost! Consider the devastation that's killing us. To say: there was my house. To recognize a branch blooming in the garden. What a snare of stars and blue sky! While now . . . *(No longer able to control herself, she suddenly bursts out, as though her lament changes into a cry)* How long have you loved him?

DONATELLA. All along. Since I saw him.

ANNA. What about him?

*(*Donatella *gestures affirmatively)*

ANNA. Did he tell you before last night?

DONATELLA. *(In a very low voice)* Yes.

ANNA. And you believed him? Right? He lied to you like all the rest! He takes pleasure in that. He makes a habit of it! He lives on it . . .

DONATELLA. Mama!

ANNA. He destroyed my sunless life, and wanted yours too! Let me scream at last! Let me tell everything, to defend you! Let me trample on the purity of your youth with the base truth! Oh, the torment of my barren nights, shivering with passion and dread! . . .

DONATELLA. No, no, no! . . .

ANNA. What terrible hours! Endless! Me crazy with grief and jealousy!

DONATELLA. Mama!

ANNA. The ignoble journeys . . . to go and snatch him from the whim of an hour's adventure . . . and then . . . the base . . . concessions . . . I would have endured anything!

DONATELLA. You loved him that much?

ANNA. What shame, right? *(Silence)* But you cannot understand the grief of feeling you're growing older day by day, hour by hour, knowing for sure the man you adore is slipping away from you, after you gave him the blood of all your blood, the flesh of all your flesh, and a heart that agonizes as if it will break!

DONATELLA. That's enough! Enough, mother! Don't tell me this. You're no longer my mother! Let me go away . . . I want to go away, now!

ANNA. Not before I have told you everything. I'm the one who wants you to stay.

DONATELLA. You frighten me. You're no longer my mother.

ANNA. I spoke to you as a poor woman without peace.

DONATELLA. Shouting and crying with rancor. I'd rather be dead!

ANNA. Donatella! Donatella!

DONATELLA. . . . and not have had this nightmare of life that strangles me and has laid an unbearable burden on my youth.

ANNA. How obstinate you are now!

DONATELLA. I'm defending myself. And I know that whatever you say will be to protect what you call your love.

ANNA. Listen to me first.

DONATELLA. I know it, even before you utter a word.

ANNA. No. Donatella.

DONATELLA. I can see it in your eyes! I can feel it in your trembling voice.

ANNA. No, Donatella.

DONATELLA. *(Almost involuntarily)* I want to go away.

ANNA. You will go, but not in this state. When you've calmed down. When your mother has persuaded you. Before you, your mother has no more tears for her sorrow. Feels no more resentment, none. A thick and heavy fog seems to envelope her and separate her from her past. And she can see only her small child . . . Oh, you don't believe that for your smile your mother, your bad mother, would give her life again? She walks, she walks and then stops, in the middle of the journey. She erases everything. She has no more flesh, heart, wounds. There's only a feeling of tenderness for you. She no longer exists for anyone, because she is so unhappy and also feels a bit like dying . . .

DONATELLA. *(In a weak voice)* Mommy . . .

ANNA. And you don't want to forgive her, when she has forgiven you so much?

(They are almost undone by the great weeping which brings them close and unites them in a single embrace. Him appears discreetly at the door, makes a gesture. Anna understands)

ANNA. Is there an answer?

HIM. Yes, Madam! . . . The groom is back. He has a letter for you.

ANNA. Will you keep her company, my friend? I'll be back soon *(leaves)*

HIM. Donatella, Mimotte wants to talk to you. He said he'll come here no matter what. Do you want to see him?

DONATELLA. No.

HIM. You won't regret giving such a curt answer later?

DONATELLA. No. We have nothing more to say to each other. We'll save useless words.

HIM. You've forgotten everything. Two hours ago, your love for him seemed eternal.

DONATELLA. It's true. But it's changed.

HIM. My poor child! You want to persuade your feelings, and your feelings want to persuade your reason! I'll call him before your mother comes back.

DONATELLA. Don't. I don't want you to.

HIM. Would you sentence a man without giving him a chance to explain his crime?

DONATELLA. He has no excuse.

HIM. Well then, listen to me. Let's resort to an expedient used in popular theater. He will answer to me, as if he were talking to you directly, and you'll stand behind that curtain to listen to him. You can't kill him without at least giving him absolution.

DONATELLA. But what are you suggesting?

HIM. See? Your own desire is about to give in.

DONATELLA. I would once again betray my mother . . .

HIM. Oh, what big words! Go over there, I tell you!

DONATELLA. My mother? Of course! *(And leaves)*

HIM. What a fool! *(Left alone, he taps his forehead as if he had had an idea, goes to the other door, calls)* Mimotte, come in.

(Mimotte comes in, somewhat shyly, somewhat clumsily)

HIM. Come in, then, and hurry up. The little one is over there. *(He points to the alcove enclosed by the drapes)* But she doesn't want to see you. She's undone like a rose in the rain.

MIMOTTE. Over there?

HIM. Yes.

MIMOTTE. Let me see her then.

HIM. Impossible. *(Comes between the drape and Mimotte)*

MIMOTTE. Donatella.

HIM. It's useless. You're capable of anything, but you won't be such a cad as to get into her bedroom. What do you want to tell her? I'll be the usual silent witness. Speak. What did you want from her? What were you hoping for?

MIMOTTE. *(Little by little, he is carried away by some kind of passionate delirium. When Him asks him a question, he always answers looking toward the alcove, where he presumes the girl to be.)* Oh, nothing that wouldn't be the honest thrill of a dream.

HIM. You're using choice words. I like it.

MIMOTTE. For just five minutes I would like her to be the same as before and would open my soul entirely to her. And she would find it a beautiful thing: love for her, redemption for her, desire for her . . . Oh, how quickly one can plunge again in the murky depths of our existence! Everything impure, unhealthy, and base comes to the surface: it submerges the best part of ourselves.

HIM. So? Is that all?

MIMOTTE. At least if I could save, from the shipwreck in which I fell, the memory of the only pure thing in my life! I loved her, you know? I loved her like I don't know what. She's my youth, despite everything. And my regret! But without ulterior motives, without any hidden thought. I understood that someday . . .

HIM. You didn't understand enough.

MIMOTTE. . . . my whole dream would dissolve like a paper castle in a children's game. And I trembled at the thought of that moment! But how could one avert it? How? How often while I held her tight, the thought of another woman would strike me suddenly! Ah, Mimotte, I caught you with the lamb of my flock! Ah, big thief of the woods, you'll leave that prey which is mine! But what to do? What to do? Renounce her?

(Him *gestures repeatedly in the negative*)

MIMOTTE. Go away, like that? To think with terror that another man, perhaps tomorrow, would hold her in his arms, would kiss her mouth, would feel her trembling like a small live plant?

(Him *gestures repeatedly in the affirmative*)

MIMOTTE. Ah, by God, no! No! It was my hourly obsession! And to save my love, I'm going to lose her! And to save my torment, my restlessness, my jealousy, I lied, I lied, I lied!

HIM. The first time you went against your instinct you lost the game . . .

MIMOTTE. You, too, understand that?

HIM. A child would understand! You were wrong.

MIMOTTE. What do you want? My entire existence has been a lie. It was very necessary for me to free myself at a certain point! One lies because this is a disease of the imagination and the mark of a sin of pride! I began to live much too soon!

HIM. Go slow with lyrical flights. Be positive.

MIMOTTE. My upbringing didn't give me the will to work . . .

HIM. Here we are, this is surely positive. Now get to the point. Anna could arrive at any moment. It wouldn't be pleasant for her to meet you.

MIMOTTE. *(Continuing)* It only gave me the restless, cold curiosity of adventure, which means that whatever one touches is broken under the impact of one's fingers.

HIM. The fever to arrive at any cost . . .

MIMOTTE. We're launched like missiles. And we'll land. All procedures have been successful, in order to survive! All honest companions, provided they're happy, all evil passersby who would lend a hand, have been welcome, so long as they would help us walk for a stretch of the road . . . We made no moral compromises with them, nor with our own conscience!

HIM. Get to the point.

MIMOTTE. But can she hear me? Can she hear me? It's as though I'm speaking to a stone wall, facing death. And this takes my breath away.

HIM. And your conscience alone can understand you, since you're speaking to her about yourself, out loud, for the first time. You must confess that nothing like this has ever happened to you before.

MIMOTTE. But does she understand? Does she approve of my truth?

HIM. *(With a scornful smile)* Yes, since she is keeping quiet.

MIMOTTE. I want to see her then. Let me by.

HIM. I told you no. You'll have to deal with me if you try. Try me.

MIMOTTE. But this is outrageous! . . .

HIM. *(Aggressive, grabbing him by the arm)* Why did you deceive her mother?

MIMOTTE. For the joy of living!

HIM. Not enough.

MIMOTTE. I hadn't reckoned with this stupid heart of mine that never manages to save itself when its time comes.

HIM. Do you believe that is sufficient justification? Do you suppose, then, that two desperate women are in there, waiting for your illuminating words? For a moment put yourself in their place. Do the proof of your mental arithmetic. Would an extenuating circumstance be enough for you? The joy of living in order to destroy!

MIMOTTE. But why have I been justifying myself in front of you for fifteen minutes? Who are you, after all?

HIM. Your remorse. Don't you recognize me?

MIMOTTE. A tired Mephistopheles!

HIM. Here you are in front of a mirror locking horns with your own unfaithful image . . .

MIMOTTE. *(Desperately)* Donatella!

HIM. It's no use calling her. She isn't here.

MIMOTTE. Behind the curtain?

HIM. *(With a laugh)* It's empty.

MIMOTTE. You speak to me as if I were a madman? By God, am I mad?

HIM. Could be. No one's there. *(Pulls the curtain wide open; the alcove seems deserted)* Look, there can't be anyone. You act too well to have an audience, puppet! The audience will come now, and you won't be able to talk anymore.

ANNA. *(Enters. Seeing Mimotte, she stops hesitantly at the door)* Sir . . .

(Mimotte is bewildered, he looks like a character in a nightmare)

HIM. *(Cynically)* He came with his remorse . . .

ANNA. A bad companion . . . *(To Mimotte)* You don't want me to teach you the way out . . . *(She draws aside, pale, marblelike)*

(Mimotte leaves hastily, confused, throwing a look of hatred toward Him. Anna clings to the curtain to keep from falling)

HIM. What's the matter, Anna?

ANNA. Nothing.

HIM. *(Supporting her, he helps her to sit down)* Is that better?

ANNA. Death came so close that I felt shivers and cold.

HIM. We'll call the doctor and the priest, then.

ANNA. I don't need them.

HIM. Better this way. So, I'll sit next to you. And I'll be at the same time confessor and practical doctor. Let me feel your pulse . . .

ANNA. *(Gives him her hand almost automatically)* I've never seen you from this angle . . . You look like an undertaker. . . . It might almost make me laugh, if I could at this point.

HIM. Try.

ANNA. Ah, ah! . . .

HIM. *(Echoing)* Ah, ah! . . . Life, what a stupid comedy! . . . *(A tragic silence)*

ANNA. What look have you tonight?

HIM. The beat of your voice leaps in the rhythm of your veins. You're almost on the threshold of happiness. And you're getting there through all kinds of despair. You'll be fully happy only when you're alone and have destroyed everything around you.

ANNA. If only my husband were here!

HIM. *(Surprised)* Oh! He'll come if I want.

ANNA. *(Displays the letter she received earlier, then crushes it and throws it away)* He wrote. He can't take the trouble. He doesn't want to. I just sent Mrs. Ronzi by car, to insist. But I'm sure he won't come.

HIM. And, why don't you tell me that?

ANNA. *(Surprised)* Tell you?

HIM. The spiritual testament . . . Speak, speak . . .

ANNA. Oh, the sweetness of hypocrisy! To lock oneself up in one's own immobility. But to go back in thought twenty years ago now, what a narrow-minded blonde I was then. Entering his museum, like a live sparrow! . . . *(Him makes some gestures of agreement)*

ANNA. What restlessness! But at times, under the collapse of my illusions, a strange voluptuousness of repose seized me. To let myself go. To be carried away by the current. Then the need to live more intensely than others would make me rise again from the storm. And then I would start over again, with patience, resignation, insistence, to seek the sky best suited to my flight, the blue sky, the infinite space . . .

HIM. The Bird of Paradise!

ANNA. Ever ready for the highest and most difficult flight. Like a rare specimen, from which legend has removed the feet, so that when it alights it won't have the strength to flap the wings that carry it back up . . .

HIM. *(Suddenly changing his voice)* And so? So what? Are you sorry? If Ardeo were listening, he might even be pleased at your repentance. But he could tell you: what do I care about these confessions? In our life together you and I don't exist anymore. We destroyed each other. Giovanni Ardeo is no longer Anna Corelli's husband. He is only the father of her daughter and can only ask you about his daughter!

ANNA. Only about her?

HIM. What have you made of her?

ANNA. A lost creature, like me, in the presence of the same man!

HIM. *(Threatening)* For this you took her away from me?

ANNA. That little mouth that babbled the first two sweet syllables to call me, cried out for that love without my even noticing it!

HIM. For this you practically snatched her from me with your claws? For this you made me a man without ideals, a being ridiculous in his sadness, full of scars and wounds?

ANNA. *(Terrified)* Ah, you speak with his voice, you speak with his voice! You frighten me! I don't want Donatella to stay here anymore . . . Let him take her back! Let him teach her to live the way I haven't been able to. Let him defend her the way I wasn't able to. *(In a stifled voice)* Take her back to him!

HIM. *(Changing the tone of his voice, he regains his cynical and elegant skepticism)* As you wish. Go and call her yourself. But be sure to persuade her first. I don't want to see any more tears . . . I'll wait for you here.

(Anna leaves)

INA RONZI. *(From the other door)* Ah, my friend! What an impossible being this professor is! There was no way to move him. He said "My house is always open to my daughter, at any hour, at any time. But I will never go to my wife's! Never, do you understand?"

HIM. *(Irritated)* We'll accompany Donatella. But then, that's it. The novel has come to an end. It's necessary to change topics because catastrophe is near and the knot is untied. I made every effort to infuse soul into all these puppets and all I could squeeze out of them was words, a false love, false maternal compassion, male egoism, a few violent little quarrels. But nothing that would even be one inch from the ground, and logical according to others, although, in my opinion . . . *(He prepares to leave)*

INA RONZI. Are you leaving?

HIM. I'm going to let the destiny I set in motion play itself out, and I'll find a change of scene by going to meet live people.

INA RONZI. What about Anna?

HIM. She's going to die one of these days, naturally and suddenly. She has a heart condition. It's incurable. And I will be a kind of bankrupt dealer pursuing the conquest of truth through prejudice of faith, custom, fashion, hypocrisy . . .

INA RONZI. I don't understand you.

HIM. I know. Yet I express myself with sufficient clarity. What could prevent Donatella from taking her fine dandy, guffawing in her mother's face, and enjoying life according to her own pleasure?

INA RONZI. *(Confused)* Her filial discretion.

HIM. *(With increasing intensity)* What could prevent Anna from kicking her daughter out on the street, where one can meet more beautiful and perhaps more honest women?

INA RONZI. *(Still uncertain, and somewhat fearful)* Her maternal discretion.

HIM. *(With increasing intensity)* And what could prevent Mimotte from taking Donatella as a plaything of his most frivolous fancy only to drop her for the first slut who might pass by?

INA RONZI. *(Bewildered)* Gentlemanly discretion.

HIM. *(With ever-increasing intensity)* And what could prevent Ardeo from saying: don't bother me anymore, once and for all! Leave me with my glass cases and my mold! I'm already somewhat embalmed myself, but stuffed with tranquillity. From now on, my whole life will be classified according to thoughts, acts, words, and it's a real delight to be a man of discipline.

INA RONZI. *(With anxiety in her whisper)* His discretion as a man of honor!

HIM. *(As if exploding)* No. What discretion are you philosophizing about? It's for morality, for so-called morality, my lady! For that false control apparatus which does not exist and sees to it that, at a certain point, the ideas of an intellect without moderation, like Anna's, are fine for others, but become absurd for her! Sees to it that she is crazy when, through love, she wants to conquer men with her tenderness and reduce them from men to gallant men or gentlemen—elevate them, that is, to her intellectual integrity—and becomes wise gradually as disillusionment slaps her in the face! Wise and sad, because wisdom is always melancholy . . . *(Regains his apparent ease)* I bid you goodbye, my little one. I'm abandoning these bankrupt subjects whose chronic course from now on can only be human . . .

INA RONZI. I'll see you to the door.

HIM. One moment.

(Anna and Donatella *enter together)*

ANNA. *(To* Ronzi*)* Well then, what did he say? Is he coming? . . .

HIM. Her father is determined to wait for her at home. The ambassadress is back . . .

ANNA. *(Discouraged, worn out)* His will be done! . . . My little one! My little one! We part, then . . .

HIM. I authorize the last scene of the melodrama.

DONATELLA. *(Clings to* Anna*)* Mommy!

ANNA. How sweet this word is on your lips tonight! You say it the way you did when I used to hold you in my arms in the evening, and you were cold, and you would promise to be good . . .

DONATELLA. Yes . . .

ANNA. With a long yes that came from your heart. *(Silence)* Can you still promise me that? Your mother wants you to be at peace. And when you're with your dad, she'll think of you with great tenderness, as if you, dear, were very close to her.

DONATELLA. What about you? . . . How can I leave you?

ANNA. *(Resigned)* One day or another you would have gone away just the same, with your girlish hope, leaving me alone with my sad experience! I've been old for so long. You don't know.

DONATELLA. It's not true . . . You're beautiful . . .

ANNA. I was indeed. I knew it. But when you, too, become like me, little by little? When you have passed from the sweet state of youth to the state of grace of old age? I don't want you to be alone. Stop your heart. Lock it. Remember what your beautiful mother was reduced to, lying before everyone's eyes because she was in love . . . Your beautiful mother who smiled on the street was all pretense. As your rosy mother who greeted everyone with a sweet smile like a promise was a pretense. Your mother is ugly. Only her love was young. And it wanted her to smile. It wanted her to be pleasing. When you see one of those petite women's faces, made up and smiling, think that under that color and that smile are almost always feelings of jealousy, choking tears, and consuming passion. And there is something atrocious about life! The inability to forget those words that kill our souls. You must forget and forgive.

DONATELLA. Mama! Mama!

ANNA. Be good to your father. He'll bring peace of mind into your life. He has the secret. In life he has proved to be right by staying dry, cold, and subtle. Me, do you see? I am a poor worn-out thing, finished . . . Ah, never fall in love! Reject love, if you can. Lock yourself up. Don't ask for happiness at any price, don't take it whenever you find it. Be fearful of your joy and suspicious of men who are all egotistical, bad, and ungrateful. We deceive ourselves that life is fun! Woe to stopping at appearances. Remember, Donatella. It's your good mama who's telling you that . . .

DONATELLA. Yes, mama . . .

ANNA. And now, leave me alone for a while . . . *(She can't take it anymore, doesn't have the strength)* I'm tired . . . I'm weary . . .

(Him takes Donatella gently by the hand, separating her away from her mother. He is speechless. He points to the door. Donatella lets herself almost be dragged along. Ronzi follows her)

ANNA. *(Looks around her, runs her hand over the eyes as if to remove traces of a bad dream).* Yes! Now I'm really alone!